D0560247

THE ENGLISHWOMAN IN AMERICA

ISABELLA BIRD

THE ENGLISHWOMAN
IN AMERICA

KÖNEMANN

© 2000 for this edition
Könemann Verlagsgesellschaft mbH
Bonner Straße 126, D–50968 Köln

Series and volume editor: Michael Hulse
Cover design: Peter Feierabend
Layout and typesetting: Birgit Beyer
Printed in Hungary
ISBN 3-8290-5804-7
10 9 8 7 6 5 4 3 2 1

CONTENTS

CHAPTER I

Prefatory and explanatory—The voyage out—The sentimental—The actual—The oblivious—The medley—Practical joking—An unwelcome companion—American patriotism—The first view—The departure.

As a general dislike of prefaces is unmistakeably evidenced by their uncut leaves, and as unknown readers could scarcely be induced to read a book by the most cogent representations of an unknown author, and as apologies for "rushing into print" are too trite and insincere to have any effect, I will merely prefix a few explanatory remarks to my first chapter.

Circumstances which it is unnecessary to dwell upon led me across the Atlantic with some relatives; and on my return, I was requested by numerous friends to give an account of my travels. As this volume has been written with a view to their gratification, there is far more of personal narrative than is likely to interest the general reader.

With respect to the people of the United States, I have given those impressions which as a traveller I formed; if they are more favourable than those of some of my predecessors, the difference may arise from my having taken out many excellent introductions, which afforded me greater facilities of seeing the best society in the States than are usually possessed by those who travel merely to see the country.

Where I have offered any opinions upon the effect produced by the institutions of America, or upon any great national question, I have done so with extreme diffidence, giving *impressions* rather than *conclusions*, feeling the great injustice of drawing general inferences from partial premises, as well as the impossibility of rightly estimating cause and effect during a brief residence in the United States. I have endeavoured to give a faithful picture of what I saw and heard, avoiding the beaten track as much as possible, and dwelling principally on those things in which I knew that my friends were most interested.

Previously to visiting the United States, I had read most of the American travels which had been published; yet from experience I can say that even those who read most on the Americans know little of them, from the disposition which leads travellers to seize and dwell upon the ludicrous points which continually present themselves.

We know that there is a vast continent across the Atlantic, first discovered by a Genoese sailing under the Spanish flag, and that for many years past it has swallowed up thousands of the hardiest of our population. Although our feelings are not particularly fraternal, we give the people inhabiting this continent the national cognomen of "*Brother Jonathan*," while we name individuals "*Yankees*." We know that they are famous for smoking, spitting, "gouging," and bowie-knives—for monster hotels, steamboat explosions, railway collisions, and repudiated debts. It is believed also that this nation is re-nowned for keeping three millions of Africans in slavery—for wooden nutmegs, paper money, and "fillibuster" expeditions—for carrying out nationally and individually the maxim

> "That they may take who have the power,
> And they may keep who can."

I went to the States with that amount of prejudice which seems the birthright of every English person, but I found that, under the knowledge of the Americans which can be attained by a traveller mixing in society in every grade, these prejudices gradually melted away. I found much which is worthy of commendation, even of imitation: that there is much which is very reprehensible, is not to be wondered at in a country which for years has been made a "cave of Adullam"—a refuge for those who have "left their country for their country's good"—a receptacle for the barbarous, the degraded, and the vicious of all other nations. It must never be forgotten that the noble, the learned, and the wealthy have shrunk from the United States; her broad lands have been peopled to a great extent by those whose stalwart arms have been their only possession.

Is it surprising, considering these antecedents, that much of arrogance, coarseness, and vulgarity should be met with? Is it not rather surprising, that a traveller should meet with so little to annoy—so few obvious departures from the rules of propriety?

An Englishman bears with patience any ridicule which foreigners cast upon him. John Bull never laughs so loudly as when he laughs at himself; but the Americans are nationally sensitive, and cannot endure that good-humoured raillery which jests at their weaknesses and foibles. Hence candid and even favourable statements of the *truth* by English travellers are received with a perfect outcry by the Americans; and the phrases, "shameful misstatements," "violation of the rights of hospitality," &c., are on every lip.

Most assuredly that spirit of envious rivalry and depreciating criticism in which many English travellers have written, is greatly to be deprecated, no less than the tone of servile adulation which some writers have adopted; but our American neighbours must recollect that they provoked both the virulent spirit and the hostile caricature by the way in which some of their most popular writers of travels have led an ungenerous onslaught against our institutions and people, and the bitter tone in which their newspaper press, headed by the *Tribune*, indulges towards the British nation.

Having made these few remarks, I must state that at the time of my visit to the States I had no intention of recording my "experiences" in print; and as my notes taken at the time were few and meagre, and have been elaborated from memory, some inaccuracies have occurred which it will not take a keen eye to detect. These must be set down to want of correct information rather than to wilful misrepresentation. The statistical information given is taken from works compiled by the Americans themselves. The few matters on which I write which did not come under my own observation, I learned

13

from trustworthy persons who have been long resident in the country.

Of Canada it is scarcely necessary to speak here. Perhaps an English writer may be inclined to adopt too eulogistic a tone in speaking of that noble and loyal colony, in which British institutions are undergoing a Transatlantic trial, and where a free people is protected by British laws. There are, doubtless, some English readers who will be interested in the brief notices which I have given of its people, its society, and its astonishing capabilities.[1]

The notes from which this volume is taken were written in the lands of which it treats: they have been amplified and corrected in the genial atmosphere of an English home. I will not offer hackneyed apologies for its very numerous faults and deficiencies; but will conclude these tedious but necessary introductory remarks with the sincere hope that my readers may receive one hundredth part of the pleasure from the perusal of this volume which I experienced among the scenes and people of which it is too imperfect a record.

Although bi-weekly steamers ply between England and the States, and many mercantile men cross the Atlantic twice annually on business, and think nothing of it, the voyage seems an important event when undertaken for the first time. Friends living in inland counties, and those who have been sea-sick in crossing the straits of Dover, exaggerate the dangers and discomforts of ocean travelling, and shake their heads knowingly about fogs and icebergs.

Then there are a certain number of boxes to be packed, and a very uncertain number of things to fill them, while clothing has to be provided suitable to a tropical summer, and a winter within the arctic circle. But a variety of minor arrangements, and even an indefinite number of leave-takings, cannot be

---

1 I must here record my grateful acknowledgments to a gentleman in a prominent public position in Canada, who has furnished me with much valuable information which I should not otherwise have obtained.

indefinitely prolonged; and at eight o'clock on a Saturday morning in 1854, I found myself with my friends on the landing-stage at Liverpool.

Whatever sentimental feelings one might be inclined to indulge in on leaving the shores of England were usefully and instantaneously annihilated by the discomfort and crush in the *Satellite* steam-tender, in which the passengers were conveyed, helplessly huddled together like a flock of sheep, to the *Canada*, an 1850-ton paddle-wheel steamer of the Cunard line, which was moored in the centre of the Mersey.

An investigation into the state-rooms, and the recital of disappointed expectations consequent on the discovery of their very small dimensions, the rescue of "regulation" portmanteaus from sailors who were running off with them, and the indulgence of that errant curiosity which glances at everything and rests on nothing, occupied the time before the arrival of the mail-boat with about two tons of letters and newspapers, which were consigned to the mail-room with incredible rapidity.

Then friends were abruptly dismissed—two guns were fired—the lashings were cast off—the stars and stripes flaunted gaily from the 'fore—the captain and pilot took their places on the paddle-boxes—the bell rang—our huge paddle-wheels revolved, and, to use the words in which the same event was chronicled by the daily press, "The Cunard royal mail steamer *Canada*, Captain Stone, left the Mersey this morning for Boston and Halifax, conveying the usual mails; with one hundred and sixty-eight passengers, and a large cargo on freight."

It was an auspiciously commenced voyage as far as appearances went. The summer sun shone brightly—the waves of the Mersey were crisp and foam-capped—and the fields of England had never worn a brighter green. The fleet of merchant-ships through which we passed was not without an interest. There were timber-ships, huge and square-sided, unmistakeably from Quebec or Miramichi—green high-sterned Dutch galliots—American ships with long black hulls and tall raking masts—and those far-famed "Black Ball" clippers, the *Marco Polo* and the *Champion of the Seas*,—in short, the ships of all nations, with their marked and distinguishing peculiarities. But the most interesting object of all was the screw troop-ship *Himalaya*, which was embarking the Scots Greys for the Crimea—that regiment which has since earned so glorious but fatal a celebrity on the bloody field of Balaklava.

It is to be supposed that to those who were crossing the Atlantic for the first time to the western hemisphere there was some degree of excitement, and that regret was among the feelings with which they saw the coast of England become a faint cloud on the horizon; but soon oblivion stole over the intellects of most of the passengers, leaving one absorbing feeling of disgust, first to the viands, next to those who could partake of them, and lastly to everything connected with the sea. Fortunately this state of things only lasted for two days, as the weather was very calm, and we ran with studding-sails set before a fair wind as far as the Nova Scotian coast.

The genius of Idleness presided over us all. There were five ample meals every day, and people ate, and walked till they could eat again; while some, extended on sofas, slept over odd volumes of novels from the ship's library, and others played at chess, cards, or backgammon from morning to night. Some of the more active spirits played "shuffle-boards," which kept the deck in an uproar; while others enjoyed the *dolce far niente* in their berths, except when the bell summoned to meals. There were weather-wise people, who smoked round the funnel all day, and prophesied foul winds every night; and pertinacious querists, who asked the captain every hour or two when we should reach Halifax. Some betted on the "run," and others on the time of reaching port; in short, every expedient was resorted to by which time could be killed.

We had about twenty English passengers; the rest were Canadians, Americans, Jews, Germans, Dutch, French, Californians, Spaniards, and Bavarians. Strict equality was preserved in this heterogeneous assembly. An Irish pork-merchant was seated at dinner next a Jew, who regarded the pig *in toto* as an abomination—a lady, a scion of a ducal family, found herself next to a French cook going out to a San Franciscan eating-house—an officer, going out to high command at Halifax, was seated next a rough Californian, who wore "nuggets" of gold for buttons; and there were contrasts even stranger than these. The most conspicuous of our fellow-voyagers was the editor of an American paper, who was writing a series of clever but scurrilous articles on England, from materials gleaned in a three weeks' tour!

Some of the Americans were very fond of practical jokes, but these were rather of a stupid description. There was a Spanish gentleman who used to promenade the deck with a dignity worthy of the Cid Rodrigo, addressing everybody he met with the question, "*Parlez-vous Français, Monsieur?*" and at the end of the voyage his stock of English only amounted to "Dice? Sixpence." One day at dinner this gentleman requested a French-speaking Californian to tell him how to ask for *du pain* in English. "My donkeys," was the prompt reply, and the joke was winked down the table, while the Spaniard was hammering away at "My donkeys" till he got the pronunciation perfect. The waiter came round, and the unhappy man, in confident but mellifluous tones, pointing to the bread, asked for "My donkeys."

Comic drinking-songs, and satires on the English, the latter to the tune of "Yankee Doodle," were sung in the saloon in the evenings round large bowls of punch, and had the effect of keeping many of the ladies on deck, when a refuge from the cold and spray would have been desirable; but with this exception the conduct of the passengers on the whole was marked by far more propriety than could have been expected from so mixed a company. If the captain had been more of a disciplinarian, even this annoyance might have been avoided.

I had the misfortune of having for my companion in my state-room an Englishwoman who had resided for some years at New York, and who combined in herself the disagreeable qualities of both nations. She was in a frequent state of intoxication, and kept gin, brandy, and beer in her berth. Whether sober or not, she was equally voluble; and as her language was not only inelegant, but replete with coarseness and profanity, the annoyance was almost insupportable. She was a professed atheist, and as such justly an object of commiseration, the weakness of her unbelief being clearly manifested by the frequency with which she denied the existence of a God.

On one day, as I was reading my Bible, she exclaimed with a profane expression, " I wish you'd pitch that book overboard, it's enough to sink the ship;" the contradiction implied in the words showing the weakness of her atheism, which, while it promises a man the impunity of non-existence, and degrades him to desire it, very frequently seduces him to live as an infidel, but to die a terrified and despairing believer.

It was a very uneventful voyage. The foul winds prophesied never blew, the icebergs kept far away to the northward, the excitement of flight from Russian privateers was exchanged for the sight of one harmless merchantman; even the fogs off Newfoundland turned out complete *myths*.

On the seventh day out the bets on the hour of our arrival at Halifax increased in number and magnitude, and a lottery was started; on the eighth we passed Cape Race, and spoke the steamer *Asia*; our rigging was tightened, and our railings polished; and in nine days and five hours from Liverpool we landed on the shores of the New World. The day previous to our landing was a Sunday, and I was pleased to observe the decorum which pervaded the ship. Service was conducted with propriety in the morning; a large proportion of the passengers read their Bibles or other religious books; punch, chess, and cards were banished from the saloon; and though we had almost as many creeds as nationalities, and some had no creed at all, yet those who might ridicule the observance of the Sabbath themselves, avoided any proceedings calculated to shock what they might term the prejudices of others.

On the next day we had a slight head wind for the first time; most of the passengers were sea-sick, and those who were not so were promenading the wet, sooty deck in the rain, in a uniform of oilskin coats and caps. The sea and sky were both of a leaden colour; and as there was nothing to enliven the prospect but the gambols of some very uncouth-looking porpoises, I was lying half asleep on a settee, when I was roused by the voice of a kind-hearted Yankee skipper, saying, "Come, get up; there's a glorious country and no mistake; a great country, a progressive country, the greatest country under the sun." The honest sailor was rubbing his hands with delight as he spoke, his broad, open countenance beaming with a perfect glow of satisfaction. I looked in the direction indicated by his finger, and beheld, not the lofty pinnacled cliffs of the "Pilgrim Fathers," but a low gloomy coast, looming through a mist.

I already began to appreciate the hearty enthusiasm with which Americans always speak of their country, designated as it is by us by the names "National vanity," and "Boastfulness." This *esprit du pays*, although it is sometimes carried to a ridiculous extent, is greatly to be preferred to the abusive manner in which an Englishman accustoms himself to speak of the glorious country to which he appears to feel it a disgrace to belong. It does one good to hear an American discourse on America, his panegyric generally concluding with the words, "We're the greatest people on the face of the earth."

At dusk, after steaming during the whole day along the low green coast of Nova Scotia, we were just outside the heads of Halifax harbour, and the setting sun was bathing the low, pine-clad hills of America in floods of purple light. A pilot came off to offer his services, but was rejected, and to my delight he hailed in a pure English accent, which sounded like a friendly welcome. The captain took his place on the paddle-box, and our speed was slackened. Two guns were fired, and their echoes rolled for many a mile among the low, purple hills, from which a soft, fragrant scent of pines was borne to us on

19

the evening breeze, reminding me of the far-distant mountains of Scotland. The tiny waves rippled towards us like diamonds, the moon and stars shone brilliantly from a summer sky, and the white smoke from our guns floated away in silver clouds.

People were tumbling over each other in their haste, and making impossible demands, each one being anxious to have his luggage produced first, though the said luggage might be at the bottom of the hold; babies, as babies always do, persisted in crying just at the wrong time; articles essential to the toilet were missing, and sixpences or half-sovereigns had found their way into impossible crevices. Invitations were given, cards exchanged, elderly ladies unthinkingly promised to make errant expeditions to visit agreeable acquaintances in California, and by the time the last words had been spoken we were safely moored at Cunard's wharf.

The evening gun boomed from the citadel. I heard the well-known British bugle; I saw the familiar scarlet of our troops; the voices which vociferated were English; the physiognomies had the Anglo-Saxon cast and complexion; and on the shores of the western hemisphere I felt myself at home. Yet, as I sprang from the boat, and set my foot for the first time on American soil, I was vexed that these familiar sights and sounds should deprive me of the pleasurable feeling of excitement which I had expected to experience under such novel circumstances.

CHAPTER II

An inhospitable reception—Halifax and the Blue Noses—The heat—Disappointed expectations—The great departed—What the Blue Noses might be—What the coach was not—Nova Scotia and its capabilities—The reads and their annoyances— A tea dinner—A night journey and a Highland cabin—A nautical catastrophe—A joyful reunion.

The Cunard steamers are powerful, punctual, and safe, their *cuisine* excellent, their arrangements admirable, till they reach Halifax, which is usually the destination of many of the passengers. I will suppose that the voyage has been propitious, and our guns have thundered forth the announcement that the news of the Old World has reached the New; that the stewards have been *fee'd* and the captain complimented; and that we have parted on the best possible terms with the Company, the ship, and our fellow-passengers. The steamer generally remains for two or three hours at Halifax to coal, and unship a portion of her cargo, and there is a very natural desire on the part of the passengers to leave what to many is at best a floating prison, and set foot on firm ground, even for an hour. Those who, like ourselves, land at Halifax for the interior, are anxious to obtain rooms at the hotel, and all who have nothing else to do hurry to the ice-shop, where the luxury of a tumbler of raspberry-cream ice can be obtained for threepence. Besides the hurried rush of those who with these varied objects in view leave the steamer, there are crowds of incomers in the shape of porters, visitors, and coalheavers, and passengers for the States, who prefer the comfort and known punctuality of the Royal Mail steamers to the delay, danger, and uncertainty of the intercolonial route, though the expense of the former is nearly double. There are the friends of the passengers, and numbers of persons who seem particularly well acquainted with the purser, who bring fruits, vegetables, meat, poultry, and lobsters.

From this description it may be imagined that there is a motley and considerable crowd; but it will scarcely be imagined that there is only one regulation, which is, that no persons may enter or depart till the mail-bags have been landed. The wharf is small and at night unlighted, and the scene which ensued on our landing about eight o'clock in the evening reminded me, not by contrast, but resemblance, of descriptions which travellers give of the disembarkation at Alexandria. Directly that the board was laid from the *Canada* to the wharf a rush both in and out took place, in which I was separated from my relations, and should have fallen had not a friend, used to the scene of disorder, come to my assistance.

The wharf was dirty, unlighted, and under repair, covered with heaps and full of holes. My friend was carrying three parcels, when three or four men made a rush at us, seized them from him, and were only compelled to relinquish them by some sharp physical arguments. A large gateway, lighted by one feeble oil-lamp at the head of the wharf, was then opened, and the crowd pent up behind it came pouring down the sloping road. There was a simultaneous rush of trucks, hand-carts, waggons, and cars, their horses at full trot or canter, two of them rushing against the gravel-heap on which I was standing, where they were upset. Struggling, shouting, beating, and scuffling, the drivers all forced their way upon the wharf, regardless of cries from the ladies and threats from the gentlemen, for all the passengers had landed and were fighting their way to an ice-shop. Porters were scuffling with each other for the possession of portmanteaus, wheels were locked, and drivers were vehemently expostulating in the rich brogue of Erin; people were jostling each other in their haste, or diving into the dimly-lighted custom-house, and it must have been fully half an hour before we had extricated ourselves from this chaos of mismanagement and disorder, by scrambling over gravel-heaps and piles of timber, into the dirty, unlighted streets of Halifax.

Dirty they were then, though the weather was very dry, for oyster-shells, fish heads and bones, potato-skins, and cabbage-stalks littered the roads; but *dirty* was a word which does not give the faintest description of the almost impassable state in which I found them, when I waded through them ankle-deep in mud some months afterwards.

We took apartments for two days at the Waverley House, a most comfortless place, yet the best inn at Halifax. Three hours after we landed, the *Canada* fired her guns, and steamed off to Boston; and as I saw her coloured lights disappear round the heads of the harbour, I did not feel the slightest regret at having taken leave of her for ever.

We remained for two days at Halifax, and saw the little which was worth seeing in the Nova-Scotian capital. I was disappointed to find the description of the lassitude and want of enterprise of the Nova-Scotians, given by Judge Halliburton, so painfully correct. Halifax possesses one of the deepest and most commodious harbours in the world, and is so safe that ships need no other guide into it than their charts. There are several small fortified islands at its mouth, which assist in its defence without impeding the navigation. These formidable forts protect the entrance, and defend the largest naval depôt which we possess in North America. The town itself, which contains about 25,000 people, is on a small peninsula, and stands on a slope rising from the water's edge to the citadel, which is heavily armed, and amply sufficient for every purpose of defence. There are very great natural advantages in the neighbourhood, lime, coal, slate, and minerals being abundant, added to which Halifax is the nearest port to Europe.

Yet it must be confessed that the Nova-Scotians are far behind, not only their neighbours in the States, but their fellow-subjects in Canada and New Brunswick. There are capacious wharfs and roomy warehouses, yet one laments over the absence of everything like trade and business. With the finest harbour in North America, with a country abounding in minerals, and coasts swarming with fish, the Nova-Scotians appear to have expunged the word *progress* from their dictionary—still live in shingle houses, in streets without side-walks, rear long-legged ponies, and talk largely about railroads, which they seem as if they would never complete, because they trust more to the House of Assembly than to their own energies. Consequently their astute and enterprising neighbours the Yankees, the acute speculators of Massachusetts and Connecticut, have seized upon the traffic which they have allowed to escape them, and have diverted it to the thriving town of Portland in Maine. The day after we landed was one of intense heat, the thermometer stood at 93° in the shade. The rays of a summer sun scorched the shingle roof of our hotel, and, penetrating the thin plank walls, made the interior of the house perfectly unbearable. There were neither sunshades nor Venetian blinds, and not a tree to shade the square white wooden house from an almost tropical heat. When I came into the parlour I found Colonel H— stretched on the sofa, almost expiring with heat, my cousin standing panting before the window in his shirt-sleeves, and his little boy lying moaning on the hearth-rug, with his shoes off, and his complexion like that of a Red Indian. One of our party had been promenading the broiling streets of Halifax without his coat! A gentleman from one of the Channel Islands, of unsophisticated manners and excellent disposition, who had landed with us *en route* to a town on the Gulf of St. Lawrence, had fancied our North American colonies for ever "locked in regions of thick-ribbed ice," and consequently was abundantly provided with warm clothing of every description. With this he was prepared to face a thermometer at twenty degrees below zero.

But when he found a torrid sun, and the thermometer at 93° in the shade, his courage failed him, and, with all his preconceived ideas overthrown by the burning experience of one day, despair seized on him, and his expressions of horror and astonishment were coupled with lamentations over the green fertility of Jersey. The colonel was obliged to report himself at head-quarters in his full uniform, which was evidently tight and hot; and after changing his apparel three times in the day, apparently without being a gainer, he went out to make certain meteorological inquiries, among others if 93° were a common temperature.

The conclusion he arrived at was, that the "climate alternates between the heat of India and the cold of Lapland."

We braved the heat at noonday in a stroll through the town, for, from the perfect dryness of the atmosphere, it is not of an oppressive nature. I saw few whites in the streets at this hour. There were a great many Indians lying by the door-steps, having disposed of their baskets, besoms, and raspberries, by the sale of which they make a scanty livelihood. The men, with their jet-black hair, rich complexions, and dark liquid brown eyes, were almost invariably handsome; and the women, whose beauty departs before they are twenty, were something in the "*Meg Merrilies*" style.

When the French first colonised this country, they called it "*Acadie*." The tribes of the Mic-Mac Indians peopled its forests, and, among the dark woods which then surrounded Halifax, they worshipped the Great Spirit, and hunted the moose-deer. Their birch-bark wigwams peeped from among the trees, their squaws urged their light canoes over the broad deep harbour, and their wise men spoke to them of the "happy hunting-grounds." The French destroyed them not, and gave them a corrupted form of Christianity, inciting their passions against the English by telling them that they were the people who had crucified the Saviour. Better had it been for them if battle or pestilence had swept them at once away.

The Mic-Macs were a fierce and warlike people, too proud to mingle with an alien race—too restless and active to conform to the settled habits of civilization. Too proud to avail themselves of its advantages, they learned its vices, and, as the snow-wreaths in spring, they melted away before the poisonous "fire-water," and the deadly curse of the white man's wars. They

25

had welcomed the "pale faces" to the "land of the setting sun," and withered up before them, smitten by their crimes.

Almost destitute of tradition, their history involved in obscurity, their broad lands filled with their unknown and nameless graves, these mighty races have passed away; they could not pass into slavery, therefore they must die.

At some future day a mighty voice may ask of those who have thus wronged the Indian, "Where is now thy brother?" It is true that frequently *we* arrived too late to save them as a race from degradation and dispersion; but as they heavily tottered along to their last home, under the burden of the woes which contact with civilization ever entails upon the aborigines, we might have spoken to them the tidings of "peace on earth and good will to men"—of a Saviour "who hath abolished death, and hath brought life and immortality to light through his gospel."

Far away amid the thunders of Niagara, surrounded by a perpetual rainbow, Iris Island contains almost the only known burying-place of the race of red men. Probably the simple Indians who buried their dead in a place of such difficult access, and sacred to the Great Spirit, did so from a wish that none might ever disturb their ashes. None can tell how long those interred there have slept their last long sleep, but the ruthless hands of the white men have profaned the last resting-place of the departed race.

There were also numerous blacks in the streets, and, if I might judge from the brilliant colours and good quality of their clothing, they must gain a pretty good living by their industry. A large number of these blacks and their parents were carried away from the States by one of our admirals in the war of 1812, and landed at Halifax.

The capital of Nova Scotia looks like a town of cards, nearly all the buildings being of wood. There are wooden houses, wooden churches, wooden wharfs, wooden slates, and, if there are side-walks, they are of wood also. I was pleased at a distance with the appearance of two churches, one of them a

Gothic edifice, but on nearer inspection I found them to be of wood, and took refuge in the substantial masonry of the really handsome Province Building and Government House. We went up to the citadel, which crowns the hill, and is composed of an agglomeration of granite walls, fosses, and casemates, mounds, ditches, barracks, and water-tanks.

If I was pleased with the familiar uniforms of the artillery-men who lounged about the barracks, I was far more so with the view from the citadel. It was a soft summer evening, and, seen through the transparent atmosphere, everything looked unnaturally near. The large town of Halifax sloped down to a lake-like harbour, about two miles wide, dotted with islands; and ranges of picturesque country spangled with white cottages lay on the other side. The lake or firth reminded me of the Gareloch, and boats were sailing about in all directions before the evening breeze. From tangled coppices of birch and fir proceeded the tinkle of the bells of numerous cows, and, mingled with the hum of the city, the strains of a military band rose from the streets to our ears.

With so many natural advantages, and such capabilities for improvement, I cannot but regret the unhappy quarrels and maladministration which threaten to leave the noble colony of Nova Scotia an incubus and excrescence on her flourishing and progressive neighbours, Canada and New Brunswick. From the *talk* about railways, steamers, and the House of Assembly, it is pleasant to turn to the one thing which has been really done, namely, the establishment of an electric telegraph line to St. John, and thence to the States. By means of this system of wires, which is rough and inexpensive to a degree which in England we should scarcely believe, the news brought by the English mail steamer is known at Boston, New York, New Orleans, Cincinnati, and all the great American cities, before it has had time to reach the environs of Halifax itself.

The telegraph costs about £20 per mile, and the wires are generally supported on the undressed stems of pines, but are often carried from tree to tree along miserable roads, or through the deep recesses of the forests.

The stores in Halifax are pretty good, all manufactured articles being sold at an advance on English prices. Books alone are cheap and abundant, being the American editions of pirated English works.

On the morning when we left Halifax I was awakened by the roll of the British drum and the stirring strains of the Highland bagpipe. Ready equipped for the tedious journey before us, from Halifax to Pictou in the north of the colony, I was at the inn-door at six, watching the fruitless attempts of the men to pile our mountain of luggage on the coach.

Do not let the word *coach* conjure up a vision of "*the good old times*," a dashing mail with a well-groomed team of active bays, harness all "spick and span," a gentlemanly-looking coachman, and a guard in military scarlet, the whole affair rattling along the road at a pace of ten miles an hour.

The vehicle in which we performed a journey of 120 miles in 20 hours deserves a description. It consisted of a huge coach-body, slung upon two thick leather straps; the sides were open, and the places where windows ought to have been were screened by heavy curtains of tarnished moose-deer hide. Inside were four cross-seats, intended to accommodate twelve persons, who were very imperfectly sheltered from the weather. Behind was a large rack for luggage, and at the back of the driving-seat was a bench which held three persons. The stage was painted scarlet, but looked as if it had not been washed for a year. The team of six strong white horses was driven by a Yankee, remarkable only for his silence. About a ton of luggage was packed on and behind the stage, and two open portmanteaus were left behind without the slightest risk to their contents.

Twelve people and a baby were with some difficulty stowed in the stage, and the few interstices were filled up with baskets, bundles, and packages. The coachman whipped his horses, and we rattled down the uneven streets of Halifax to a steam ferry-boat, which conveyed the stage across to Dartmouth, and was so well arranged that the six horses had not to alter their positions.

Our road lay for many miles over a barren, rocky, undulating country, covered with var and spruce trees, with an undergrowth of raspberry, wild rhododendron, and alder. We passed a chain of lakes extending for sixteen miles, their length varying from one to three miles, and their shores covered with forests of gloomy pine. People are very apt to say that Nova Scotia is sterile and barren, because they have not penetrated into the interior. It is certainly rather difficult of access, but I was by no means sorry that my route lay through it. The coast of Nova Scotia is barren, and bears a very distinct resemblance to the east of Scotland. The climate, though severe in winter and very foggy, is favourable both to health and vegetation. The peach and grape ripen in the open air, and the cultivation of corn and potatoes amply repays the cultivator. A great part of the country is still covered with wood, evidently a second growth, for, wherever the trees of the fir tribe are cut down or destroyed by fire, hard-wood trees spring up.

So among the maple, the American elm, and the purple-blossomed sumach, the huge scorched and leafless stems of pines would throw up their giant arms as if to tell of some former conflagration. In clearings among these woods, slopes of ground are to be seen covered with crops of oats and maize, varied with potatoes and pumpkins. Wherever the ground is unusually poor on the surface, mineral treasures abound. There are beds of coal of vast thickness; iron in various forms is in profusion, and the supply of gypsum is inexhaustible. Many parts of the country are very suitable for cattle-rearing, and there are "water privileges" without end in the shape of numerous rivers. I have seldom seen finer country in the colonies than the large tract of cleared undulating land about Truro, and I am told that it is far exceeded by that in the neighbourhood of Windsor. Wherever apple-trees were planted they seemed to flourish, and the size and flavour of their fruit evidences a short, hot summer. While the interior of the country is so fertile, and is susceptible of a high degree of improvement, it is scarcely fair in the Nova-Scotians to account for their backwardness by pointing strangers to their sterile and iron-bound coast. But they are a moral, hardy, and loyal people; none of our colonial fellow-subjects are more attached to the British crown, or more ready to take up arms in its defence.

I was greatly pleased with much that I heard, and with the little I saw of the Nova-Scotians. They seemed temperate, sturdy, and independent, and the specimens we had of them in the stage were civil, agreeable, and intelligent.

After passing the pretty little village of Dartmouth, we came upon some wigwams of birch-bark among the trees. Some squaws, with papooses strapped upon their backs, stared vacantly at us as we passed, and one little barefooted Indian, with a lack of apparel which showed his finely moulded form to the best advantage, ran by the side of the coach for two or three miles, bribed by coppers which were occasionally thrown to him.

A dreary stage of eighteen miles brought us to Shultze's, a road-side inn by a very pretty lake, where we were told the *"coach breakfasted."* Whether Transatlantic coaches can perform this, to us, unknown feat, I cannot pretend to say, but *we* breakfasted. A very coarse repast was prepared for us, consisting of stewed salt veal, country cheese, rancid salt butter, fried eggs, and barley bread; but we were too hungry to find fault either with it, or with the charge made for it, which equalled that at a London hotel. Our Yankee coachman, a man of monosyllables, sat next to me, and I was pleased to see that he regaled himself on tea instead of spirits.

We packed ourselves into the stage again with great difficulty, and how the forty-eight limbs fared was shown by the painful sensations experienced for several succeeding days. All the passengers, however, were in perfectly good humour, and amused each other during the eleven hours spent in this painful way. At an average speed of six miles an hour we travelled over roads of various descriptions, plank, corduroy, and sand; up long heavy hills, and through swamps swarming with mosquitoes.

Everyone has heard of corduroy roads, but how few have experienced their miseries! They are generally used for traversing swampy ground, and are formed of small pine-trees deprived of their branches, which are laid across the track alongside each other. The wear and tear of travelling soon separates these, leaving gaps between; and when, added to this, one trunk rots away, and another sinks down into the swamp, and another tilts up, you may imagine such a jolting as only leather springs could bear. On the very worst roads, filled with deep holes, or covered with small granite boulders, the stage only swings on the straps. Ordinary springs, besides dislocating the joints of the passengers, would be wrenched and broken after a few miles travelling.

Even as we were, faces sometimes came into rather close proximity to each other and to the side railings, and heads sustained very unpleasant collisions. The amiable man who was so disappointed with the American climate suffered very much from the journey. He said he had thought a French diligence the climax of discomfort, but a "stage was misery, oh torture!" Each time that we had rather a worse jolt than usual the poor man groaned, which always drew forth a chorus of laughter, to which he submitted most good-humouredly. Occasionally he would ask the time, when someone would point maliciously to his watch, remarking, "Twelve hours more," or "Fifteen hours more," when he would look up with an expression of despair. The bridges wore a very un-English feature. Over the small streams or brooks they consisted of three pines covered with planks, without any parapet—with sometimes a plank out, and sometimes a hole in the middle. Over large streams they were wooden erections of a most peculiar kind, with high parapets; their insecurity being evidenced by the notice, "Walk your horses, according to law,"—a notice generally disregarded by our coachman, as he trotted his horses over the shaking and rattling fabric.

We passed several small streams, and one of a large size, the Shubenacadie, a wide, slow, muddy river, flowing through willows and hedges, like the rivers in the fen districts of England. At the mouth of the Shubenacadie the tides rise and fall forty feet.

In Nova Scotia the animals seemed to be more carefully lodged than the people. Wherever we changed horses, we drove into a lofty shed, opening into a large stable with a boarded floor scrupulously clean, generally containing twenty horses. The rigour of the climate in winter necessitates such careful provision for the support of animal life. The coachman went into the stable and chose his team, which was brought out, and then a scene of kicking, biting, and screaming ensued, ended by the most furious kickers being put to the wheel; and after a certain amount of talking, and settling the mail-bags, the ponderous vehicle moved off again, the leaders always rearing for the first few yards.

For sixty miles we were passing through woods, the trees sometimes burned and charred for several miles, and the ground all blackened round them. We saw very few clearings, and those there were consisted merely of a few acres of land, separated from the forest by rude "snake-fences." Stumps of trees blackened by fire stood up among the oat-crops; but though they look extremely untidy, they are an unavoidable evil for two or three years, till the large roots decay.

Eleven hours passed by not at all wearisomely to me, though my cousins and their children suffered much from cramp and fatigue, and at five, after an ascent of three hours, we began to descend towards a large tract of cultivated undulating country, in the centre of which is situated a large settlement called Truro. There, at a wretched hostelry, we stopped to dine, but the meal by no means answered to our English ideas of dinner. A cup of tea was placed by each plate; and after the company, principally consisting of agricultural settlers, had made a substantial meal of mutton, and the potatoes for which the country is famous, they solaced themselves with this beverage. No intoxicating liquor was placed upon the table,[1] and I observed the same temperate habits at the inns in New Brunswick, the city of St. John not excepted. It was a great pleasure to me to find that the intemperance so notoriously prevalent among a similar class in England was so completely discouraged in Nova Scotia. The tea was not tempting to an English palate; it was stewed, and sweetened with molasses.

While we were waiting for a fresh stage and horses, several waggons came up, laden with lawyers, storekeepers, and ship-carpenters, who with their families were flying from the cholera at St. John, New Brunswick.

I enjoyed the next fifty miles exceedingly, as I travelled outside on the driving-seat, with plenty of room to expatiate. The coachman was a very intelligent settler, pressed into the service, because Jengro, the French Canadian driver, had indulged in a fit of intoxication in opposition to a temperance meeting held at Truro the evening before.

Our driver had not tasted spirits for thirty years, and finds that a cup of hot tea at the end of a cold journey is a better stimulant than a glass of grog.

It was just six o'clock when we left Truro; the shades of evening were closing round us, and our road lay over fifty miles of nearly uninhabited country; but there was so much to learn and hear, that we kept up an animated and unflagging conversation hour after hour. The last cleared land was passed by seven, and we entered the forest, beginning a long and tedious ascent of eight miles. At a post-house in the wood we changed horses, and put on some lanterns, not for the purpose of assisting ourselves, but to guide the boy-driver of a waggon or "extra," who, having the responsibility of conducting four

1 I write merely of what fell under my own observation, for there has been so much spirit-drinking in Nova Scotia, that the legislature has deemed it expedient to introduce the "Maine Law," with its stringent and somewhat arbitrary provisions.

horses, came clattering close behind us. The road was hilly, and often ran along the very edge of steep declivities, and our driver, who did not know it well, and was besides a cautious man, drove at a most moderate pace.

Not so the youthful Jehu of the light vehicle behind. He came desperately on, cracking his whip, shouting "G'lang, Gee'p," rattling down hill, and galloping up, and whirling round corners, in spite of the warning "Steady, whoa!" addressed to him by our careful escort. Once the rattling behind entirely ceased, and we stopped, our driver being anxious for the safety of his own team, as well as for the nine passengers who were committed on a dark night to the care of a boy of thirteen. The waggon soon came clattering on again, and remained in disagreeably close proximity to us till we arrived at Pictou.

At ten o'clock, after another long ascent, we stopped to water the horses, and get some refreshment, at a shanty kept by an old Highland woman, well known as "*Nancy Stuart of the Mountain.*" Here two or three of us got off, and a comfortable meal was soon provided, consisting of tea, milk, oat-cake, butter, and cranberry and raspberry jam. This meal we shared with some handsome, gloomy-looking, bonneted Highlanders, and some large ugly dogs. The room was picturesque enough, with blackened rafters, deer and cow horns hung round it, and a cheerful log fire. After tea I spoke to Nancy in her native tongue, which so delighted her, that I could not induce her to accept anything for my meal. On finding that I knew her birthplace in the Highlands, she became quite talkative, and on wishing her good bye with the words "*Oiche mhaith dhuibh; Beannachd luibh!*"[1] she gave my hand a true Highland grasp with both of hers; a grasp bringing back visions of home and friends, and "the bonnie North countrie."

A wild drive we had from this place to Pictou. The road lay through forests which might have been sown at the beginning

1 Good night; blessings be with you.

of time. Huge hemlocks threw high their giant arms, and from between their dark stems gleamed the bark of the silver birch. Elm, beech, and maple flourished; I missed alone the oak of England. The solemn silence of these pathless roads was broken only by the note of the distant bull-frog; meteors fell in streams of fire, the crescent moon occasionally gleamed behind clouds from which the lightning flashed almost continually, and the absence of any familiar faces made me realize at length that I was a stranger in a strange land.

After the subject of the colony had been exhausted, I amused the coachman with anecdotes of the supernatural—stories of ghosts, wraiths, apparitions, and second sight; but he professed himself a disbeliever, and I thought I had failed to make any impression on him, till at last he started at the crackling of a twig, and the gleaming whiteness of a silver birch. He would have liked the stories better, he confessed at length, if the night had not been quite so dark.

The silence of the forest was so solemn, that, remembering the last of the Mohicans, we should not have been the least surprised if an Indian war-whoop had burst upon our startled ears.

We were travelling over the possessions of the Red men.

Nothing more formidable occurred than the finding of three tipsy men laid upon the road; and our coachman had to alight and remove them before the vehicle could proceed.

We reached Pictou at a quarter past two on a very chilly starlight morning, and by means of the rude telegraph, which runs along the road, comfortable rooms had been taken for us at an inn of average cleanliness.

Here we met with a storekeeper from Prince Edward Island, and he told us that the parents of my cousins, whom we were about to visit, knew nothing whatever of our intended arrival, and supposed their children to be in Germany.

As a colonial dinner is an aggregate of dinner and tea, so a colonial breakfast is a curious complication of breakfast and dinner, combining, I think, the advantages of both. It is only an extension of the Highland breakfast; fish of several sorts, meat, eggs, and potatoes, buckwheat fritters and Johnny cake, being served with the tea and coffee.

Pictou may be a flourishing town some day: it has extensive coal mines; one seam of coal is said to be thirty feet thick. At present it is a most insignificant place, and the water of the harbour is very shallow. The distance from Pictou to Charlotte Town, Prince Edward Island, is sixty miles, and by this route, through Nova Scotia and across Northumberland Strait, the English mail is transmitted once a fortnight.

A fearful catastrophe happened to the *Fairy Queen*, a small mail steamer plying between these ports, not long ago. By some carelessness, she sprang a leak and sank; the captain and crew escaping to Pictou in the ship's boats, which were large enough to have saved all the passengers. Here they arrived, and related the story of the wreck, in the hope that no human voice would ever tell of their barbarity and cowardice. Several perished with the ill-fated vessel, among whom were Dr. Mackenzie, a promising young officer, and two young ladies, one of whom was coming to England to the married. A few of the passengers floated off on the upper deck and reached the land in safety, to bear a terrible testimony to the inhumanity which had left their companions to perish. A voice from the dead could not have struck greater horror into the heart of the craven captain than did that of those whom he never expected to meet till the sea should give up her dead. The captain was committed for manslaughter, but escaped the punishment due to his offence, though popular indignation was strongly excited against him. We were told to be on board the *Lady le Marchant* by twelve o'clock, and endured four hours' detention on her broiling deck, without any more substantial sustenance than was afforded to us by some pine-apples. We were five hours in crossing Northumberland Strait—five hours of the greatest possible discomfort. We had a head-wind and a rough chopping sea, which caused the little steamer to pitch unmercifully. After gaining a distant view of Cape Breton

Island, I lay down on a mattress on deck, in spite of the persecutions of an animated friend, who kindly endeavoured to rouse me to take a first view of Prince Edward Island.

When at last, in the comparative calmness of the entrance to Charlotte Town harbour, I stood up to look about me, I could not help admiring the peaceful beauty of the scene. Far in the distance were the sterile cliffs of Nova Scotia and the tumbling surges of the Atlantic, while on three sides we were surrounded by land so low that the trees upon it seemed almost growing out of the water. The soil was the rich red of Devonshire, the trees were of a brilliant green, and sylvan lawns ran up amongst them. The light canoes of the aborigines glided gracefully on the water, or lay high and dry on the beach; and two or three miles ahead the spires and houses of the capital of the island lent additional cheerfulness to the prospect.

We were speedily moored at the wharf, and my cousins, after an absence of eight years, were anxiously looking round for some familiar faces among the throng on the shore. They had purposely avoided giving any intimation to their parents of their intended arrival, lest anything should occur to prevent the visit; therefore they were entirely unexpected. But, led by the true instinct of natural affection, they were speedily recognised by those of their relatives who were on the wharf, and many a joyful meeting followed which must amply have compensated for the dreary separation of years.

It was in an old-English looking, red brick mansion, encircled by plantations of thriving firs—warmly welcomed by relations whom I had never seen, for the sake of those who had been my long-tried friends—surrounded by hearts rejoicing in the blessings of unexpected re-union, and by faces radiant with affection and happiness—that I spent my first evening in the "Garden of British America."

CHAPTER III

Popular ignorance—The garden island—Summer and winter contrasted—A wooden capital—Island politics, and their consequences—Gossip—"Blowin-time"—Religion and the clergy—The servant nuisance—Colonial society—An evening party—An island premier—Agrarian outrage—A visit to the Indians—The pipe of peace—An Indian coquette—Country hospitality—A missionary—A novel mode of lobster-fishing— Uncivilised life—Far away in the woods—Starvation and dishonesty—An old Highlander and a Highland welcome— Hopes for the future.

I was showing a collection of autographs to a gentleman at a party in a well-known Canadian city, when the volume opened upon the majestic signature of Cromwell. I paused as I pointed to it, expecting a burst of enthusiasm. *"Who is Cromwell?"* he asked; an ignorance which I should have believed counterfeit had it not been too painfully and obviously genuine.

A yeoman friend in England, on being told that I had arrived safely at Boston, after encountering great danger in a gale, *"reckoned that it was somewhere down in Lincolnshire."*

With these instances of ignorance, and many more which I could name, fresh in my recollection, I am not at all surprised that few persons should be acquainted with the locality of a spot of earth so comparatively obscure as Prince Edward Island. When I named my destination to my friends prior to my departure from England, it was supposed by some that I was going to the Pacific, and by others that I was going to the north-west coast of America, while one or two, on consulting their maps, found no such island indicated in the part of the ocean where I described it to be placed.

Now, Prince Edward Island is the abode of seventy thousand human beings. It *had* a garrison, though now the loyalty of its inhabitants is considered a sufficient protection. It *has* a Governor, a House of Assembly, a Legislative Council, and a

Constitution. It has a wooden Government House, and a stone Province Building. It has a town of six thousand people, and an extensive shipbuilding trade, and, lastly, it has a prime minister. As it has not been tourist-ridden, like Canada or the States, and is a *terra incognita* to many who are tolerably familiar with the rest of our North American possessions, I must briefly describe it, though I am neither writing a guide-book nor an emigrant's directory.

This island was discovered by Sebastian Cabot in 1497, and more than two centuries afterwards received the name of St. John, by which it is still designated in old maps. It received the name of Prince Edward Island in compliment to the illustrious father of our Queen, who bestowed great attention upon it. It has been the arena of numerous conflicts during the endless wars between the French and English. Its aboriginal inhabitants have here, as in other places, melted away before the whites. About three hundred remain, earning a scanty living by shooting and fishing, and profess the Romish faith.

This island is 140 miles in length, and at its widest part 34 in breadth. It is intersected by creeks; every part of its coast is indented by the fierce flood of the Gulf of St. Lawrence, and no part of it is more than nine miles distant from some arm of the sea. It bears the name throughout the British provinces of the "Garden of British America." That this title has been justly bestowed, none who have ever visited it in summer will deny.

While Nova Scotia, New Brunswick, and the banks of the St. Lawrence are brown, even where most fertile, this island is clothed in brilliant green. I suppose that the most elevated land in it is less than 400 feet above the level of the sea; there is not a rock in any part of it, and the stones which may be very occasionally picked up in the recesses of the forest cause much speculation in the minds of the curious and scientific. The features of this country are as soft as the soil. The land is everywhere gently undulating, and, while anything like a hill is unknown, it has been difficult to find a piece of ground sufficiently level for a cricket-field. The north shore is extremely pretty; it has small villages, green clearings, fine harbours, with the trees growing down to the water's edge, and shady streams.

The land is very suitable for agricultural purposes, as also for the rearing of sheep; but the island is totally destitute of mineral wealth. It is highly favoured in climate. The intense heat of a North American summer is here tempered by a cool sea-breeze; fogs are almost unknown, and the air is dry and bracing. Instances of longevity are very common; fever and consumption are seldom met with, and the cholera has never visited its shores. Wages are high, and employment abundant; land is cheap and tolerably productive; but though a competence may always be obtained, I never heard of anyone becoming rich through agricultural pursuits. Shipbuilding is the great trade of the island, and the most profitable one. Everywhere, even twenty miles inland, and up among the woods, ships may be seen in course of construction. These vessels are sold in England and in the neighbouring colonies; but year by year, as its trade increases, the island requires a greater number for its own use.

In summer, the island is a very agreeable residence; the sandy roads are passable, and it has a bi-weekly communication with the neighbouring continent. Shooting and fishing may be enjoyed in abundance, and the Indians are always ready to lend assistance in these sports. Bears, which used to be a great attraction to the more adventurous class of sportsmen, are, however, rapidly disappearing.

In winter, I cannot conceive a more dull, cheerless, and desolate place than Prince Edward Island. About the beginning of December steam communication with the continent ceases, and those who are leaving the island hurry their departure. Large stocks of fuel are laid in, the harbour is deserted by the shipping, and all out-door occupations gradually cease. Before Christmas the frost commences, the snow frequently lies six feet deep, and soon the harbours and the adjacent ocean freeze, and the island is literally "locked in regions of thick-ribbed ice" for six long months. Once a fortnight during the winter an ice-boat crosses Northumberland Strait, at great hazard, where it is only nine miles wide, conveying the English mail; but sometimes all the circumstances are not favourable, and the letters are delayed for a month—the poor islanders being locked meanwhile in their icebound prison, ignorant of the events which may be convulsing the world. Charlotte Town, the capital of the island and the seat of government, is very prettily situated on a capacious harbour, which *was* defended by several heavy guns. It is a town of shingles, but looks very well from the sea. With the exception of Quebec, it is considered the prettiest town in British America; but while Quebec is a city built on a rock, Charlotte Town closely borders upon a marsh, and its drainage has been very much neglected.

There are several commons in the town, the grass of which is of a peculiarly brilliant green, and, as these are surrounded by houses, they give it a cheerful appearance. The houses are small, and the stores by no means pretentious. The streets are unlighted, and destitute of side-walks; there is not an attempt at paving, and the grips across them are something fearful. "Hold on" is a caution as frequently given as absolutely necessary. I have travelled over miles of corduroy road in a springless waggon, and in a lumber waggon, drawn by oxen, where there was no road at all, but I never experienced anything like the merciless joint-dislocating jolting which I met with in Charlotte Town. This island metropolis has two or three weekly papers of opposite sides in politics, which vie with each other in gross personalities and scurrilous abuse.

The colony has "responsible government," a Governor, a Legislative Council, and a House of Assembly, and storms in politics are not at all unfrequent. The members of the Lower House are elected by nearly universal suffrage, and it is considered necessary that the "Premier" should have a majority in it. This House is said to be on a par with Irish poor-law guardian meetings for low personalities and vehement vituperation.

41

The genius of Discord must look complacently on this land. Politics have been a fruitful source of quarrels, mis-representation, alienation, and division. The opposition parties are locally designated "*snatchers*" and "*snarlers*," and no love is lost between the two. It is broadly affirmed that half the people on the island do not speak to the other half. And, worse than all, religious differences have been brought up as engines wherewith to wreak political animosities. I never saw a community in which people appeared to hate each other so cordially. The flimsy veil of etiquette does not conceal the pointed sneer, the malicious inuendo, the malignant back-biting, and the unfounded slander. Some of the forms of society are observed in the island—that extreme of civilisation vulgarly called "*cutting*" is common; morning calls are punctiliously paid and returned, and there are occasional balls and tea-parties. Quebec is described as being the hottest and coldest town in the world, Paris the gayest, London the richest; but I should think that Charlotte Town may bear away the palm for being the most gossiping.

There is a general and daily flitting about of its inhabitants after news of their neighbours—all that is said and done within a three-mile circle is reported, and, of course, a great deal of what has neither been said nor done. There are certain people whose business it is to make mischief, and mischief-making is a calling in which it does not require much wit to be successful.

The inhabitants are a sturdy race, more than one-half of them being of Scotch descent. They are prevented from attaining settled business-like habits by the long winter, which puts a stop to all out-door employment. This period, when amusement is the only thing thought of, is called in the colonies "blowin-time." All the country is covered with snow, and the inhabitants have nothing to do but sleigh about, play ball on the ice, drive the young ladies to quilting frolics and snow picnics, drink brandy-and-water, and play at whist for sixpenny points.

The further you go from Charlotte Town, the more primitive and hospitable the people become; they warmly welcome a stranger, and seem happy, moral, and contented. This island is the only place in the New World where I met with any who believed in the supernatural. One evening I had been telling some very harmless ghost stories to a party by moonlight, and one of my auditors, a very clever girl, fancied during the night that she saw something stirring in her bedroom. In the idea that the ghost would attack her head rather than her feet, she tied up her feet in her *bonnet-de-nuit*, put them upon the pillow, and her head under the quilt—a novel way of cheating a spiritual visitant.

There are numerous religious denominations in the colony, all enjoying the same privileges, or the absence of any. I am not acquainted with the number belonging to each, but would suppose the Roman Catholics to be the most dominant, from the way in which their church towers over the whole town. There are about eleven Episcopalian clergymen, overworked and underpaid. Most of these are under the entire control of the Bishop of Nova Scotia, and are removable at his will and pleasure. This *will* Bishop Binney exercises in a very capricious and arbitrary manner.

Some of these clergymen are very excellent and laborious men. I may particularise Dr. Jenkins, for many years chief minister of Charlotte Town, whose piety, learning, and Christian spirit would render him an ornament to the Church of England in any locality. Even among the clergy, some things might seem rather peculiar to a person fresh from England. A clergyman coming to a pause in his sermon, one of his auditors from the floor called up "Propitiation;" the preacher thanked him, took the word, and went on with his discourse.

The difficulty of procuring servants, which is felt from the Government House downwards, is one of the great objections to this colony. The few there are know nothing of any individual department of work,—for instance, there are neither cooks nor housemaids, they are strictly "*helps*,"—the mistress being expected to take more than her fair share of the work. They come in and go out when they please, and, if anything dissatisfies them, they ask for their wages, and depart the same day, in the certainty that their labour will command a higher price in the United States. It is not an uncommon thing for a gentleman to be obliged to do the work of gardener, errand-boy, and groom. A servant left at an hour's notice, saying, "she had never been so insulted before," because her master requested her to put on shoes when she waited at table; and a gentleman was obliged to lie in bed because his servant had taken all his shirts to the wash, and had left them while she went to a "frolic" with her lover.

The upper class of society in the island is rather exclusive, but it is difficult to say what qualification entitles a man to be received into "society." The *entrée* at Government House is not sufficient; but a uniform is powerful, and wealth is omnipotent. The present governor, Mr. Dominick Daly, is a man of great suavity of manner. He has a large amount of *finesse*, which is needful in a colony where people like the supposition that they govern themselves, but where it is absolutely necessary that a firm hand should hold the reins. The island is prospering under its new form of "responsible government;" its revenue is increasing; it is out of debt; and Mr. Daly, whose tenure of power has been very short, will without doubt considerably develop its resources. Mrs. Daly is an invalid, but her kindness makes her deservedly popular, together with her amiable and affable daughters, the elder of whom is one of the most beautiful girls whom I saw in the colonies.

I remained six weeks in this island, being detained by the cholera, which was ravaging Canada and the States. I spent the greater part of this time at the house of Captain Swabey, a near relation of my father's, at whose house I received every hospitality and kindness. Captain Swabey is one of the most influential inhabitants of the island, as, since the withdrawal of the troops, the direction of its defences has been intrusted to him, in consideration of his long experience in active service. He served in the land forces which assisted Nelson at the siege of Copenhagen. He afterwards served with distinction through the Peninsular war, and, after receiving a ball in the knee at Vittoria, closed his military career at the battle of Waterloo. It is not a little singular that Mr. Hensley, another of the principal inhabitants, and a near neighbour of Captain Swabey's, fought at Copenhagen under Lord Nelson, where part of his cheek-bone was shot away.

While I was there, the governor gave his first party, to which, as a necessary matter of etiquette, all who had left cards at Government House were invited. I was told that I should not see such a curious mixture anywhere else, either in the States or in the colonies. There were about a hundred and fifty persons present, including all the officers of the garrison and customs, and the members of the government. The "prime minister," the Hon. George Coles, whose name is already well known in the colonies, was there in all the novel glories of office and "red-tapeism."

I cannot say that this gentleman looked at all careworn; indeed the cares of office, even in England, have ceased to be onerous, if one may judge from the ease with which a premier of seventy performs upon the parliamentary stage; but Mr. Coles looked particularly the reverse. He is justified in his complacent appearance, for he has a majority in the house, a requisite scarcely deemed essential in England, and the finances of the colony are flourishing under his administration. He is a self-made and self-educated man, and by his own energy, industry, and perseverance, has raised himself to the position which he now holds; and if his manners have not all the finish of polite society, and if he does sometimes say "Me and the governor," his energy is not less to be admired.

Another member of the government appeared in a yellow waistcoat and brown frock-coat; but where there were a great many persons of an inferior class it was only surprising that there should be so few inaccuracies either in dress or deportment. There were some very pretty women, and almost all were dressed with simplicity and good taste. The island

45

does not afford a band, but a pianist and violinist played most perseveringly, and the amusements were kept up with untiring spirit till four in the morning.

The governor and his family behaved most affably to their guests, and I was glad to observe that in such a very mixed company not the slightest vulgarity of manner was perceptible.

It may be remarked, however, that society is not on so safe a footing as in England. Such things as duels, but of a very bloodless nature, have been known: people occasionally horsewhip and kick each other; and if a gentleman indulges in the pastime of breaking the windows of another gentleman, he receives a bullet for his pains. Some time ago, a gentleman connected with a noble family in Scotland, emigrated to the island with a large number of his countrymen, to whom he promised advantageous arrangements with regard to land. He was known by the name of Tracadie. After his tenants had made a large outlay upon their farms, Tracadie did not fulfil his agreements, and the dissatisfaction soon broke forth into open outrage.

Conspiracies were formed against him, his cows and carts were destroyed, and night after night the country was lighted by the flames of his barns and mills. At length he gave loaded muskets to some of his farm-boys, telling them to shoot any-one they saw upon his premises after dusk. The same evening he went into his orchard, and was standing with his watch in his hand waiting to set it by the evening gun, when the boys fired, and he fell severely wounded. When he recovered from this, he was riding out one evening, when he was shot through the hat and hip by men on each side of the road, and fell weltering in blood. So detested was he, that several persons passed by without rendering him any assistance. At length one of his own tenantry, coming by, took him into Charlotte Town in a cart, but was obliged shortly afterwards to leave the island, to escape from the vengeance which would have overtaken the succourer of a tyrant. Tracadie was shot at five or six different times. Shortly after my arrival in the island,

46

he went to place his daughter in a convent at Quebec, and died there of the cholera.

One day, with a party of youthful friends, I crossed the Hillsboro' Creek, to visit the Indians. We had a large heavy boat, with cumbrous oars, very ill balanced, and a most inefficient crew, two of them being boys either very idle or very ignorant, and, as they kept tumbling backwards over the thwarts, one gentleman and I were left to do all the work. On our way we came upon an Indian in a bark canoe, and spent much of our strength in an ineffectual race with him, succeeding in nothing but in getting aground. We had very great difficulty in landing, and two pretty squaws indulged in hearty laughter at our numerous failures.

After scrambling through a wood, we came upon an Indian village, consisting of fifteen wigwams. These are made of poles, tied together at the upper end, and are thatched with large pieces of birch-bark. A hole is always left at the top to let out the smoke, and the whole space occupied by this primitive dwelling is not larger than a large circular dining-table. Large fierce dogs, and uncouth, terrified-looking, lank-haired children, very scantily clothed, abounded by these abodes. We went into one, crawling through an aperture in the bark. A fire was burning in the middle, over which was suspended a kettle of fish. The wigwam was full of men and squaws, and babies, or "papooses," tightly strapped into little trays of wood. Some were waking, others sleeping, but none were employed, though in several of the *camps* I saw the materials for baskets and bead-work. The eyes of all were magnificent, and the young women very handsome, their dark complexions and splendid hair being in many instances set off by a scarlet handkerchief thrown loosely round the head.

We braved the ferocity of numerous dogs, and looked into eight of these abodes; Mr. Kenjins, from the kind use he makes of his medical knowledge, being a great favourite with the Indians, particularly with the young squaws, who seemed thoroughly to understand all the arts of coquetry. We were

47

going into one wigwam when a surly old man opposed our entrance, holding out a calabash, vociferous voices from the interior calling out, "Ninepence, ninepence!" The memory of *Uncas* and *Magua* rose before me, and I sighed over the degeneracy of the race. These people are mendicant and loquacious. When you go in, they begin a list of things which they want—blankets, powder, tobacco, &c.; always concluding with, "Tea, for God's sake!" for they have renounced the worship of the Great Spirit for a corrupted form of Christianity.

We were received in one *camp* by two very handsome squaws, mother and daughter, who spoke broken English, and were very neat and clean. The floor was thickly strewn with the young shoots of the var, and we sat down with them for half an hour. The younger squaw, a girl of sixteen, was very handsome and coquettish. She had a beautiful cap, worked in beads, which she would not put on at the request of any of the ladies; but directly Mr. Kenjins hinted a wish to that effect, she placed it coquettishly on her head, and certainly looked most bewitching. Though only sixteen, she had been married two years, and had recently lost her twins. Mr. Kenjins asked her the meaning of an Indian phrase. She replied in broken English, "What one little boy say to one little girl: I love you." "I suppose your husband said so to you before you were married? "Yes, and he say so now," she replied, and both she and her mother laughed long and uncontrollably. These Indians retain few of their ancient characteristics, except their dark complexions and their comfortless nomade way of living. They are not represented in the Legislative Assembly.

Very different are the Indians of Central America, the fierce Sioux, Comanches, and Blackfeet. In Canada West I saw a race differing in appearance from the Mohawks and Mic-Macs, and retaining to a certain extent their ancient customs. Among these tribes I entered a wigwam, and was received in sullen silence. I seated myself on the floor with about eight Indians; still not a word was spoken. A short pipe was then lighted and offered to me. I took, as previously directed, a few whiffs of the fragrant weed, and then the pipe was passed round the circle, after which the oldest man present began to speak.[1] This pipe is the celebrated calumet, or pipe of peace, and it is considered even among the fiercest tribes as a sacred obligation.

A week before I left Prince Edward Island I went for a tour of five days in the north-west of the island with Mr. and Miss Kenjins. This was a delightful change, an uninterrupted stream of novelty and enjoyment. It was a relief from Charlotte Town, with its gossiping morning calls, its malicious stories, its political puerilities, its endless discussions on servants, turnips, and plovers; it was a bound into a region of genuine kindness and primitive hospitality.

We left Charlotte Town early on a brilliant morning, in a light waggon, suitably attired for "roughing it in the bush." Our wardrobes, a draught-board, and a number of books (which we never read), were packed into a carpet-bag of most diminutive proportions. We took large buffalo robes with us, in case we should not be able to procure a better shelter for the night than a barn. We were for the time being perfectly congenial, and determined on thoroughly enjoying ourselves. We sang, and rowed, and fished, and laughed, and made others laugh, and were perfectly happy, never knowing and scarcely caring where we should obtain shelter for the night. Our first day's dinner was some cold meat and bread, eaten in a wood, our horse eating his oats by our side; and we made drinking-cups, in Indian fashion, of birch-tree bark—cups of Tantalus, properly speaking, for very little of the water reached our lips. While engaged in drawing some from a stream, the branch on which I leaned gave way, and I fell into the water, a mishap which amused my companions so much that they could not help me out.

After a journey of thirty miles our further course was stopped by a wide river, with low wooded hills and

---

[1] "Why has our white sister visited the wigwams of her red brethren?" was the salutation with which they broke silence—a question rather difficult to answer.

promontories, but there was no ferry-boat, so, putting up our horse in a settler's barn, we sat on the beach till a cranky, leaky boat, covered with fish-scales, was with some difficulty launched, and a man took us across the beautiful stream. This kindly individual came for us again the next morning, and would accept nothing but our thanks for his trouble. The settler in whose barn we had left our horse fed him well with oats, and was equally generous. The people in this part of the island are principally emigrants from the north of Scotland, who thus carry Highland hospitality with them to their distant homes. After a long walk through a wood, we came upon a little church, with a small house near it, and craved a night's hospitality. The church was one of those strongholds of religion and loyalty which I rejoice to see in the colonies. There, Sabbath after Sabbath, the inhabitants of this peaceful locality worship in the pure faith of their forefathers: here, when "life's fitful fever" is over, they sleep in the hallowed ground around these sacred walls. Nor could a more peaceful resting-place be desired: from the graveyard one could catch distant glimpses of the Gulf of St. Lawrence, and tall pine-trees flung their dark shadows over the low green graves.

Leaving our friends in the house, we went down to a small creek running up into the woods, the most formidable *"longer fences"* not intercepting our progress. After some ineffectual attempts to gain possession of a log-canoe, we launched a leaky boat, and went out towards the sea. The purple beams of the setting sun fell upon the dark pine woods, and lay in long lines upon the calm waters of the Gulf of St. Lawrence. It was a glorious evening, and the scene was among the fairest which I saw in the New World. On our return we found our host, the missionary, returned from his walk of twenty-two miles, and a repast of tea, wheaten scones, raspberries, and cream, awaited us. This good man left England twenty-five years ago, and lived for twenty in one of the most desolate parts of Newfoundland. Yet he has retained his vivid interest in England, and kept us up till a late hour talking over its church and people. Contented in his isolated position, which is not without its severe hardships, this good missionary pursues his useful course unnoticed by the world as it bustles along; his sole earthly wish seems to be that he may return to England to die.

The next morning at seven we left his humble home, where such hospitality had awaited us, and be accompanied us to the river. He returned to his honourable work—I shortly afterwards went to the United States—another of the party is with the Turkish army in the Crimea—and the youngest is married in a distant land. For several hours we passed through lovely scenery, on one of the loveliest mornings I ever saw. We stopped at the hut of an old Highland woman, who was "*terribly glad*" to see us, and gave us some milk; and we came up with a sturdy little barefooted urchin of eight years old, carrying a basket. "What's your name?" we asked. "*Mr. Crozier,*" was the bold and complacent reply.

At noon we reached St. Eleanor's, rather a large village, where we met with great hospitality for two days at the house of a keeper of a small store, who had married the lively and accomplished daughter of an English clergyman. The two Irish servant-girls were ill, but she said she should be delighted to receive us if we would help her to do the household work. The same afternoon we drove to the house of a shipbuilder at a little hamlet called Greenshore, and went out lobster-fishing in his beautiful boat. The way of fishing for these creatures was a novel one to me, but so easy that a mere novice may be very successful. We tied *sinks* to mackerel, and let them down in six fathoms water. We gently raised them now and then, and, if we felt anything pulling the bait, raised it slowly up. Gently, gently, or the fish suspects foul play; but soon, just under the surface, I saw an immense lobster, and one of the gentlemen caught it by the tail and threw it into the boat. We fished for an hour, and caught fifteen of these esteemed creatures, which we took to the house in a wheelbarrow. At night we drove to St. Eleanor's, taking some of our spoil with us, and immediately adjourned to the kitchen, a large, unfinished place built of logs, with a clay floor and huge smoke-stained rafters. We sat by a large stove in the centre, and looked as if we had never known civilised life. Miss Kenjins and I sat on either side of the fireplace in broad-brimmed straw hats, Mrs. Maccallummore in front, warming the feet of the unhappy baby, who had been a passive spectator of the fishing; the three gentlemen stood round in easy attitudes, these, be it remembered, holding glasses of brandy and water; and the two invalid servants stood behind, occasionally uttering suppressed shrieks as Mr. Oppe took one out of a heap of lobsters and threw it into a caldron of boiling water on the stove. This strange scene was illuminated by a blazing pine-knot. Mr. Kenjins laughingly reminded me of the elegant drawing-room in which he last saw me in England—"Look on this picture and on that."

On the Sunday we crossed the Grand River, on a day so stormy that the ferryman would not take the "*scow*" across. We rowed ourselves over in a crazy boat, which seemed about to fill and sink when we got to the middle of the river, and attended service at Port Hill, one of the most desolate-looking places I ever saw. We saw Lenox Island, where on St. Ann's day all the island Indians meet and go through ceremonies with the Romish priests.

We remained for part of the next day with our hospitable friends at St. Eleanor's, and set out on an exploring expedition in search of a spring which Mr. K. remembered in his childish days. We went down to a lonely cabin to make inquiries, and were told that "none but the old people knew of it—it was far away in the woods." Here was mystery; so, leaving the waggon, into the woods we went to seek for it, and far away in the woods we found it, and now others besides the "old people" know of it.

We struck into the forest, an old, untrodden forest, where generations of trees had rotted away, and strange flowers and lichens grew, and bats flew past us in the artificial darkness; and there were snakes too, ugly spotted things, which hissed at us, and put out their double tongues, and then coiled themselves away in the dim recesses of the forest. But on we went, climbing with difficulty over prostrate firs, or breaking through matted juniper, and still the spring was not, though we were "far away in the woods." But still we climbed on, through swamp and jungle, till we tore our dresses to pieces, and our hats got pulled off in a tree and some of our hair with them; but at last we reached the spring. It was such a scene as one might have dreamed of in some forest in a fabulous Elysium. It was a large, deep basin of pure white sand, covered with clear water, and seven powerful springs, each about a foot high, rose from it; and trees had fallen over it, and were covered with bright green moss, and others bent over it ready to fall; and above them the tall hemlocks shut out the light, except where a few stray beams glittered on the pure transparent water.

And here it lay in lonely beauty, as it had done for centuries, probably known only to the old people and to the wandering Indians. In enterprising England a town would have been built round it, and we should have had cheap excursions to the "Baths of St. Eleanor's."

In the evening we went to the house of Mr. Oppe at Bedeque, but not finding him at home we presumed on colonial hospitality so far as to put our horse in the stable and unpack our clothes; and when Mr. Oppe returned he found us playing at draughts, and joined us in a hearty laugh at our coolness. Our fifth and last day's journey was a long one of forty miles, yet near Cape Traverse our horse ran away down a steep hill, and across a long wooden bridge without a parapet, thereby placing our lives in imminent jeopardy. After travelling for several hours we came to a lone house, where we hoped to get some refreshment both for ourselves and the horse, but found the house *locked*, a remarkable fact, as in this island robbery is almost unknown. We were quite exhausted with hunger, and our hearts sank when we found every door and window closed. We then, as an act of mercy, stole a sheaf of oats from a neighbouring field, and cut the ears off for the horse with our penknives, after which we, in absolute hunger, ate as many grains as we could clean from the husks, and some fern, which we found very bitter. We looked very much like a group of vagrants sitting by the road-side, the possession of the oats being disputed with us by five lean pigs. When after another hour we really succeeded in getting something more suitable for human beings, we ate like famished creatures.

While I was walking up a long hill, I passed a neat cabin in a garden of pumpkins, placed in a situation apparently chosen from its extreme picturesqueness. Seeing an old man, in a suit of grey frieze and a blue bonnet, standing at the gate, I addressed him with the words, "*Cia mar thasibh an diugh.*" "*Slan gu robh math agaibh. Cia mar thasibh an fein,*"[1] was the delighted reply, accompanied with a hearty shake of both hands. He was from Snizort, in the Isle of Skye, and, though he had attained competence in the land of his adoption, he mourned the absence of his native heather. He asked me the usual Highland question, "Tell me the news;" and I told him all that I could recollect of those with whom he was familiar. He spoke of the Cuchullin Hills, and the stern beauty of Loch Corruisk, with tears in his eyes. "Ah," he said, "I have no wish but to see them once again. Who is the lady with you—the lily?" he asked, for he spoke English imperfectly, and preferred his own poetical tongue. "May your path be always bright, lady!" he said, as he shook my hand warmly at parting; "and ye'll come and see me when ye come again, and bring me tales from the old country." The simple wish of Donnuil Dhu has often recurred to me in the midst of gayer scenes and companions. It brought to mind memories of many a hearty welcome received in the old man's Highland home, and of those whose eyes were then looking upon the Cuchullin Hills.

After this expedition, where so much kindness had been experienced, Charlotte Town did not appear more delightful than before, and, though sorry to take leave of many kind

1 "How are you today?" "Very well, thank you. I hope you are well."

relatives and friends, I was glad that only one more day remained to me in the island.

I cordially wish its people every prosperity. They are loyal, moral, and independent, and their sympathies with England have lately been evidenced by their liberal contributions to the Patriotic Fund. When their trade and commerce shall have been extended, and when a more suitable plan has been adopted for the support of religion; when large portions of waste land have been brought under cultivation, and local resources have been farther developed, people will be too much occupied with their own affairs to busy themselves, as now, either with the affairs of others, or with the puerile politics of so small a community; and then the island will deserve the title which has been bestowed on it, *"The Garden of British America."*

CHAPTER IV

The ravages of the cholera having in some degree ceased, I left
Prince Edward Island for the United States, and decided to
endure the delays and inconveniences of the intercolonial
route for the purpose of seeing something of New Brunswick
on my way to Boston.

The journey from the island to the States is in itself by no
means an easy one, and is rendered still more difficult by the
want of arrangement on the part of those who conduct the
transit of travellers. The inhabitants of our eastern colonies do
not understand the value of time, consequently the uncertain
arrivals and departures of the *Lady Le Marchant* furnish matter
for numerous speculations. From some circumstances which
had occurred within my knowledge—one being that the
captain of this steamer had *forgotten* to call for the continental
mails—I did not attach much importance to the various times
which were fixed definitely for her sailing between the hours
of four and ten.

A cloudy, gloomy night had succeeded to the bright blaze of
an August day, and midnight was fast approaching before the
signal-bell rang. Two friends accompanied me as far as
Bedeque, and, besides the gentleman under whose escort I
was to travel, there were twelve island gentlemen and two
ladies, all supposed to be bound, like myself, for Boston. All
separate individualities were, however, lost amid the confusion

of bear-skin and waterproof coats and the impenetrable darkness which brooded both on wharf and steamer.

An amusing scene of bungling marked our departure from Charlotte Town. The captain, a sturdy old Northumbrian seaman, thoroughly understood his business; but the owners of the ship compelled him to share its management with a very pertinacious pilot, and the conflicting orders given, and the want of harmony in the actions produced, gave rise to many reflections on the evils of divided responsibility. On the night in question some mysterious spell seemed to bind us to the shores of Prince Edward Island. In an attempt to get the steamer off she ran stern foremost upon the bowsprit of a schooner, then broke one of the piles of the wharf to pieces, crushing her fender to atoms at the same time. Some persons on the pier, compassionating our helplessness, attempted to *stave* the ship off with long poles, but this well-meant attempt failed, as did several others, until someone suggested to the captain the very simple expedient of working the engines, when the steamer moved slowly away, smashing the bulwarks of a new brig, and soon in the dark and murky atmosphere the few lights of Charlotte Town ceased to be visible.

The compass was then required, but the matches in the ship hung fire; and when a passenger at length produced a light, it was discovered that the lamp in the binnacle was without that essential article, oil. Meanwhile no one had ascertained what had caused the heavy smash at the outset, and certain timid persons, in the idea that a hole had been knocked in the ship's side, were in continual apprehension that she would fill and sink. To drown all such gloomy anticipations we sang several songs, among others the appropriate one, "Isle of Beauty, fare thee well." The voices rapidly grew more faint and spiritless as we stood farther out to sea, a failure which might have been attributed to grief at leaving old friends on the chance of making new ones, had not hints and questions been speedily interchanged, such as

"Do you like the sea?" "Are you feeling comfortable?" "Would you prefer being downstairs?"—and the like.

Cloaks and pillows became more thought of than either songs or friends; indefinable sensations of melancholy rendered the merriest of the party silent, and a perfect deluge of rain rendered a retreat into the lower regions a precautionary measure which even the boldest were content to adopt. Below, in addition to the close overpowering odour of cabins without any ventilation, the smell of the bilge-water was sufficient in itself to produce nausea. The dark den called the ladies' cabin, which was by no means clean, was the sleeping abode of twelve people in various stages of discomfort, and two babies.

I spent a very comfortless four hours, and went on deck at dawn to find a thick fog, a heavy rain, the boards swimming with soot and water, and one man cowering at the wheel. Most of the gentlemen, induced by the discomfort to the early risers, came up before we reached Bedeque, in oilskin caps, coats, and leggings, wearing that expression on their physiognomies peculiar to Anglo-Saxons in the rain.

The K——s wished me to go ashore here, but the skipper, who seemed to have been born with an objection on the tip of his tongue, dissuaded me, as the rain was falling heavily, and the boat was a quarter full of water; but as my clothes could not be more thoroughly saturated than they were, I landed; and even at the early hour of six we found a blazing log-fire in the shipbuilder's hospitable house, and "Biddy," more the "Biddy" of an Irish novelist than a servant in real life, with her merry face, rich brogue, and potato-cakes, welcomed us with many expressions of commiseration for our drowned plight.

Who that has ever experienced the miseries of a voyage in a dirty, crowded, and ill-ventilated little steamer, has not also appreciated the pleasure of getting upon the land even for a few minutes? The consciousness of the absence of suffocating sensations, and of the comfort of a floor which does not move under the feet—of space, and cleanliness, and warmth—soon produce an oblivion of all past miseries; but if the voyage has not terminated, and the relief is only temporary, it enhances the dread of future ones to such an extent that, when the captain came to the door to fetch me, I had to rouse all my energies before I could leave a blazing fire to battle with cold and rain again. The offer of a cup of tea, which I would have supposed irresistible, would not induce him to permit me to finish my breakfast, but at length his better nature prevailed, and he consented to send the boat a second time.

After allowing my pocket to be filled with "notions" by the generous "Biddy," I took leave of Miss Kenjins, who is good, clever, and agreeable enough to redeem the young-ladyhood of the island—nor was there enough of pleasant promise for the future to compensate for the regret I felt at leaving those who had received a stranger with such kindness and hospitality.

I jumped into the boat, where I stood with my feet in the water, in company with several gentlemen with dripping umbrellas, whose marked want of nasal development rendered Disraeli's description of "flat-nosed Franks" peculiarly appropriate. The rain poured down as rain never pours in England; and under these very dispiriting circumstances I began my travels over the North American continent.

I went down to my miserable berth, and vainly tried to sleep, the discomfort and mismanagement which prevailed leading my thoughts by force of contrast to the order, cleanliness, and regularity of the inimitable line of steamers on the West Highland coast. Wherever the means of locomotion are concerned, these colonies are very far behind either the "old country" or their enterprising neighbours in Canada; and at present they do not appear conscious of the deficiencies which are sternly forced upon a traveller's observation.

The prospect which appeared through the door was not calculated to please, as it consisted of a low, dark, and suffocating cabin, filled with men in suits of oilskin, existing in a steamy atmosphere, loaded with the odours of india-rubber, tobacco, and spirits. The stewardess was ill, and my companions were groaning; unheeded babies were crying; and the only pleasing feature in the scene was the gruff old pilot, ubiquitous in kindness, ever performing some act of humanity. At one moment he was holding smelling-salts to some exhausted lady—at another carrying down a poor Irishwoman, who, though a steerage passenger, should not, he said, be left to perish from cold and hunger—and again, feeding some crying baby with bread and milk. My clothes were completely saturated, and his good offices probably saved me from a severe illness by covering me up with a blanket.

At twelve we reached Shediac in New Brunswick, a place from which an enormous quantity of timber is annually exported. It is a village in a marsh, on a large bay surrounded by low wooded hills, and presents every appearance of unhealthiness. Huge square-sided ships, English, Dutch, and Austrian, were swallowing up rafts of pine which kept arriving from the shore. The water on this coast is shallow, and, though our steamer was not of more than 150 tons burthen, we were obliged to anchor nearly two miles from shore.

Shediac had recently been visited by the cholera, and there was an infectious melancholy about its aspect, which, coupled with the fact that I was wet, cold, and weary, and with the discovery that my escort and I had not two ideas in common, had a tendency to produce anything but a lively frame of mind.

We and our luggage were unceremoniously trundled into two large boats, some of the gentlemen, I am sorry to say, forcing their way into the first, in order to secure for themselves inside places in the stage. An American gentleman offered our rowers a dollar if they could gain the shore first, but they failed in doing so, and these very ungallant individuals hired the first waggon, and drove off at full speed to the Bend on the Petticodiac river, confident in the success of their scheme. What was their surprise and mortification to find that a gentleman of our party, who said he was "an old stager, and up to a dodge or two," had leisurely telegraphed from Shediac for nine places! Thus, on their arrival at the Bend, the delinquents found that, besides being both censured and laughed at for their selfishness, they had lost their places, their dinners, and their tempers.

As we were rowing to shore, the captain told us that our worst difficulty was yet to come—an insuperable one, he added, to corpulent persons. There was no landing-place for boats, or indeed for anything, at low water, and we had to climb up a wharf ten feet high, formed of huge round logs placed a foot apart from each other, and slippery with sea-grass. It is really incredible that, at a place through which a considerable traffic passes, as being on the high road from Prince Edward Island to the United States, there should be a more inconvenient landing-place than I ever saw at a Highland village.

Large, high, springless waggons were waiting for us on this wharf, which, after jolting us along a bad road for some distance, deposited us at the door of the inn at Shediac, where we came for the first time upon the track of the cholera, which had recently devastated all the places along our route. Here we had a substantial dinner of a very homely description, and, as in Nova Scotia, a cup of tea sweetened with molasses was placed by each plate, instead of any intoxicating beverage.

After this meal I went into the "house-room," or parlour, a general "rendezvous" of lady visitors, babies, unmannerly children, Irish servant-girls with tangled hair and bare feet, colonial gossips, "cute" urchins, and not unfrequently of those curious-looking beings, pauper-emigrant lads from Erin, who do a little of everything and nothing well, denominated stable-helps.

Here I was assailed with a host of questions as to my country, objects in travelling, &c., and I speedily found that being from the "old country" gave me a *status* in the eyes of the colonial ladies. I was requested to take off my cloak to display the pattern of my dress, and the performance of a very inefficient country *modiste* passed off as the latest Parisian fashion. My bonnet and cloak were subjected to a like scrutiny, and the pattern of the dress was taken, after which I was allowed to resume my seat.

Interrogatories about England followed, and I was asked if I had seen the queen? The hostess "guessed" that she must be a "tall grand lady," and one pretty damsel that "she must dress beautiful, and always wear the crown out of doors." I am afraid that I rather lessened the estimation in which our gracious liege lady was held by her subjects when I replied that she dressed very simply on ordinary occasions; had never, I believed, worn the crown since her coronation, and was very little above my height. They inquired about the royal children, but evinced more curiosity about the princess-royal than with respect to the heir to the throne.

One of the querists had been at Boston, but guessed that "London must be a pretty considerable touch higher." Most, however, could only compare it in idea with St. John, N. B., and listened with the greatest appearance of interest to the wonders which I narrated of the extent, wealth, and magnificence of the British metropolis. Altogether I was favourably impressed by their intelligence, and during my short journey through New Brunswick I formed a higher opinion of the uneducated settlers in this province than of those in Nova Scotia. They are very desirous to possess a reputation for being, to use their borrowed phraseology, "Knowing 'coons, with their eye-teeth well cut." It would be well if they borrowed from their neighbours, the Yankees, something more useful than their slang, which renders the vernacular of the province rather repulsive. The spirit of enterprise, which has done so much for the adjacent state of Maine, has not yet displayed itself in New Brunswick in the completion of any works of practical utility; and though the soil in many places has great natural capabilities, these have not been taken due advantage of.

There are two modes of reaching St. John from Shediac, one by stage, the other by steamer; and the ladies and children, fearful of the fatigue of a land journey, remained to take the steamer from the Bend. I resolved to stay under Mr. Sandford's escort, and go by land, one of my objects being to see as much of the country as possible; also my late experiences of colonial steamboat travelling had not been so agreeable as to induce me to brave the storms of the Bay of Fundy in a crazy vessel, which had been injured only two nights before by a collision in a race. On the night on which some of my companions sailed the *Creole's* engines were disabled, and she remained in a helpless condition for four hours, so I had a very fortunate escape.

Taking leave of the amusingly miscellaneous party in the "house-room," I left Shediac for the Bend, in company with seven persons from Prince Edward Island, in a waggon drawn by two ponies, and driven by the landlord, a shrewd specimen of a colonist.

This mode of transit deserves a passing notice. The waggon consisted of an oblong shallow wooden tray on four wheels; on this were placed three boards resting on high unsteady props, and the machine was destitute of springs. The ponies were thin, shaggy, broken-kneed beings, under fourteen hands high, with harness of a most meagre description, and its cohesive qualities seemed very small, if I might judge from the frequency with which the driver alighted to repair its parts with pieces of twine, with which his pockets were stored, I suppose in anticipation of such occasions.

These poor little animals took nearly four hours to go fourteen miles, and even this rate of progression was only kept up by the help of continual admonitions from a stout leather thong.

It was a dismal evening, very like one in England at the end of November—the air cold and damp—and I found the chill from wet clothes and an east wind anything but agreeable. The country also was extremely uninviting, and I thought its aspect more gloomy than that of Nova Scotia. Sometimes we traversed swamps swarming with bullfrogs, on corduroy roads which nearly jolted us out of the vehicle, then dreary levels abounding in spindly hacmetac, hemlock, and birch-trees; next we would go down into a cedar-swamp alive with mosquitoes. Dense forests, impassable morasses, and sedgy streams always bounded the immediate prospect, and the clearings were few and far between. Nor was the conversation of my companions calculated to beguile a tedious journey; it was on "*snatchings*," "*snarlings*," and other puerilities of island politics, corn, sugar, and molasses.

About dusk we reached the Bend, a dismal piece of alluvial swampy-looking land, drained by a wide, muddy river, called the Petticodiac, along the shore of which a considerable shipbuilding village is located. The tide here rises and falls twenty-four feet, and sixty at the mouth of the river, in the Bay of Fundy. It was a dispiriting view—acres of mud bare at low water, and miles of swamp covered with rank coarse grass, intersected by tide-streams, which are continually crossed on rotten wooden bridges without parapets. This place had recently been haunted by fever and cholera.

As there was a slight incline into the village, our miserable ponies commenced a shambling trot, the noise of which brought numerous idlers to the inn-door to inquire the news. This inn was a rambling, unpainted erection of wood, opposite to a "cash, credit, and barter store," kept by an enterprising Caledonian—an additional proof of the saying which ascribes ubiquity to "Scots, Newcastle grindstones, and Birmingham buttons." A tidy, bustling landlady, very American in her phraseology, but kind in her way, took me under her especial protection, as forty men were staying in the house, and there was an astonishing paucity of the softer sex; indeed, in all my subsequent travels I met with an undue and rather disagreeable preponderance of the "lords of the creation."

Not being inclined to sit in the "parlour" with a very motley company, I accompanied the hostess into the kitchen, and sat by the fire upon a chopping-block, the most luxurious seat in the apartment. Two shoeless Irish girls were my other companions, and one of them, hearing that I was from

England, inquired if I were acquainted with "one Mike Donovan, of Skibbereen!" The landlady's daughter was also there, a little, sharp-visaged, precocious torment of three years old, who spilt my ink and lost my thimble; and then, coming up to me, said, "Well, stranger, I guess you're kinder tired." She very unceremoniously detached my watch from my chain, and, looking at it quite with the eye of a *connoisseur*, "guessed it must have cost a pretty high figure"! After she had filled my purse with ink, for which misdemeanour her mother offered no apology, I looked into the tea-room, which presented the curious spectacle of forty men, including a number of ship-carpenters of highly respectable appearance, taking tea in the silent, business-like way in which Transatlantic meals are generally despatched. My own meal, which the landlady evidently intended should be a very luxurious one, consisted of stewed tea, sweetened with molasses, soft cheese instead of butter, and dark rye-bread.

The inn was so full that my hostess said she could not give me a bed—rather an unwelcome announcement to a wayworn traveller—and with considerable complacency she took me into a large, whitewashed, carpetless room, furnished with one chair, a small table, and my valise. She gave me two buffalo robes, and left me, hoping I should be comfortable! Rather disposed to quarrel with a hardship which shortly afterwards I should have laughed at, I rolled up my cloak for a pillow, wrapped myself in a buffalo-skin, and slept as soundly as on the most luxurious couch. I was roused early by a general thumping and clattering, and, making the hasty toilette which one is compelled to do when destitute of appliances, I found the stage at the early hour of six ready at the door; and, to my surprise, the coachman was muffled up in furs, and the morning was intensely cold.

This vehicle was of the same construction as that which I have already described in Nova Scotia; but, being narrower, was infinitely more uncomfortable. Seven gentlemen and two ladies went inside, in a space where six would have been disagreeably crowded. Mr. Sandford preferred the outside, where he could smoke his cigar without molestation. The road was very hilly, and several times our progress was turned into retrogression, for the horses invariably refused to go up hill, probably, poor things! because they felt their inability to drag the loaded wain up the steep declivities which we continually met with. The passengers were therefore frequently called upon to get out and walk—a very agreeable recreation, for the ice was the thickness of a penny; the thermometer stood at 35°; there was a piercing north-east wind; and though the sun shone from a cloudless sky, his rays had scarcely any power. We breakfasted at eight, at a little wayside inn, and then travelled till midnight with scarcely any cessation.

The way would have been very tedious had it not been enlivened by the eccentricities of Mr. Latham, an English passenger. After breakfast the conversation in the stage was pretty general, led by the individual aforesaid, who *lectured* and *preached*, rather than conversed. Few subjects were untouched by his eloquence; he spoke with equal ease on a difficult point in theology, and on the conformation of the sun. He lectured on politics, astronomy, chemistry, and anatomy with great fluency and equal incorrectness. In describing the circulation of the blood, he said, "It's a purely metaphysical subject;" and the answering remark, "It is the most purely physical," made him vehemently angry. He spoke of the sun by saying, "I've studied the sun; I know it as well as I do this field; it's a dark body with a luminous atmosphere, and a climate more agreeable than that of the earth"—thus announcing as a fact what has been timidly put forward as a theory only by our greatest astronomers.

Politics soon came on the *tapis*, when he attacked British institutions violently, with an equal amount of ignorance and presumption, making such glaring misstatements that I felt bound to contradict them; when he, not liking to be lowered in the estimation of his companions, contested the points in a way which closely bordered upon rudeness.

He made likewise a very pedantic display of scientific knowledge, in virtue of an occasional attendance at meetings of mechanics' institutes, and asked the gentlemen—for "We're all gentlemen here"—numerous questions, to which they could not reply, when one of the party took courage to ask him why fire burned. "Oh, because of the hydrogen in the air, of course," was the complacent answer. "I beg your pardon, but there is no hydrogen in atmospheric air."—"There is; I know the air well: it is composed one-half of hydrogen, the other half of nitrogen and oxygen." "You're surely confounding it with water."—"No, I am as well acquainted with the composition of water as with that of air; it is composed of the same gases, only in different proportions." This was too monstrous, and his opponent, while contradicting the statement, could not avoid a hearty laugh at its absurdity, in which the others joined without knowing why, which so raised the choler of this irascible gentleman, that it was most difficult to smooth matters. He contended that he was right and the other wrong; that his propositions were held by all chemists of eminence on both sides of the water; that, though he had not verified the elements of these fluids by analysis, he was perfectly acquainted with their nature; that the composition of air was a mere theory, but that his opponent's view was not held by any *savans* of note. The latter merely replied, "When you next light a candle you may be thankful that there is no hydrogen in the air; " after which there was a temporary cessation of hostilities.

But towards night, being still unwarned by the discomfitures of the morning, he propounded some questions which his companions could not answer; among which was, "Why are there black sheep?" How he would have solved this difficult problem in natural history, I do not know. Mystification sat on all faces, when the individual who had before attacked Mr. Latham's misstatements, took up the defence of the puzzled colonists by volunteering to answer the question if he would explain how "impossible roots enter equations." No reply was given to this, when, on some of the gentlemen urging him, perhaps rather mischievously, to answer, he retorted angrily,—"I'm master of mathematics as well as of other sciences; but I see there's an intention to make fun of me. I don't choose to be made a butt of, and I'll show you that I can be as savage as other people." This threat had the effect of producing a total silence for the remainder of the journey; but Mr. Latham took an opportunity of explaining to me that in this speech he intended no personal allusion, but had found it necessary to check the ill-timed mirth in the stage. In spite of his presumption and pedantry, he never lost an opportunity of showing kindness. I saw him last in the very extremity of terror, during a violent gale off the coast of Maine.

For the first fifty miles after leaving the Bend, our road lay through country as solitary and wild as could be conceived—high hills, covered with endless forests of small growth. I looked in vain for the gigantic trees so celebrated by travellers in America. If they ever grew in this region, they now, in the shape of ships, are to be found on every sea where England's flag waves. Occasionally the smoke of an Indian wigwam would rise in a thin blue cloud from among the dark foliage of the hemlock; and by the primitive habitation one of the aboriginal possessors of the soil might be seen, in tattered habiliments, cleaning a gun or repairing a bark canoe, scarcely deigning an apathetic glance at those whom the appliances of civilisation and science had placed so immeasurably above him. Then a squaw, with a papooses trapped upon her back, would peep at us from behind a tree; or a half-clothed urchin would pursue us for coppers, contrasting strangely with the majesty of *Uncas*, or the sublimity of *Chingachgook*; portraits which it is very doubtful if Cooper ever took from life.

In the few places where the land had been cleared the cultivation was tolerable and the houses comfortable, surrounded generally by cattle-sheds and rich crops of Tartarian oats. The potatoes appeared to be free from disease, and the pumpkin crop was evidently abundant and in good condition. Sussex Valley, along which we passed for thirty miles, is green, wooded, and smilingly fertile, being watered by a clear rapid river. The numerous hay-meadows, and the neat appearance of the arable land, reminded me of England. It is surprising, considering the advantages possessed by New Brunswick, that it has not been a more favourite resort of emigrants. It seems to me that one great reason of this must be the difficulty and expense of land-travelling, as the province is destitute of the means of internal communication in the shape of railways and canals. It contains several navigable rivers, and the tracts of country near the St. John, the Petticodiac, and the Miramichi rivers are very fertile, and adapted for cultivation. The lakes and minor streams in the interior of the province are also surrounded by rich land, and the capacious bays along the coast abound with fish. New Brunswick possesses "responsible government," and has a Governor, an Executive Council, a Legislative Council, and a House of Assembly. Except that certain expenses of defence, &c., are borne by the home government, which would protect the colony in the event of any predatory incursions on the part of the Americans, it has all the advantages of being an independent nation; and it is believed that the Reciprocity Treaty, recently concluded with the United States, will prove of great commercial benefit.

Yet the number of emigrants who have sought its shores is comparatively small, and these arrivals were almost exclusively of the labouring classes, attracted by the extraordinarily high rates of wages, and were chiefly absorbed by mechanical employments. The numbers landed in 1853 were 3762, and, in 1854, 3618. With respect to the general affairs of New Brunswick, it is very satisfactory to observe that the provincial revenue has increased to upwards of £200,000 per annum.

Fredericton, a town of about 9000 inhabitants, on the St. John river, by which it has a daily communication with the city of St. John, 90 miles distant, by steamer, is the capital and seat of government. New Brunswick has considerable mineral wealth; coal and iron are abundant, and the climate is less foggy than that of Nova Scotia; but these great natural advantages are suffered to lie nearly dormant. The colonists are very hardy and extremely loyal; but the vice of drinking, so prevalent in northern climates, has recently called for legislative interference.

We stopped at the end of every stage of eighteen miles to change horses, and at one of the little inns an old man brought to the door of the stage a very pretty, interesting-looking girl of fifteen years old, and placed her under my care, requesting me to "see her safely to her home in St. John, and not allow any of the gentlemen to be rude to her." The latter part of the instructions was very easy to fulfil, as, whatever faults the colonists possess, they are extremely respectful in their manners to ladies. But a difficulty arose, or rather what would have been a difficulty in England, for the stage was full both inside and out, and all the passengers were desirous to reach Boston as speedily as possible. However, a gentleman from New England, seeing the anxiety of the young girl to reach St. John, got out of the stage, and actually remained at the little roadside inn for one whole day and two nights, in order to accommodate a stranger. This act of kindness was performed at great personal inconvenience, and the gentleman who showed it did not appear to attach the slightest merit to it. The novelty of it made a strong impression upon me, and it fully bore out all that I had read or heard of the almost exaggerated deference to ladies which custom requires from American gentlemen.

After darkness came on, the tedium of a journey of twenty hours, performed while sitting in a very cramped posture, was almost insupportable, and the monotony of it was only broken by the number of wooden bridges which we crossed, and the driver's admonition, "Bridge dangerous; passengers get out and walk." The night was very cold and frosty, and so productive of aguish chills, that I was not at all sorry for the compelled pedestrianism entailed upon me by the insecure state of these bridges.

My young charge seemed extremely timid while crossing them, and uttered a few suppressed shrieks when curious splitting noises, apparently proceeding from the woodwork, broke the stillness; nor was I altogether surprised at her emotions when, as we were walking over a bridge nearly half a mile in length, I was told that a coach and six horses had disappeared through it a fortnight before, at the cost of several broken limbs.

While crossing the St. John, near the pretty town of Hampton, one of our leaders put both his forefeet into a hole, and was with difficulty extricated.

Precisely at midnight the stage clattered down the steep streets of the city of St. John, to which the ravages of the cholera had recently given such a terrible celebrity. After a fruitless pilgrimage to three hotels, we were at length received at Waverley House, having accomplished a journey of one hundred miles in twenty hours! On ringing my bell, it was answered by a rough porter, and I soon found that *waiting* chambermaids are not essential at Transatlantic hotels; and the female servants, or rather *helps*, are of a very superior class. A friend of mine, on leaving an hotel at Niagara, offered a *douceur* in the shape of half a dollar to one of these, but she drew herself up, and proudly replied, "American ladies do not receive money from gentlemen." Having left my keys at the Bend, I found my valise a useless incumbrance, rather annoying after a week of travelling.

We spent the Sunday at St. John, and, the opportune arrival of my keys enabling me to don some habiliments suited to the day, I went to the church, where the service, with the exception of the sermon, was very well performed. A solemn thanksgiving for the removal of the cholera was read, and was rendered very impressive by the fact that most of the congregation were in new mourning. The Angel of Death had long hovered over the doomed city, which lost rather more than a tenth of its population from a disease which in the hot summer of America is nearly as fatal and terrible as the plague. All who could leave the town fled; but many carried the disease with them, and died upon the road. The hotels, shipyards, and stores were closed, bodies rudely nailed up in boards were hurried about the streets, and met with hasty burial outside the city, before vital warmth had fled; the holy ties of natural affection were disregarded, and the dying were left alone to meet the King of Terrors, none remaining to close their eyes; the ominous clang of the death-bell was heard both night and day, and a dense brown fog was supposed to brood over the city, which for five weeks was the abode of the dying and the dead.

A temporary regard for religion was produced among the inhabitants of St. John by the visit of the pestilence; it was scarcely possible for the most sceptical not to recognise the overruling providence of God: and I have seldom seen more external respect for the Sabbath and the ordinances of religion than in this city.

The preponderance of the rougher sex was very strongly marked at Waverley House. Fifty gentlemen sat down to dinner, and only three ladies, inclusive of the landlady. Fifty-three cups of tea graced the table, which was likewise ornamented with six boiled legs of mutton, numerous dishes of splendid potatoes, and corn-cobs, squash, and pumpkin-pie, in true colonial abundance.

I cannot forbear giving a conversation which took place at a meal at this inn, as it is very characteristic of the style of persons whom one continually meets with in travelling in these colonies: "I guess you're from the Old Country?" commenced my *vis-à-vis*; to which recognition of my nationality I humbly bowed. "What do you think of us here down east?" "I have been so short a time in these provinces, that I cannot form any just opinion." "Oh, but you must have formed some; we like to know what Old Country folks think of us." Thus asked, I could not avoid making some reply, and said, "I think there is a great want of systematic enterprise in these colonies; you do not avail yourselves of the great natural advantages which you possess." "Well, the fact is, old father

Jackey Bull ought to help us, or let us go off on our own hook right entirely." "You have responsible government, and, to use your own phrase, you are on 'your own hook' in all but the name." "Well, I guess as we are; *we're a long chalk above the Yankees*, though them is fellers as thinks nobody's got their eye teeth cut but themselves."

The self-complacent ignorance with which this remark was made was ludicrous in the extreme. He began again: "What do you think of Nova Scotia and the 'Blue Noses'? Halifax is a grand place, sure*ly!*" "At Halifax I found the best inn such a one as no respectable American would condescend to sleep at, and a town of shingles, with scarcely any sidewalks. The people were talking largely of railways and steamers, yet I travelled by the mail to Truro and Pictou in a conveyance that would scarcely have been tolerated in England two centuries ago. The people of Halifax possess the finest harbour in North America, yet they have no docks, and scarcely any shipping. The Nova-Scotians, it is known, have iron, coal, slate, limestone, and freestone, and their shores swarm with fish, yet they spend their time in talking about railways, docks, and the House of Assembly, and end by walking about doing nothing."

"Yes," chimed in a Boston sea-captain, who had been our fellow-passenger from Europe, and prided himself upon being a "thorough-going down-easter," "it takes as long for a Blue Nose to put on his hat as for one of our free and enlightened citizens to go from Bosting to New *Orleens*. If we don't whip all creation it's a pity! Why, stranger, if you were to go to Connecticut, and tell 'em what you've been telling this ere child, they'd guess you'd been with *Colonel Crockett*."

"Well, I proceeded, in answer to another question from the New-Brunswicker, "if you wish to go to the north of your own province, you require to go round Nova Scotia by sea. I understand that a railway to the Bay of Chaleur has been talked about, but I suppose it has ended where it began; and, for want of a railway to Halifax, even the Canadian traffic has been diverted to Portland."

73

"We want to invest some of our surplus revenue," said the captain. "It'll be a good spec when Congress buys these colonies; some of our ten-horse power chaps will come down, and, before you could whistle 'Yankee Doodle,' we'll have a canal to Bay Varte, with a town as big as Newhaven at each end. The Blue Noses will look kinder streaked then, I guess." The New-Brunswicker retorted, with some fierceness, that the handful of British troops at Fredericton could "chaw up" the whole American army; and the conversation continued for some time longer in the same boastful and exaggerated strain on each side, but the above is a specimen of colonial arrogance and American conceit.

The population of New Brunswick in 1851 was 193,800; but it is now over 210,000, and will likely increase rapidly, should the contemplated extension of the railway system to the province ever take place; as in that case the route to both the Canadas by the port of St. John will probably supersede every other. The spacious harbour of St. John has a sufficient depth of water for vessels of the largest class, and its tide-fall of about 25 feet effectually prevents it from being frozen in the winter.

The timber trade is a most important source of wealth to the colony—the timber floated down the St. John alone, in the season of 1852, was of the value of £405,208 sterling. The saw-mills, of which by the last census there were 584, gave employment to 4302 hands. By the same census there were 87 ships, with an average burthen of 400 tons each, built in the year in which it was taken, and the number has been on the increase since. These colonial-built vessels are gradually acquiring a very high reputation; some of our finest clippers, including one or two belonging to the celebrated "White Star" line, are by the St. John builders. Perhaps, with the single exception of Canada West, no colony offers such varied inducements to emigrants.

I saw as much of St. John as possible, and on a fine day was favourably impressed with it. It well deserves its cognomen, "The City of the Rock," being situated on a high, bluff, rocky peninsula, backed on the land-side by steep barren hills. The harbour is well sheltered and capacious, and the suspension-bridge above the falls very picturesque. The streets are steep, wide, and well paved, and the stores are more pretentious than those of Halifax. There is also a very handsome square, with a more respectable fountain in it than those which excite the ridicule of foreigners in front of our National Gallery. It is a place where a large amount of business is done, and the shipyards alone give employment to several thousand persons.

Yet the lower parts of the town are dirty in the extreme. I visited some of the streets near the water before the cholera had quite disappeared from them, nor did I wonder that the pestilence should linger in places so appropriate to itself; for the roadways were strewn to a depth of several inches with sawdust, emitting a foul decomposing smell, and in which lean pigs were *routing* and fighting.

Yet St. John wears a lively aspect. You see a thousand boatmen, raftmen, and millmen, some warping dingy scows, others loading huge square-sided ships; busy gangs of men in fustian jackets, engaged in running off the newly sawed timber; and the streets bustling with storekeepers, lumber-merchants, and market-men; all combining to produce a chaos of activity very uncommon in the towns of our North American colonies. But too often, murky-looking wharfs, storehouses, and half-dismantled ships, are enveloped in drizzling fog—the fog rendered yet more impenetrable by the fumes of coal-tar and sawdust; and the lower streets swarm with a demoralised population. Yet the people of St. John are so far beyond the people of Halifax, that I heartily wish them success and a railroad.

The air was ringing with the clang of a thousand saws and hammers, when, at seven on the morning of a brilliant August day, we walked through the swarming streets bordering upon the harbour to the *Ornevorg* steamer, belonging to the United States, built for Long Island Sound, but now used as a coasting steamer. All my preconceived notions of a steamer were here at fault. If it were like anything in nature, it was like Noah's ark, or, to come to something post-diluvian, one of those covered hulks, or "ships in ordinary," which are to be seen at Portsmouth and Devonport.

She was totally unlike an English ship, painted entirely white, without masts, with two small black funnels alongside each other; and several erections one above another for decks, containing multitudes of windows about two feet square. The fabric seemed kept together by two large beams, which added to the top-heavy appearance of the whole affair. We entered by the paddle-box (which was within the outer casing of the ship), in company with a great crowd, into a large square uncarpeted apartment, called the "Hall," with offices at the sides for the sale of railway and dinner tickets. Separated from this by a curtain is the ladies' saloon, a large and almost *too* airy apartment extending from the Hall to the stern of the ship, well furnished with sofas, rocking-chairs, and marble tables. A row of berths runs along the side, hung with festooned drapery of satin damask, the curtains being of muslin, embroidered with rose-coloured braid.

Above this is the general saloon, a large, handsomely furnished room, with state rooms running down each side, and opening upon a small deck fourteen feet long, also covered; the roof of this and of the saloon, forming the real or hurricane deck of the ship, closed to passengers, and twelve feet above which works the beam of the engine. Below the Hall, running the whole length of the ship, is the gentlemen's cabin, containing 170 berths. This is lighted by artificial light, and is used for meals. An enclosure for the engine occupies the centre, but is very small, as the machinery of a high-pressure engine is without the encumbrances of condenser and air-pump. The engines drove the unwieldy fabric through the calm water at the rate of fifteen miles an hour. I have been thus minute in my description, because this one will serve for all the steamers in which I subsequently travelled in the United States and Canada.

The city of St. John looked magnificent on its lofty steep; and for some time we had some very fine coast scenery; lofty granite cliffs rising abruptly from the water, clothed with forests, the sea adjoining them so deep, that we passed them, as proved by actual demonstration, within a stone's throw. At one we arrived at Eastport, in Maine, a thriving-looking place, and dinner was served while we were quiescent at the wharf. The stewardess hunted up all the females in the ship, and, preceding them downstairs, placed them at the head of the table; then, and not an instant before, were the gentlemen allowed to appear, who made a most obstreperous rush at the viands. There were about 200 people seated in a fetid and dimly-lighted apartment, at a table covered over with odoriferous viands—pork stuffed with onions, boiled legs of mutton, boiled chickens and turkeys, roast geese, beef-steaks, yams, tomatoes, squash, mush, corn-cobs, johnny cake, and those endless dishes of pastry to which the American palate is so partial. I was just finishing a plate of soup when a waiter touched me on the shoulder—"Dinner ticket, or fifty cents;" and almost before I had comprehended the mysteries of American money sufficiently to pay, other people were eating their dessert. So simple, however, is the coinage of the United States, that in two days I understood it as well as our own. Five dollars equal an English sovereign, and one hundred cents make a dollar, and with this very moderate amount of knowledge one can conduct one's pecuniary affairs all over the Union. The simplicity of the calculation was quite a relief to me after the relative values of the English sovereign in the colonies, which had greatly perplexed me: 25s. 6d. in New Brunswick, 25s. in Nova Scotia, and 30s. in Prince Edward Island. I sat on deck till five, when I went down to my berth. As the evening closed in gloomily, the sea grew coarser, and I heard the captain say, "We are likely to have a very fresh night of it." At seven a wave went down the companion-way, and washed half the tea-things off the table, and before I fell asleep, the mate put his head through the curtain to say, "It's a rough night, ladies, but there's no danger;" a left-handed way of giving courage, which of course frightened the timid. About eleven I was awoke by confused cries, and in my dawning consciousness everything seemed going to pieces. The curtain was undrawn, and I could see the hall continually swept by the waves.

Everything in our saloon was loose; rocking-chairs were careering about the floor and coming into collision; the stewardess, half-dressed, was crawling about from berth to berth, answering the inquiries of terrified ladies, and the ship was groaning and straining heavily; but I slept again, till awoke at midnight by a man's voice shouting "Get up, ladies, and dress, but don't come out till you're called; the gale's very heavy." Then followed a scene. People, helpless in illness a moment before, sprang out of their berths and hastily huddled on their clothes; mothers caught hold of their infants with a convulsive grasp; some screamed, others sat down in apathy, while not a few addressed agonised supplications to that God, too often neglected in times of health and safety, to save them in their supposed extremity.

Crash went the lamp, which was suspended from the ceiling, as a huge wave struck the ship, making her reel and stagger, and shrieks of terror followed this event, which left us in almost total darkness. Rush came another heavy wave, sweeping up the saloon, carrying chairs and stools before it, and as rapidly retiring. The hall was full of men, clinging to the supports, each catching the infectious fear from his neighbour. Wave after wave now struck the ship. I heard the captain say the sea was making a clean breach over her, and order the deck-load overboard. Shortly after, the water, sweeping in from above, put out the engine-fires, and, as she settled down continually in the trough of the sea, and lay trembling there as though she would never rise again, even in my ignorance I knew that she had "no way on her" and was at the mercy of the waters. I now understood the meaning of "blowing great guns." The wind sounded like continual discharges of heavy artillery, and the waves, as they struck the ship, felt like cannon-balls. I could not get up and dress, for, being in the top berth, I was unable to get out in consequence of the rolling of the ship, and so, being unable to mend matters, I lay quietly, the whole passing before me as a scene. I had several times been called on to anticipate death from illness; but here, as I heard the men outside say, "She's going down, she's water-logged, she can't hold together," there was a different prospect of sinking down among the long trailing weeds in the cold, deep waters of the Atlantic. Towards three o'clock, a wave, striking the ship, threw me against a projecting beam of the side, cutting my head severely and stunning me, and I remained insensible for three hours. We continued in great danger for ten hours, many expecting each moment to be their last, but in the morning the gale moderated, and by most strenuous exertions at the pumps the water was kept down till assistance was rendered, which enabled us about one o'clock to reach the friendly harbour of Portland in Maine, with considerable damage and both our boats stove. Deep thankfulness was expressed by many at such an unlooked-for termination of the night's terrors and adventures; many the resolutions expressed not to trust the sea again.

We were speedily moored to the wharf at Portland, amid a forest of masts; the stars and stripes flaunted gaily overhead in concert with the American eagle; and as I stepped upon those shores on which the sanguine suppose that the Anglo-Saxon race is to renew the vigour of its youth, I felt that a new era of my existence had begun.

CHAPTER V

First experiences of American freedom—The "striped pig" and
"Dusty Ben"—A country mouse—What the cars are like—
Beauties of New England—The land of apples—A Mammoth
hotel—The rusty inkstand exiled—Eloquent eyes—
Alone in a crowd.

The city of Portland, with its busy streets, and crowded wharfs, and handsome buildings, and railway *depôts*, rising as it does on the barren coast of the sterile State of Maine, fully bears out the first part of an assertion which I had already heard made by Americans, "We're a great people, the greatest nation on the face of the earth."

A polite custom-house officer asked me if I had anything contraband in my trunks, and on my reply in the negative they were permitted to pass without even the formality of being uncorded. "Enlightened citizens" they are truly, I thought, and, with the pleasant consciousness of being in a perfectly free country, where everyone can do as he pleases, I entered an hotel near the water and sat down in the ladies' parlour. I had not tasted food for twenty-five hours, my clothes were cold and wet, a severe cut was on my temple, and I felt thoroughly exhausted. These circumstances, I thought, justified me in ringing the bell and asking for a glass of wine. Visions of the agreeable refreshment which would be produced by the juice of the grape appeared simultaneously with the waiter. I made the request, and he brusquely replied, "You can't have it, *it's contrary to law.*" In my half-drowned and faint condition the refusal appeared tantamount to positive cruelty, and I remembered that I had come in contact with the celebrated "*Maine Law.*" That the inhabitants of the State of Maine are not "*free*" was thus placed practically before me at once. Whether they are "*enlightened*" I doubted at the time, but leave the question of the prohibition of fermented liquors to be decided by abler social economists than myself.

I was hereafter informed that to those who go downstairs, and ask to see the "*striped pig*," wine and spirits are produced; that a request to speak with "*Dusty Ben*" has a like effect, and that, on asking for "*sarsaparilla*" at certain stores in the town, the desired stimulant can be obtained. Indeed it is said that the consumption of this drug is greater in Maine than in all the other States put together. But in justice to this highly respectable State, I must add that the drunkenness which forced this stringent measure upon the legislature was among the thousands of English and Irish emigrants who annually land at Portland. My only companion here was a rosy-cheeked, simple country girl, who was going to Kennebunk, and, never having been from home before, had not the slightest idea what to do. Presuming on my antiquated appearance, she asked me "to take care of her, to get her ticket for her, for she daren't ask those men for it, and to let her sit by me in the car." She said she was so frightened with something she'd seen that she didn't know how she should go in the cars. I asked her what it was. "Oh," she said, "it was a great thing, bright red, with I don't know how many wheels, and a large black top, and bright shining things moving about all over it, and smoke and steam coming out of it, and it made such an awful noise it seemed to shake the earth."

At half-past three we entered the cars in a long shed, where there were no officials in uniform as in England, and we found our way in as we could. "All aboard!" is the signal for taking places, but on this occasion a loud shout of "Tumble in for your lives!" greeted my amused ears, succeeded by "Go a-head!" and off we went, the engineer tolling a heavy bell to notify our approach to the passengers in *the streets along which we passed*. America has certainly flourished under her motto "Go a-head!" but the cautious "All right!" of an English guard, who waits to start till he is sure of his ground being clear, gives one more confidence. I never experienced the same amount of fear which is expressed by *Bunn* and other writers, for, on comparing the number of accidents with the number of miles of railway open in America, I did not find the disadvantage in point of safety on her side. The cars are a complete novelty to an English eye. They are twenty-five feet long, and hold about sixty persons; they have twelve windows on either side, and two and a door at each end; a passage runs down the middle, with chairs to hold two each on either side. There is a small saloon for ladies with babies at one end, and a filter containing a constant supply of iced water. There are rings along the roof for a rope which passes through each car to the engine, so that anything wrong can be communicated instantly to the engineer. Every car has eight solid wheels, four being placed close together at each end, all of which can be locked by two powerful breaks. At each end of every car is a platform, and passengers are "prohibited from standing upon it at their peril," as also from passing from car to car while the train is in motion; but as no penalty attaches to this law, it is incessantly and continuously violated, "free and enlightened citizens" being at perfect liberty to imperil their own necks; and "poor, ignorant, benighted Britishers" soon learn to follow their example. Persons are for ever passing backwards and forwards, exclusive of the conductor whose business it is, and water-carriers, book, bonbon, and peach venders. No person connected with these railways wears a distinguishing dress, and the stations, or "depôts" as they are called, are generally of the meanest description, mere wooden sheds, with a ticket-office very difficult to discover. If you are so fortunate as to find a man standing at the door of the baggage-car, he attaches copper plates to your trunks, with a number and the name of the place you are going to upon them, giving you labels with corresponding numbers. By this excellent arrangement, in going a very long journey, in which you are obliged to change cars several times, and cross rivers and lakes in steamers, you are relieved of all responsibility, and only require at the end to give your checks to the hotel-porter, who regains your baggage without any trouble on your part.

This plan would be worthily imitated at our termini in England, where I have frequently seen "unprotected females" in the last stage of frenzy at being pushed out of the way, while some persons unknown are running off with their possessions.

When you reach a *depôt*, as there are no railway porters, numerous men clamour to take your effects to an hotel, but, as many of these are thieves, it is necessary to be very careful in only selecting those who have hotel-badges on their hats.

An emigrant-car is attached to each train, but there is only one class: thus it may happen that you have on one side the President of the Great Republic, and on the other the *gentleman* who blacked your shoes in the morning. The Americans, however, have too much respect for themselves and their companions to travel except in good clothes, and this mingling of all ranks is far from being disagreeable, particularly to a stranger like myself, one of whose objects was to see things in their everyday dress. We must be well aware that in many parts of England it would be difficult for a lady to travel unattended in a second-class, impossible in a third-class carriage; yet I travelled several thousand miles in America, frequently alone, from the house of one friend to another's, and never met with anything approaching to incivility; and I have often heard it stated that a lady, no matter what her youth or attractions might be, could travel alone through every State in the Union, and never meet with anything but attention and respect.

I have had considerable experience of the cars, having travelled from the Atlantic to the Mississippi, and from the Mississippi to the St. Lawrence, and found the company so agreeable in its way, and the cars themselves so easy, well ventilated, and comfortable, that, were it not for the disgusting practice of spitting upon the floors in which the lower classes of Americans indulge, I should greatly prefer them to our own exclusive carriages, denominated in the States "'*coon sentry-boxes.*" Well, we are seated in the cars; a man shouts "Go a-head!" and we are off, the engine ringing its heavy bell, and thus begin my experiences of American travel.

I found myself in company with eleven gentlemen and a lady from Prince Edward Island, whom a strange gregarious instinct had thus drawn together. The engine gave a hollow groan, very unlike our cheerful whistle, and, soon moving through the town, we reached the open country.

Fair was the country that we passed through in the States of Maine, New Hampshire, and Massachusetts. Oh very fair! smiling, cultivated, and green, like England, but far happier; for slavery which disgraces the New World, and poverty which desolates the Old, are nowhere to be seen.

There were many farmhouses surrounded by the nearly finished harvest, with verandahs covered with vines and roses; and patriarchal-looking family groups seated under them, engaged in different employments, and enjoying the sunset, for here it was gorgeous summer. And there were smaller houses of wood painted white, with bright green jalousies, in gardens of pumpkins, and surrounded by orchards. Apples seemed almost to grow wild; there were as many orchards as corn-fields, and apple and pear trees grew in the very hedgerows.

And such apples! not like our small, sour, flavourless *things*, but like some southern fruit; huge balls, red and yellow, such as are caricatured in wood, weighing down the fine large trees. There were heaps of apples on the ground, and horses and cows were eating them in the fields, and rows of freight-cars at all the stations were laden with them, and little boys were selling them in the cars; in short, where were they not? There were smiling fields with verdant hedgerows between them, unlike the untidy snake-fences of the colonies, and meadows like parks, dotted over with trees, and woods filled with sumach and scarlet maple, and rapid streams hurrying over white pebbles, and villages of green-jalousied houses, with churches and spires, for here all places of worship have spires; and the mellow light of a declining sun streamed over this varied scene of happiness, prosperity, and comfort; and for a moment I thought—O traitorous thought!—that the New England was fairer than the Old.

84

Nor were the more material evidences of prosperity wanting, for we passed through several large towns near the coast—Newbury Port, Salem, and Portsmouth—with populations varying from 30,000 to 50,000 souls. They seemed bustling, thriving places, with handsome stores, which we had an opportunity of observing, as in the States the cars run right into the streets along the carriage-way, traffic being merely diverted from the track while the cars are upon it.

Most of the railways in the States have only one track or line of rails, with occasional sidings at the stations for the cars to pass each other. A fence is by no means a matter of necessity, and two or three animals are destroyed every day from straying on the line. The engines, which are nearly twice the size of ours, with a covered enclosure for the engineer and stoker, carry large *fenders* or guards in front, to lift incumbrances from the track. At eight o'clock we found ourselves passing over water, and between long rows of gas-lights, and shortly afterwards the cars stopped at Boston, the Athens of America. Giving our baggage-checks to the porter of the American House, we drove to that immense hotel, where I remained for one night. It was crammed from the very basement to the most undesirable locality nearest the moon; I believe it had seven hundred inmates. I had arranged to travel to Cincinnati, and from thence to Toronto, with Mr. and Mrs. Walrence, but on reaching Boston I found that they feared fever and cholera, and, leaving me to travel alone from Albany, would meet me at Chicago. Under these circumstances I remained with my island friends for one night at this establishment, a stranger in a land where I had few acquaintances, though I was well armed with letters of introduction. One of these was to Mr. Amy, a highly respected merchant of Boston, who had previously informed me by letter of the best route to the States, and I immediately despatched a note to him, but he was absent at his country-house, and I was left to analyse the feeling of isolation inseparable from being alone in a crowd. Having received the key of my room, I took my supper in an immense hall, calculated for dining 400 persons. I next went into the ladies' parlour, and felt rather out of place among so many richly dressed females; for as I was proceeding to write a letter, a porter came in and told me that writing was not allowed in that saloon. "Freedom again," thought I. On looking round I did feel that my antiquated goose-quill and rusty-looking inkstand were rather out of place. The carpet of the room was of richly flowered Victoria pile, rendering the heaviest footstep noiseless; the tables were marble on gilded pedestals, the couches covered with gold brocade. At a piano of rich workmanship an elegantly dressed lady was seated, singing "And will you love me always?"—a question apparently satisfactorily answered by the speaking eyes of a bearded Southerner, who was turning over the pages for her. A fountain of antique workmanship threw up a *jet d'eau* of iced water, scented with *eau de Cologne*; and the whole was lighted by four splendid chandeliers interminably reflected, for the walls were mirrors divided by marble pillars. The room seemed appropriate to the purposes to which it was devoted— music, needlework, conversation, and flirting. With the single exception of the rule against writing in the ladies' saloon, a visitor at these immense establishments is at perfect liberty to do as he pleases, provided he pays the moderate charge of two dollars, or 8*s.* a day. This includes, even at the best hotels, a splendid *table-d'hôte*, a comfortable bedroom, lights, attendance, and society in abundance. From the servants one meets with great attention, not combined with deference of manner, still less with that obsequiousness which informs you by a suggestive bow, at the end of your visit, that it has been meted out with reference to the probable amount of half-sovereigns, shillings, and sixpences at your disposal.

It will not be out of place here to give a sketch of the peculiarities of the American hotel system, which constitutes such a distinctive feature of life in the States, and is a requirement arising out of the enormous extent of their territory, and the nomade life led by vast numbers of the most restless and energetic people under the sun.

"People will turn hastily over the pages when they come to this" was the remark of a lively critic on reading this announcement; but while I promise my readers that hotels shall only be described *once*, I could not reconcile it to myself not to give them information on "Things as they are in America," when I had an opportunity of acquiring it.

The American House at Boston, which is a fair specimen of the best class of hotels in the States, though more frequented by mercantile men than by tourists, is built of grey granite, with a frontage to the street of 100 feet. The ground floor to the front is occupied by retail stores, in the centre of which a lofty double doorway denotes the entrance, marked in a more characteristic manner by groups of gentlemen smoking before it. This opens into a lofty and very spacious hall, with a chequered floor of black and white marble; there are lounges against the wall, covered over with buffalo-skins; and, except at meal-times, this capacious apartment is a scene of endless busy life, from two to three hundred gentlemen constantly thronging it, smoking at the door, lounging on the settees, reading the newspapers, standing in animated groups discussing commercial matters, arriving, or departing. Piles of luggage, in which one sees with dismay one's light travelling valise crushed under a gigantic trunk, occupy the centre; porters seated on a form wait for orders; peripatetic individuals walk to and fro; a confused Babel of voices is ever ascending to the galleries above; and at the door, hacks, like the "*eilwagon*" of Germany, are ever depositing fresh arrivals. There is besides this a private entrance for ladies. Opposite the entrance is a counter, where four or five clerks constantly attend, under the superintendence of a cashier, to whom all applications for rooms are personally made. I went up to this functionary, wrote my name in a book, he placed a number against it, and, giving me a key with a corresponding number attached, I followed a porter down a long corridor, and up to a small clean room on the third story, where to all intents and purposes my identity was lost—merged in a mere numeral. At another side of the hall is the bar, a handsomely decorated apartment, where lovers of such beverages can procure "toddy," "nightcaps," "mint julep," "gin sling," &c. On the door of my very neat and comfortable bedroom was a printed statement of the rules, times of meals and charge per diem. I believe there are nearly 300 rooms in this house, some of them being bedrooms as large and commodious as in a private mansion in England.

On the level of the entrance is a magnificent eating saloon, principally devoted to male guests, and which is 80 feet long. Upstairs is a large room furnished with a rare combination of splendour and taste, called "The Ladies' Ordinary," where families, ladies, and their invited guests take their meals. Breakfast is at the early hour of seven, and remains on the table till nine; dinner is at one, and tea at six. At these meals "every delicacy of the season" is served in profusion; the daily bill of fare would do credit to a banquet at the Mansion House; the *chef de cuisine* is generally French, and an epicure would find ample scope for the gratification of his palate. If people persist in taking their meals in a separate apartment, they are obliged to pay dearly for the indulgence of their exclusiveness. There are more than 100 waiters, and the ladies at table are always served first, and to the best pieces.

Though it is not part of the hotel system, I cannot forbear mentioning the rapidity with which the Americans despatch their meals. My next neighbour has frequently risen from his seat after a substantial and varied dinner while I was sending away my soup-plate. The effect of this at a *table-d'hôte*, where 400 or 600 sit down to dine, is unpleasant, for the swing-door is incessantly in motion. Indeed, the utter absence of repose is almost the first thing which strikes a stranger. The incessant sound of bells and gongs, the rolling of hacks to and from the door, the arrivals and departures every minute, the trampling of innumerable feet, the flirting and talking in every corridor, make these immense hotels more like a human beehive than anything else.

The drawing-rooms are always kept very hot by huge fires of anthracite coal, and the doors are left open to neutralise the effect. The temperance at table filled me with surprise. I very seldom saw any beverage but pure iced-water. There are conveniences of all descriptions for the use of the guests. The wires of the electric telegraph, constantly attended by a clerk, run into the hotel; porters are ever ready to take your messages into the town; pens, paper, and ink await you in recesses in the lobbies; a man is ever at hand to clean and brush soiled boots—in short, there is every contrivance for abridging your labour in mounting upstairs. But the method of avoiding the confusion and din of two or three hundred bells must not be omitted. All the wires from the different rooms centre at one bell, which is located in a case in the lobby, with the mechanism seen on one side through a sheet of plate-glass. The other side of the case is covered with numbers in rows. By each number is a small straight piece of brass, which drops and hangs down when the bell is sounded, displaying the number to the attention of the clerk, who sends a waiter to the apartment, and places the piece of brass in its former position.

Steam laundries are connected with all the large hotels. At American House the laundry is under the management of a clerk, who records all the minor details. The linen is cleansed in a churn-like machine moved by steam, and wrung by a novel application of the principle of centrifugal force; after which the articles are dried by being passed through currents of hot air, so that they are washed and ironed in the space of a few minutes. The charge varies from six to ten shillings a dozen. There are also suites of hot and cold baths, and barbers' shops.

Before I understood the mysteries of these hotels, I used to be surprised to see gentlemen travelling without even carpet-bags, but it soon appeared that razors and hair-brushes were superfluous, and that the possessor of one shirt might always pass as the owner of half a dozen, for, while taking a bath, the magic laundry would reproduce the article in its pristine glories of whiteness and starch. Every attention to the comfort and luxury of the guest is paid at American House, and its spirited proprietor, Mr. Rice, deserves the patronage which the travelling public so liberally bestow upon him. On ringing my bell it was answered by a garçon, and it is rather curious seldom or never to see a chambermaid.

CHAPTER VI

*A suspected bill—A friend in need—All aboard for the Western
cars—The wings of the wind—American politeness—A
loquacious conductor—Three minutes for refreshments—A
conversation on politics—A confession—The emigrant car—
Beauties of the woods—A forest on fire—Dangers of the cars—
The Queen City of the West.*

I rose the morning after my arrival at five, hoping to leave
Boston for Cincinnati by the *Lightning Express*, which left at
eight. But on summoning the cashier (or rather *requesting* his
attendance, for one never *summons* anyone in the States), and
showing him my bill of exchange drawn on Barclay and
Company of London, he looked at *me*, then at *it*, suspiciously,
as if doubting whether the possessor of such a little wayworn
portmanteau could be the *bonâ fide* owner of such a sum as
the figures represented. "There's so much bad paper going
about, we can't possibly accommodate you," was the dis-
couraging reply; so I was compelled patiently to submit to the
detention.

I breakfasted at seven in the ladies' ordinary, without
exchanging a syllable with anyone, and soon after my kind
friend, Mr. Amy, called upon me. He proved himself a friend
indeed, and his kindness gave me at once a favourable
impression of the Americans. First impressions are not always
correct, but I am happy to say they were fully borne out in this
instance by the uniform kindness and hospitality which I
experienced during my whole tour. Mr. Amy soon procured
me the money for my bill, all in five-dollar notes, and I was glad
to find the exchange greatly in favour of England. He gave me
much information about my route, and various cautions which
I found very useful, and then drove me in a light "waggon"
round the antiquated streets of Boston, crowded with the
material evidences of prosperity, to his pretty villa three miles
distant, in one of those villages of ornamental dwelling-houses

91

which render the appearance of the environs of Boston peculiarly attractive. I saw a good deal of the town in my drive, but, as I returned to it before leaving the States, I shall defer my description of it, and request my readers to dash away at once with me to the "far west," the goal alike of the traveller and the adventurer, and the El Dorado of the emigrant's misty ideas.

Leaving American House with its hall swarming like a hive of bees, I drove to the *depôt* in a hack with several fellow-passengers, Mr. Amy, who was executing a commission for me in the town, having promised to meet me there, but, he being detained, I arrived alone, and was deposited among piles of luggage, in a perfect Babel of men vociferating, "Where are you for?" "Lightning Express!" "All aboard for the Western cars," &c. Someone pounced upon my trunks, and was proceeding to weigh them, when the stage-driver stepped forward and said, "It's a lady's luggage," upon which he relinquished his intention. He also took my ticket for me, handed me to the cars, and then withdrew, wishing me a pleasant journey, his prompt civility having assisted me greatly in the chaotic confusion which attends the departure of a train in America. The cars by which I left were guaranteed to take people to Cincinnati, a distance of 1000 miles, in 40 hours, allowing time for refreshments! I was to travel by five different lines of railway, but this part of the railway system is so well arranged that I only took a ticket once, rather a curious document—a strip of paper half a yard long, with passes for five different roads upon it; thus, whenever I came upon a fresh line, the conductor tore off a piece, giving me a ticket in exchange. Tickets are not only to be procured at the stations, but at several offices in every town, in all the steamboats, and in the cars themselves. For the latter *luxury*, for such it must certainly be considered, as it enables one to step into the cars at the last moment without any preliminaries, one only pays five cents extra.

The engine tolled its heavy bell, and soon we were amid the beauties of New England; rocky hills, small lakes, rapid streams, and trees distorted into every variety of the picturesque. At the next station from Boston the Walrences joined me. We were to travel together, with our ulterior destination a settlement in Canada West, but they would not go to Cincinnati; there were lions in the street; cholera and yellow fever, they said, were raging; in short, they left me at Springfield, to find my way in a strange country as best I might; our *rendezvous* to be Chicago.

At Springfield I obtained the first seat in the car, generally the object of most undignified elbowing, and had space to admire the beauties among which we passed. For many miles we travelled through a narrow gorge, between very high precipitous hills, clothed with wood up to their summits; those still higher rising behind them, while the track ran along the very edge of a clear rushing river. The darkness which soon came on was only enlivened by the sparks from the wood fire of the engine, so numerous and continuous as to look like a display of fireworks. Just before we reached Albany a very respectable-looking man got into the car, and, as his manners were very quiet and civil, we entered into conversation about the trade and manufactures of the neighbourhood. When we got out of the cars on the east side of the river, he said he was going no farther, but, as I was alone, he would go across with me, and see me safe into the cars on the other side. He also offered to carry my reticule and umbrella, and look after my luggage. His civility so excited my suspicions of his honesty, that I did not trust my luggage or reticule out of my sight, mindful of a notice posted up at all the stations, "Beware of swindlers, pickpockets, and luggage-thieves."

We emerged from the cars upon the side of the Hudson river, in a sea of mud, where, had not my friend offered me his arm, as Americans of every class invariably do to an "unprotected female" in a crowd, I should have been borne down and crushed by the shoals of knapsack-carrying pedestrians and truck-pushing porters who swarmed down upon the dirty wharf. The transit across occupied fully ten minutes, in consequence of the numerous times the engine had to be reversed, to avoid running over the small craft which infest this stream. My volunteer escort took me through a crowd through which I could not have found my way alone, and put me into the cars which started from the side of a street in Albany, requesting the conductor, whose countenance instantly prepossessed me in his favour, to pay me every attention on the route. He remained with me until the cars started, and told me that when he saw ladies travelling alone he always made a point of assisting them. I shook hands with him at parting, feeling real regret at losing so kind and intelligent a companion. This man was a working engineer.

Some time afterwards, while travelling for two successive days and nights in an unsettled district in the west, on the second night, fairly overcome with fatigue, and unable, from the crowded state of the car, to rest my feet on the seat in front, I tried unsuccessfully to make a pillow for my head by rolling up my cloak, which attempts being perceived by a working mechanic, he accosted me thus: "Stranger, I guess you're almost used up? Maybe you'd be more comfortable if you could rest your head." Without further parley he spoke to his companion, a man in a similar grade in society; they both gave up their seats, and rolled a coat round the arm of the chair, which formed a very comfortable sofa; and these two men stood for an hour and a half, to give me the advantage of it, apparently without any idea that they were performing a deed of kindness. I met continually with these acts of hearty unostentatious good nature. I mention these in justice to the lower classes of the United States, whose rugged exteriors and uncouth vernacular render them peculiarly liable to be misunderstood.

The conductor quite verified the good opinion which I had formed of him. He turned a chair into a sofa, and lent me a buffalo robe (for, hot though the day had been, the night was intensely cold), and several times brought me a cup of tea. We were talking on the peculiarities and amount of the breakage power on the American lines as compared with ours, and the interest of the subject made him forget to signal the engine-driver to stop at a station. The conversation concluded, he looked out of the window. "Dear me," he said, "we ought to have stopped three miles back; likely there was no one to get out!"

At midnight I awoke shivering with cold, having taken nothing for twelve hours; but at two we stopped at something called by courtesy a station, and the announcement was made, "Cars stop three minutes for refreshments." I got out; it was pitch dark; but I, with a young lady, followed a lantern into a frame-shed floored by the bare earth. Visions of Swindon and Wolverton rose before me, as I saw a long table supported on rude trestles, bearing several cups of steaming tea, while a dirty boy was opening and frizzling oysters by a wood fire on the floor. I swallowed a cup of scalding tea; some oysters were put upon my plate; "Six cents" was shouted by a nasal voice in my ear, and, while hunting for the required sum, "All aboard" warned me to be quick; and, jumping into the cars just as they were in motion, I left my untasted supper on my plate. After "Show your tickets," frequently accompanied by a shake, had roused me several times from a sound sleep, we arrived at Rochester, an important town on the Gennessee Falls, surrounded by extensive clearings, then covered with hoar frost.

Here we were told to get out, as there were twenty minutes for breakfast. But whither should we go when we had got out? We were at the junction of several streets, and five engines, with cars attached, were snorting and moving about. After we had run the gauntlet of all these, I found men ringing bells, and negroes rushing about, tumbling over each other, striking gongs, and all shouting "The cheapest house in all the world—house for all nations—a splenderiferous breakfast for 20 cents!" and the like. At length, seeing an unassuming placard, "Hot breakfast, 25 cents," I ventured in, but an infusion of mint was served instead of the China leaf; and I should be afraid to pronounce upon the antecedents of the steaks. The next place of importance we reached was Buffalo, a large thriving town on the south shore of Lake Erie. There had been an election for Congress at some neighbouring place the day before, and my *vis-à-vis*, the editor of a Buffalo paper, was arguing vociferously with a man on my right.

At length he began to talk to me very vivaciously on politics, and concluded by asking me what I thought of the late elections. Wishing to put an end to the conversation, which had become tedious, I replied that I was from England. "English! you surprise me!" he said; "you've not the *English accent* at all." "What do you think of our government?" was his next question. "Considering that you started free, and had to form your institutions in an enlightened age, that you had the estimable parts of our constitution to copy from, while its faults were before you to serve as beacons, I think your constitution ought to be nearer perfection than it is." "I think our constitution is as near perfection as anything human can be; we are the most free, enlightened, and progressive people under the sun," he answered, rather hotly; but in a few minutes resuming the conversation with his former companion, I overheard him say, "I think I shall give up politics altogether; *I don't believe we have a single public man who is not corrupt.*" "A melancholy result of a perfect constitution, and a humiliating confession for an American," I observed.

The conversations in the cars are well worth a traveller's attention. They are very frequently on politics, but often one hears stories such as the world has become familiarised with from the early pages of Barnum's Autobiography, abounding in racy anecdote, broad humour, and cunning imposition. At Erie we changed cars, and I saw numerous emigrants sitting on large blue boxes, looking disconsolately about them; the Irish physiognomy being the most predominant. They are generally so dirty that they travel by themselves in a partially lighted van, called the Emigrants' car, for a most trifling payment. I once got into one by mistake, and was almost sickened by the smell of tobacco, spirits, dirty fustian, and old leather, which assailed my olfactory organs. Leaving Erie, beyond which the lake of the same name stretched to the distant horizon, blue and calm like a tideless sea, we entered the huge forests on the south shore, through which we passed, I suppose, for more than 100 miles. My next neighbour was a stalwart, bronzed Kentucky farmer, in a palm-leaf hat, who, strange to say, never made any demonstrations with his bowie-knife, and, having been a lumberer in these forests, pointed out all the objects of interest.

The monotonous sublimity of these primeval woods far exceeded my preconceived ideas. We were locked in among gigantic trees of all descriptions, their huge stems frequently rising without a branch for a hundred feet; then breaking into a crown of the most luxuriant foliage. There were walnut, hickory, elm, maple, beech, oak, pine, and hemlock trees, with many others which I did not know, and the only undergrowth, a tropical-looking plant, with huge leaves, and berries like bunches of purple grapes. Though it was the noon of an unclouded sun, all was dark, and still, and lonely; no birds twittered from the branches; no animals enlivened the gloomy shades; no trace of man or of his works was there, except the two iron rails on which we flew along, unfenced from the forest, and those trembling electric wires, which will only cease to speak with the extinction of man himself.

Very occasionally we would come upon a log shanty, that most picturesque of human habitations; the walls formed of large logs, with the interstices filled up with clay, and the roof of rudely sawn boards, projecting one or two feet, and kept in their places by logs placed upon them. Windows and doors there were none, but, where a door was *not*, I generally saw four or five shoeless, ragged urchins, whose light tangled hair and general aspect were sufficient to denote their nationality. Sometimes these cabins would be surrounded by a little patch of cleared land, prolific in Indian corn and pumpkins; the brilliant orange of the latter contrasting with the charred stumps among which they grew; but more frequently the lumberer supported himself solely by his axe. These dwellings are suggestive, for they are erected by the pioneers of civilization; and if the future progress of America be equal in rapidity to its past, in another fifty years the forests will have been converted into lumber and firewood—rich and populous cities will have replaced the cabins and shanties—and the children of the urchins who gazed vacantly upon the cars will have asserted their claims to a voice in the councils of the nation.

The rays of the sun never penetrate the forest, and evening was deepening the gloom of the artificial twilight, when gradually we became enveloped in a glare, redder, fiercer, than that of moonlight; and looking a-head I saw the forest on fire, and that we were rushing into the flames. "Close the windows, there's a fire a-head," said the conductor; and after obeying this *commonplace* direction, many of the passengers returned to the slumbers which had been so unseasonably disturbed. On, on we rushed—the flames encircled us round—we were enveloped in clouds of stifling smoke—crack, crash went the trees—a blazing stem fell across the line—the fender of the engine pushed it aside—the flames hissed like tongues of fire, and then, leaping like serpents, would rush up to the top of the largest tree, and it would blaze like a pineknot. There seemed no egress; but in a few minutes the raging, roaring conflagration was left behind. A forest on fire from a distance looks very much like 'Punch's' picture of a naval review; a near view is the height of sublimity.

The dangers of the cars, to my inexperience, seemed by no means over with the escape from being roasted alive. A few miles from Cleveland they rushed down a steep incline, apparently into Lake Erie; but in *reality* upon a platform supported on piles, so narrow that the edges of the cars hung over it, so that I saw nothing but water. A gale was blowing, and drove the surf upon the platform, and the spray against the windows, giving such a feeling of insecurity, that for a moment I wished myself in one of our "'coon sentry-boxes." The cars were very full after leaving Cleveland, but I contrived to sleep soundly till awakened by the intense cold which attends dawn.

It was a glorious morning. The rosy light streamed over hills covered with gigantic trees, and park-like glades watered by the fair Ohio. There were bowers of myrtle, and vineyards ready for the vintage, and the rich aromatic scent wafted from groves of blossoming magnolias told me that we were in a different clime, and had reached the sunny south. And before us, placed within a perfect amphitheatre of swelling hills, reposed a huge city, whose countless spires reflected the beams of the morning sun—the creation of yesterday— Cincinnati, the *Queen City of the West.* I drove straight to Burnet House, almost the finest edifice in the town, and after travelling a thousand miles in forty-two hours, without either water or a hair-brush, it was the greatest possible luxury to be able to remove the accumulations of soot, dust, and cinders of two days and nights. I spent three days at Clifton, a romantic village three miles from Cincinnati, at the hospitable house of Dr. M'Ilvaine, the Bishop of Ohio; but it would be an ill return for the kindness which I there experienced to give details of my visit, or gratify curiosity by describing family life in one of the "homes of the New World."

CHAPTER VII

*The Queen City continued—Its beauties—Its inhabitants
human and equine—An American church—Where chairs and
bedsteads come from—Pigs and pork—A peep into Kentucky—
Popular opinions respecting slavery—The curse of America.*

The important towns in the United States bear designations of
a more poetical nature than might be expected from so
commercial a people. New York is the Empire City—
Philadelphia the City of Brotherly Love—Cleveland the Forest
City—Chicago the Prairie City—and Cincinnati the Queen City
of the West. These names are no less appropriate than poetical,
and none more so than that applied to Cincinnati. The view
from any of the terraced heights round the town is
magnificent. I saw it first bathed in the mellow light of a
declining sun. Hill beyond hill, clothed with the rich verdure of
an almost tropical clime, slopes of vineyards just ready for the
wine-press,[1] magnolias with their fragrant blossoms, and that
queen of trees the beautiful ilanthus, the "tree of heaven" as it
is called; and everywhere foliage so luxuriant that it looked as
if autumn and decay could never come. And in a hollow near
us lay the huge city, so full of life, its busy hum rising to the
height where I stood; and 200 feet below, the beautiful
cemetery, where its dead await the morning of the resurrection. Yet, while contrasting the trees and atmosphere
here with the comparatively stunted, puny foliage of England,
and the chilly skies of a northern clime, I thought with Cowper
respecting my own dear, but far distant land—

---

1 Grapes are grown in such profusion in the Southern and Western States, that I have seen
damaged bunches thrown to the pigs. Americans find it difficult to understand how highly this
fruit is prized in England. An American lady, when dining at Apsley House, observed that the
Duke of Wellington was cutting up a cluster of grapes into small bunches, and she wondered
that this illustrious man should give himself such unnecessary trouble. When the servant
handed round the plate containing these, she took them all, and could not account for the
amused and even censuring looks of some of the other guests, till she heard that it was
expected that she should have helped herself to one bunch only of the hothouse treasure.

"England, with all thy faults I love thee still—
My country!—

I would not yet exchange thy sullen skies,
And fields without a flower, for warmer France
With all her vines, nor for Ausonia's groves,
Her golden fruitage, or her myrtle bowers."

The change in the climate was great from that in which I had shivered a week before, with a thermometer at 33° in the sun; yet I did not find it oppressive here at 105° in the shade, owing to the excessive dryness of the air. The sallow complexions of the New Englanders were also exchanged for the fat ruddy faces of the people of Ohio, the "*Buckeyes*," as their neighbours designate them. The town of Cincinnati, situated on the navigable stream of the Ohio, 1600 miles from the sea, is one of the most remarkable monuments of the progress of the West. A second Glasgow in appearance, the houses built substantially of red brick, six stories high—huge sign-boards outside each floor denoting the occupation of its owner or lessee—heavily-laden drays rumbling along the streets—quays at which steamboats of fairy architecture are ever lying—massive warehouses and rich stores—the side-walks a perfect throng of foot-passengers—the roadways crowded with light carriages, horsemen with palmetto hats and high-peaked saddles, galloping about on the magnificent horses of Kentucky—an air of life, wealth, bustle, and progress—are some of the characteristics of a city which stands upon ground where sixty years ago an unarmed white man would have been tomahawked as he stood. The human aspect is also curious. Palmetto hats, light blouses, and white trowsers form the prevailing costume even of the clergy, while Germans smoke chibouks and luxuriate in their shirt-sleeves—southerners, with the enervated look arising from residence in a hot climate, lounge about the streets—dark-browed Mexicans, in *sombreras* and high slashed boots, dash about on small active horses with

Mamelouk bits—rovers and adventurers from California and the Far West, with massive rings in their ears, swagger about in a manner which shows their country and calling, and females richly dressed are seen driving and walking about, from the fair-complexioned European to the negress or mulatto. The windows of the stores are arranged with articles of gaudy attire and heavy jewellery, suited to the barbaric taste of many of their customers; but inside I was surprised to find the richest and most elegant manufactures of Paris and London. A bookseller's store, an aggregate of two or three of our largest, indicated that the culture of the mind was not neglected.

The number of carriages, invariably drawn by two horses, astonished me. They were the "*red horses*" of Kentucky and the jet black of Ohio, splendid, proud-looking animals, looking as if they could never tire or die. Except the "trotting baskets" and light waggons, principally driven by "swells" or "Young Americans," all the vehicles were covered, to preserve their inmates from the intense heat of the sun. In the evening hundreds, if not thousands, of carriages are to be seen in the cemetery and along the roads, some of the German ladies driving in low dresses and short sleeves. As everybody who has one hundred yards to go drives or rides, rings are fastened to all the side-walks in the town to tether the horses to. Many of the streets are planted with the ilanthus-tree, and frequently one comes upon churches of tasteful architecture, with fretted spires pointing to heaven.

I went upon the Ohio, lessened by long drought into a narrow stream, in a most commodious high-pressure steam-boat, and deemed myself happy in returning uninjured; for beautiful and fairy-like as these vessels are, between their own explosive qualities and the "snags and sawyers" of the rivers, their average existence is only five years!

Cincinnati in 1800 was a wooden village of 750 inhabitants; it is now a substantially-built brick town, containing 200,000 people, and thousands of fresh settlers are added every year. There are nearly 50,000 Germans, and I believe 40,000 Irish, who distinctly keep up their national characteristics. The Germans almost monopolise the handicraft trades, where they find a fruitful field for their genius and industry; the Irish are here, as everywhere, hewers of wood and drawers of water; they can do nothing but dig, and seldom rise in the social scale; the Germans, as at home, are a thinking, sceptical, theorising people: in politics, Socialists—in religion, Atheists. The Irish are still the willing and ignorant tools of an ambitious and despotic priesthood. And in a land where no man is called to account for his principles, unless they proceed to physical development, these errors grow and luxuriate. The Germans, in that part of the town almost devoted to themselves, have succeeded in practically abolishing the Sabbath, as they utterly ignore that divine institution even as a day of rest, keeping their stores open the whole day. The creeds which they profess are "Socialism" and "Universalism," and at stated periods they assemble to hear political harangues, and address invocations to universal deity. Skilled, educated, and intellectual, they are daily increasing in numbers, wealth, and political importance, and constitute an influence of which the Americans themselves are afraid.

The Irish are a turbulent class, for ever appealing to physical force, influencing the elections, and carrying out their "clan feuds" and "faction fights." The Germans, finding it a land like their own, of corn and vineyards, have named the streets in their locality in Cincinnati after their towns in the Old World, to which in idea one is frequently carried back.

On Sunday, after passing through this continental portion of the town, I found all was order and decorum in the strictly American part, where the whole population seemed to attend worship of one form or another. The church which I attended was the most beautiful place of worship I ever saw; it had neither the hallowed but comfortless antiquity of our village churches, nor the glare and crush of our urban temples; it was of light Norman architecture, and lighted by windows of rich stained glass. The pews were wide, the backs low, and the doors and mouldings were of polished oak; the cushions and linings were of crimson damask, and light fans for *real use* were hung in each pew. The pulpit and reading-desk, both of carved oak and of a tulip shape, were placed in front of the communion-rails, on a spacious platform ascended by three steps—this, the steps, and the aisles of the church were carpeted with beautiful Kidderminster carpeting. The singing and chanting were of a very superior description, being managed, as also a very fine-toned organ, by the young ladies and gentlemen of the congregation. The ladies were more richly dressed and in brighter colours than the English, and many of them in their features and complexions bore evident traces of African and Spanish blood. The gentlemen universally wore the moustache and beard, and generally blue or green frock-coats, the collars turned over with velvet. The responses were repeated without the assistance of a clerk, and the whole service was conducted with decorum and effect.

The same favourable description may apply generally to the churches of different denominations in the United States; coldness and discomfort are not considered as incentives to devotion; and the houses of worship are ever crowded with regular and decorous worshippers.

Cincinnati is the outpost of manufacturing civilization, though large, important, but at present unfinished cities are rapidly springing up several hundred miles farther to the west. It has regular freight steamers to New Orleans, St. Louis, and other places on the Missouri and Mississippi; to Wheeling and Pittsburgh, and thence by railway to the great Atlantic cities, Philadelphia and Baltimore, while it is connected with the Canadian lakes by railway and canal to Cleveland. Till I thoroughly understood that Cincinnati is the centre of a circle embracing the populous towns of the south, and the increasing populations of the lake countries and the western territories, with their ever-growing demand for the fruits of manufacturing industry, I could not understand the utility of the vast establishments for the production of household goods which arrest the attention of the visitor to the Queen City.

There is a furniture establishment in Baker Street, London, which employs perhaps eighty hands, and we are rather inclined to boast of it, but we must keep silence when we hear of a factory as large as a Manchester cotton-mill, five stories high, where 260 hands are constantly employed in making chairs, tables, and bedsteads.

At the factory of Mitchell and Rammelsberg common chairs are the principal manufacture, and are turned out at the rate of 2500 a week, worth from £1 to £5 a dozen. Rocking-chairs, which are only made in perfection in the States, are fabricated here, also chests of drawers, of which 2000 are made annually. Baby-rocking cribs, in which the brains of the youth of America are early habituated to perpetual restlessness, are manufactured here in surprising quantities. The workmen at this factory (most of whom are native Americans and Germans, the English and Scotch being rejected on account of their intemperance) earn from 12 to 14 dollars a week. At another factory 1000 bedsteads, worth from £1 to £5 each, are completed every week. There are vast boot and shoe factories, which would have shod our whole Crimean army in a week, at one of which the owner pays 60,000 dollars or £12,000 in wages annually! It consumes 5000 pounds weight of boot-nails per annum! The manufactories of locks and guns, tools, and carriages, with countless other appliances of civilized life, are on a similarly large scale. Their products are to be found among the sugar plantations of the south, the diggers of California, the settlers in Oregon, in the infant cities of the far West, the tent of the hunter, and the shanty of the emigrant; in one word, wherever demand and supply can be placed in conjunction.

And while the demand is ever increasing as the tide of emigration rolls westward, so the inventive brains of the Americans are ever discovering some mechanical means of abridging manual labour, which seldom or ever meets the demand. The saws, axes, and indeed all cutting tools made at respectable establishments in the States, are said to be superior to ours. On going into a hardware store at Hamilton in Upper

Canada, I saw some English spades and axes, and I suppose my face expressed some of the admiration which my British pride led me to feel; for the owner, taking up some spades and cutting-tools of Cincinnati manufacture, said, "We can only sell these; the others are bad workmanship, and won't stand two days' hard work."

Articles of English manufacture are not seen in considerable quantities in the wholesale stores, and even the import of foreign wines has been considerably diminished by the increasingly successful culture of the grape in Ohio, 130,000 gallons of wine having been produced in the course of the year. Wines resembling hock, claret, and champagne are made, and good judges speak very highly of them.

Cincinnati is famous for its public libraries and reading-rooms. The Young Men's Mercantile Library Association has a very handsome suite of rooms opened as libraries and reading-rooms, the number of books amounting to 16,000, these, with upwards of 100 newspapers, being well selected by a managing committee; none of our English works of good repute being a-wanting. The facility with which English books are reprinted in America, and the immense circulation which they attain in consequence of their cheapness, greatly increases the responsibility which rests upon our authors as to the direction which they give, whether for good or evil, to the intelligent and inquiring minds of the youth of America—minds ceaselessly occupied, both in religion and politics, in investigation and inquiry—in overturning old systems before they have devised new ones.

I believe that the most important religious denominations in Cincinnati are the Episcopalian, the Baptist, and the Wesleyan. The first is under the superintendence of the learned and pious Bishop M'Ilvaine, whose apostolic and untiring labours have greatly advanced the cause of religion in the State of Ohio. There is a remarkable absence of sectarian spirit, and the ministers of all orthodox denominations act in harmonious combination for the general good.

But after describing the beauty of her streets, her astonishing progress, and the splendour of her shops, I must not close this chapter without stating that the Queen City bears the less elegant name of Porkopolis; that swine, lean, gaunt, and vicious-looking, riot through her streets; and that, on coming out of the most splendid stores, one stumbles over these disgusting intruders. Cincinnati is the city of pigs. As there is a railway system and a hotel system, so there is also a *pig system*, by which this place is marked out from any other. Huge quantities of these useful animals are reared after harvest in the corn-fields of Ohio, and on the beech-mast and acorns of its gigantic forests. At a particular time of year they arrive by thousands—brought in droves and steamers to the number of 500,000—to meet their doom, when it is said that the Ohio runs red with blood! There are huge slaughter-houses behind the town, something on the plan of the *abattoirs* of Paris—large wooden buildings, with numerous pens, from whence the pigs march in single file along a narrow passage, to an apartment where each, on his entrance, receives a blow with a hammer, which deprives him of consciousness, and in a short time, by means of numerous hands, and a well-managed caldron system, he is cut up ready for pickling. The day on which a pig is killed in England constitutes an era in the family history of the year, and squeals of a terrific description announce the event to the neighbourhood. There is not time or opportunity for such a process at Porkopolis, and the first notification which the inhabitants receive of the massacre is the thousand barrels of pork on the quays, ready to be conveyed to the Atlantic cities, for exportation to the European markets. At one establishment 12,000 pigs are killed, pickled, and packed every fall; and in the whole neighbourhood, as I have heard in the cars, the "hog crop" is as much a subject of discussion and speculation as the cotton crop of Alabama, the hop-picking of Kent, or the harvest in England.

Kentucky, the land, by reputation, of "red horses, bowie-knives, and gouging," is only separated from Ohio by the river

Ohio; and on a day when the thermometer stood at 103° in the shade I went to the town of Covington. Marked, wide, and almost inestimable, is the difference between the free state of Ohio and the slave-state of Kentucky. They have the same soil, the same climate, and precisely the same natural advantages; yet the total absence of progress, if not the appearance of retrogression and decay, the loungers in the streets, and the peculiar appearance of the slaves, afford a contrast to the bustle on the opposite side of the river, which would strike the most unobservant. I was credibly informed that property of the same real value was worth 300 dollars in Kentucky and 3000 in Ohio! Free emigrants and workmen will not settle in Kentucky, where they would be brought into contact with compulsory slave-labour; thus the development of industry is retarded, and the difference will become more apparent every year, till possibly some great changes will be forced upon the legislature. Few English people will forget the impression made upon them by the first sight of a slave—a being created in the image of God, yet the *bonâ fide* property of his fellow-man. The first I saw was an African female, the slave of a lady from Florida, with a complexion black as the law which held her in captivity. The subject of slavery is one which has lately been brought so prominently before the British people by Mrs. Beecher Stowe, that I shall be pardoned for making a few remarks upon it. Powerfully written as the book is, and much as I admire the benevolent intentions of the writer, I am told that the effect of the volume has been prejudicial, and this assertion is borne out by persons well acquainted with the subject in the free states. A gentleman very eminent in his country, as having devoted himself from his youth to the cause of abolition, as a steadfast pursuer of one grand principle, together with other persons, say that "'Uncle Tom's Cabin' had thrown the cause back for many years!"[1] The excitement on the

1 It must be observed that I do not offer any opinion of my own upon 'Uncle Tom's Cabin,' or upon the estimation in which it is held in the United States; but in order to answer questions

subject still continues in England, though it found a safety-valve in the Stafford House manifesto, and the received impression, which no force of fact can alter, is, that slave-owners are divided into but two classes—brutalised depraved "*Legrees*," or enthusiastic, visionary "*St. Clairs*"—the former, of course, predominating.

Slavery, though under modifications which rendered it little more than the apprenticeship of our day, was *permitted* under the Mosaic dispensation; but it is contrary to the whole tenor of Christianity; and a system which lowers man as an intellectual and responsible being is no less morally than politically wrong. That it is a political mistake is plainly evidenced by the retarded development and apparent decay of the Southern States, as compared with the ceaseless material progress of the North and West. It cannot be doubted that in Alabama, Florida, and Louisiana, "*Legrees*" are to be found, for cruelty is inherent in base natures; we have "*Legrees*" in our factories and coal-pits; but in England their most terrible excesses are restrained by the strong arm of law, which, *when appealed to*, extends its protection to the feeblest and most helpless. What then must such men become in the isolated cotton or sugar plantations of the South, distant from the restraints which public opinion exercises, and where the evidence of a slave is inadmissible in a court of justice? The full extent of the cruelties practised will never be known, until revealed at the solemn tribunal of the last day. But we dare not hope that such men are rare, though circumstances of self-interest combine to form a class of slave-owners of a higher grade. These are men who look upon their slaves as we do upon our cows and horses—as mere animal property, of greater or less value according to the care which is taken of them. The slaves of these persons are well clothed, lodged, and fed; they are not overworked, and dancing, singing, and other

which have frequently been put to me upon the subject, I have just given the substance of the remarks which have been made upon it by abolitionists in the Northern States.

amusements, which increase health and cheerfulness, are actively promoted. But the system is one which has for its object the transformation of reason into instinct—the lowering of a rational being into a machine scarcely more intelligent in appearance than some of our own ingeniously-contrived steam-engines. Religious teaching is withheld, reading is forbidden, and the instruction of a slave in it punished as a crime, lest he should learn that freedom is his birthright.

A third and very large class of slave-owners is to be found, who, having inherited their property in slaves, want the means of judiciously emancipating them. The negroes are not in a condition to receive freedom in the reckless way in which some abolitionists propose to bestow it upon them. They must be prepared for it by instruction in the precepts of religion, by education, and by the reception of those principles of self-reliance, without which they have not the moral perception requisite to enable them to appreciate the blessings of freedom; and this very ignorance and obtuseness is one of the most telling arguments against the system which produces it. The want of this previous preparation has been frequently shown, particularly in Kentucky, where whole bodies of emancipated slaves, after a few days' experience of their new condition, have entreated for a return to servitude. These slave-owners of whom I now speak deeply deplore the circumstances under which they are placed, and, while wanting the spirit of self-sacrifice, and the moral courage, which would lead them, by manumitting their slaves, to enter into a novel competition with slave-labour on other estates, do their best to ameliorate the condition in which the Africans are placed, encouraging them, by the sale of little articles of their own manufacture, to purchase their freedom, which is granted at a very reduced rate. I had opportunities of conversing with several of these freed negroes, and they all expressed attachment to their late owners, and spoke of the mildness with which they were treated, saying that the great threat made use of was to send them "*down south.*"

The slaves in the northern slave States are a thoughtless, happy set, spending their evenings in dancing or singing to the banja; and 'Oh, carry me back to Old Virginny,' or 'Susannah, don't you cry for me,' may be heard on summer evenings rising from the maize and tobacco grounds of Kentucky. Yet, whether naturally humane instincts may lead to merciful treatment of the slave, or the same result be accomplished by the rigorous censorship of public opinion in the border States, apart from the abstract question of slavery, that system is greatly to be reprobated which gives *power without responsibility*, and permits the temporal, yes, the eternal well-being of another to depend upon the will and caprice of a man, when the victim of his injustice is deprived of the power of appeal to an earthly tribunal. Instances of severe treatment on one side, and of kindness on the other, cannot fairly be brought as arguments for or against the system; it must be justified or condemned by the undeviating law of moral right as laid down in divine revelation. Slavery existed in 1850 in 15 out of 31 States, the number of slaves being 3,204,345, connected by sympathy and blood with 433,643 coloured persons, nominally free, but who occupy a social position of the lowest grade. It is probable that this number will increase, as it has hitherto done, in a geometrical ratio, which will give 6,000,000 in 1875, of a people dangerous from numbers merely, but doubly, trebly so in their consciousness of oppression, and in the passions which may incite them to a terrible revenge. America boasts of freedom, and of such a progress as the world has never seen before; but while the tide of the Anglo-Saxon race rolls across her continent, and while we contemplate with pleasure a vast nation governed by free institutions, and professing a pure faith, a hand, faintly seen at present, but destined ere long to force itself upon the attention of all, points to the empires of a by-gone civilisation, and shows that they had their periods in which to rise, flourish, and decay, and that slavery was the main cause of that decay. The exasperating reproaches addressed to the Americans, in ignorance of the real difficulties of dealing with the case, have done much harm in inciting that popular clamour which hurries on reckless legislation. The problem is one which occupies the attention of thinking and Christian men on both sides of the Atlantic, but still remains a gigantic evil for philanthropists to mourn over, and for politicians to correct.

An unexceptional censure ought not to be pronounced without a more complete knowledge of the subject than can be gained from novels and newspapers; still less ought this censure to extend to America as a whole, for the people of the Northern States are more ardent abolitionists than ourselves—more consistent, in fact, for they have no white slaves, no oppressed factory children, the cry of whose wrongs ascends daily into the ears of an avenging Judge. Still, blame must attach to *them* for the way in which they place the coloured people in an inferior social position, a rigid system of exclusiveness shutting them out from the usual places of amusement and education. It must not be forgotten that England bequeathed this system to her colonies, though she has nobly blotted it out from those which still own her sway; that it is encouraged by the cotton lords of Preston and Manchester; and that the great measure of negro emancipation was carried, not by the violent declamation and ignorant railings of men who sought popularity by exciting the passions of the multitude, but by the persevering exertions and practical Christian philanthropy of Mr. Wilberforce and his coadjutors. It is naturally to be expected that a person writing a book on America would offer some remarks upon this subject, and raise a voice, however feeble, against so gigantic an evil. The conclusions which I have stated in the foregoing pages are derived from a careful comparison and study of facts which I have learned from eminent speakers and writers both in favour of and against the slave-system.

CHAPTER VIII

*The hickory stick—Chawing up ruins—A forest scene—A
curious questioner—Hard and soft shells—Dangers of a ferry—
The western prairies—Nocturnal detention—The Wild West
and the Father of Rivers—Breakfast in a shed—What is an
alligator?—Physiognomy, and its uses—The ladies' parlour—A
Chicago hotel, its inmates and its horrors—A water-drinking
people—The Prairie City—Progress of the West.*

A bright September sun glittered upon the spires of Cincinnati
as I reluctantly bade it adieu, and set out in the early morning
by the cars to join my travelling companions, meaning to make
as long a *détour* as possible, or, as a "down-east" lady might say,
to "make a pretty considerable circumlocution." Fortunately I
had met with some friends, well acquainted with the country,
who offered to take me round a much larger circle than I had
contemplated; and with a feeling of excitement such as I had
not before experienced, we started for the Mississippi and the
western prairies *en route* to Detroit.

Bishop M'Ilvaine, anxious that a very valued friend of his in
England should possess something from Ohio, had cut down
a small sapling, which, when divested of its branches and
otherwise trimmed, made a very formidable-looking bludgeon
or cudgel, nearly four feet long. This being too lengthy for my
trunks was tied to my umbrella, and on this day in the cars
excited no little curiosity, several persons eyeing it, then me, as
if wondering in what relation we stood to each other. Finally
they took it up, minutely examining it, and tapping it as if to
see whether anything were therein concealed. It caused me
much amusement, and, from its size, some annoyance, till at
length, wishing to leave it in my room at a Toronto hotel while
I went for a visit of a few days, the waiter brought it down to
the door, asking me "if I wished to take the *cudgel?*" After this
I had it shortened, and it travelled in my trunk to New York,
where it was given to a carver to be fashioned into a walking-

113

stick; and, unless the tradesman played a Yankee trick, and substituted another, it is now, after surviving many dangers by sea and land, in the possession of the gentleman for whom it was intended.

Some amusing remarks were made upon England by some of the "Buckeyes," as the inhabitants of Ohio are called. On trying to persuade a lady to go with me to St. Louis, I observed that it was *only* five hundred miles. "Five hundred miles!" she replied; "why, you'd tumble off your paltry island into the sea before you so far!" Another lady, who got into the cars at some distance from Cincinnati, could not understand the value which we set upon ruins. "We should chaw them up," she said, "make roads or bridges of them, unless Barnum transported them to his museum: we would never keep them on our own hook as you do." "You value them yourselves," I answered; "anyone would be '*lynched*' who removed a stone of Ticonderoga." It was an unfortunate speech, for she archly replied, "Our only ruins are British fortifications, and we go to see them because they remind us that we whipped the nation which whips all the world." The Americans, however, though they may talk so, would give anything if they could appropriate a Kenilworth Castle, or a Melrose or a Tintern Abbey, with its covering of ivy, and make it sustain some episode of their history. But though they can make railways, ivy is beyond them, and the purple heather disdains the soil of the New World. A very amusing ticket was given me on the Mad River line. It bore the command, "Stick this check in your ——," the blank being filled up with a little engraving of a hat; consequently I saw all the gentlemen with small pink embellishments to the covering of their heads.

We passed through a large and very beautiful portion of the State of Ohio; the soil, wherever cultivated, teeming with crops, and elsewhere with a vegetation no less beautiful than luxuriant; a mixture of small weed prairies, and forests of splendid timber. Extensive districts of Ohio are still without inhabitants, yet its energetic people have constructed within a period of five years half as many miles of railroad as the whole of Great Britain contains; they are a "*great people*," they do "*go a-head*," these Yankees. The newly cleared soil is too rich for wheat for many years; it grows Indian corn for thirty in succession, without any manure. Its present population is under three millions, and it is estimated that it would support a population of ten millions, almost entirely in agricultural pursuits. We were going a-head, and in a few hours arrived at Forest the junction of the Clyde, Mad River, and Indiana lines.

Away with all English ideas which may be conjured up by the word *junction*—the labyrinth of iron rails, the smart policeman at the points, the handsome station, and elegant refreshment-rooms. Here was a dense forest, with merely a clearing round the rails, a small shanty for the man who cuts wood for the engine, and two sidings for the trains coming in different directions. There was not even a platform for passengers, who, to the number of two or three hundred, were standing on the clearing, resting against the stumps of trees. And yet for a few minutes every day the bustle of life pervades this lonely spot, for here meet travellers from east, west, and south; the careworn merchant from the Atlantic cities, and the hardy trapper from the western prairies. We here changed cars for those of the Indianapolis line, and, nearly at the same time with three other trains, plunged into the depths of the forest.

"You're from down east, I guess?" said a sharp nasal voice behind me.—This was a supposition first made in the Portland cars, when I was at a loss to know what distinguishing and palpable peculiarity marked me as a "down-easter." Better informed now, I replied, "I am." "Going west?"—"Yes." "Travelling alone?"—"No." "Was you raised down east?"—"No, in the Old Country." "In the little old island? well, you are kinder glad to leave it, I guess? Are you a widow?"—"No." "Are you travelling on business?"—"No." "What business do you follow?"—"None." "Well, now, what are you travelling for?"—"Health and pleasure." "Well, now, I guess you're pretty considerable rich. Coming to settle out west, I suppose?"—"No,

I'm going back at the end of the fall." "Well, now, if that's not a pretty tough hickory-nut! I guess you Britishers are the queerest critturs as ever was raised!" I considered myself quite fortunate to have fallen in with such a querist, for the Americans are usually too much taken up with their own business to trouble themselves about yours, beyond such questions as, "Are you bound west, stranger?" or, "You're from down east, I guess." "Why do you take me for a *down-easter?*" I asked once. "Because you speak like one," was the reply; the frequent supposition that I was a New Englander being nearly as bad as being told that I "had not the English accent at all." I was glad to be taken for an American, as it gave me a better opportunity of seeing things as they really are. An English person going about staring and questioning, with a note-book in his hand, is considered "fair game," and consequently is "*crammed*" on all subjects; stories of petticoated table-legs, and fabulous horrors of the bowie-knife, being among the smallest of the absurdities swallowed.

Our party consisted of five persons besides myself, two elderly gentlemen, the niece of one of them, and a young married couple. They knew the governor of Indiana, and a candidate for the proud position of Senator, also our fellow travellers; and the conversation assumed a political character; in fact, they held a long parliament, for I think the discussion lasted for three hours. Extraordinary, and to me unintelligible names, were bandied backwards and forwards; I heard of "Silver Grays," but my companions were not discussing a breed of fowls; and of "Hard Shells," and "Soft Shells," but the merits of eggs were not the topic. "Whigs and Democrats" seemed to be analogous to our Radicals, and "Know-Nothings" to be a respectable and constitutional party. Whatever minor differences my companions had, they all seemed agreed in hating the "Nebraska men" (the advocates of an extension of slavery), who one would have thought, from the epithets applied to them, were a set of thieves and cut-throats. A gentleman whose whole life had been spent in opposition to

116

the principles which they are bringing forward was very violent, and the pretty young lady, Mrs. Wood, equally so.

After stopping for two hours at a wayside shed, we set out again at dark for La Fayette,[1] which we reached at nine. These Western cars are crammed to overflowing, and, having to cross a wide stream in a ferry-boat, the crush was so terrible, that I was nearly knocked down; but as American gentlemen freely use their canes where a lady is in the case, I fared better than some of my fellow-passengers, who had their coattails torn and their toes barbarously crushed in the crowd. The steam ferry-boat had no parapet, and the weakest were pushed to the side; the centre was filled up with baggage, carts, and horses; and vessels were moored along the river, with the warps crossing each other, to which we had to bow continually to avoid decapitation. When we reached the wharf, quantities of people were waiting to go to the other side; and directly the gangway-board was laid, there was a simultaneous rush of two opposing currents, and, the insecure board slipping, they were all precipitated into the water. Fortunately it was not deep, so they merely underwent its cooling influences, which they bore with admirable equanimity, only one making a bitter complaint, that he had spoiled his "*go-to-meetins.*" The farther west we went, the more dangerous the neighbourhood became. At all the American stations there are placards warning people to beware of pickpockets; but from Indiana westward they bore the caution, "Beware of pickpockets, swindlers, and luggage-thieves." At many of the *depôts* there is a general rush for the last car, for the same reason that there is a scramble for the stern cabins in a steamer,—viz. the explosive qualities of the boilers.

We travelled the whole of that night, our fellow-passengers becoming more extravagant in appearance at every station, and morning found us on the prairies. Cooper influences our youthful imaginations by telling us of the prairies—Mayne Reid

1 From the frequent recurrence of the same names, the great distance travelled over, the short halt we made at any place, and the absence of a railway guide, I have been unable to give our route from Cincinnati to Chicago with more than an approximation to correctness.

makes us long to cross them; botanists tell us of their flowers, sportsmen of their buffaloes[1]—but without seeing them few people can form a correct idea of what they are really like.

The sun rose over a monotonous plain covered with grass, rank, high, and silky-looking, blown before the breeze into long, shiny waves. The sky was blue above, and the grass a brownish green beneath; wild pigeons and turkeys flew over our heads; the horizontal line had not a single inequality; all was hot, unsuggestive, silent, and monotonous. This was the grass prairie.

A belt of low timber would bound the expanse, and on the other side of it a green sea would open before us, stretching as far as the eye could reach—stationary billows of earth, covered with short green grass, which, waving beneath the wind, completed the oceanic illusion. This was the rolling prairie.

Again a belt of timber, and a flat surface covered with flowers, brilliant even at this season of the year; though, of the most gorgeous, nothing remained but the withered stalks. The ground was enamelled with lilies, the helianthus and cineraria flourished, and the deep-green leaves and blue blossom of the lupin contrasted with the prickly stem and scarlet flower of the euphorbia. For what purpose was "the wilderness made so gay where for years no eye sees it," but to show forth his goodness who does what he will with his own? This was the weed prairie, more fitly termed "the Garden of God."

These three kinds of prairie were continually alternating with belts of timber and small lakes; but few signs of population were apparent during that long day's journey. We occasionally stopped for water at shanties on the prairies, and took in two or three men; but this vast expanse of fertile soil still must remain for many years a field for the enterprise of the European races.

Towards evening we changed cars again, and took in stores of refreshment for our night's journey, as little could be

---

1 At the present time no wild animals are to be found east of the Mississippi; so effectually has civilization changed the character of the ancient hunting-grounds of the Indians.

procured along the route. What strange people now crammed the cars! Traders, merchants, hunters, diggers, trappers, and adventurers from every land, most of them armed to the teeth, and not without good reason; for within the last few months, Indians, enraged at the aggressions of the white men, have taken a terrible revenge upon western travellers. Some of their rifles were of most costly workmanship, and were nursed with paternal care by their possessors. On the seat in front of me were two "prairie-men," such as are described in the 'Scalp-Hunters,' though of an inferior grade to St. Vrain. Fine specimens of men they were; tall, handsome, broad-chested, and athletic, with aquiline noses, piercing grey eyes, and brown curling hair and beards. They wore leathern jackets, slashed and embroidered, leather smallclothes, large boots with embroidered tops, silver spurs, and caps of scarlet cloth, worked with somewhat tarnished gold thread, doubtless the gifts of some fair ones enamoured of the handsome physiognomies and reckless bearing of the hunters. Dulness fled from their presence; they could tell stories, whistle melodies, and sing comic songs without weariness or cessation: fortunate were those near enough to be enlivened by their drolleries during the tedium of a night detention. Each of them wore a leathern belt—with two pistols stuck into it—gold earrings, and costly rings. Blithe, cheerful souls they were, telling racy stories of Western life, chivalrous in their manners, and free as the winds.

There were Californians dressed for the diggings, with leather pouches for the gold-dust; Mormons on their way to Utah; and restless spirits seeking for that excitement and variety which they had sought for in vain in civilized life! And conveying this motley assortment of human beings, the cars dashed along, none of their inmates heeding each other, or perhaps Him

"——who heeds and holds them all
In his large love and boundless thought."

At eleven we came to an abrupt pause upon the prairie. After waiting quietly for some time without seeing any vestiges of a station, my friends got out to inquire the cause of the detention, when we found that a freight-train had broken down in front, and that we might be *détenus* for some time, a mark for Indian bullets! Refreshments were produced and clubbed together; the "prairie-men" told stories; the hunters looked to their rifles, and polished their already resplendent chasing; some Mexicans sang Spanish songs, a New Englander 'Yankee Doodle;' some *guessed*, others *calculated*, till at last all grew sleepy: the trappers exhausted their stories, the singers their songs, and a Mormon, who had been setting forth the peculiar advantages of his creed, the patience of his auditors— till at length sonorous sounds, emitted by numerous nasal organs, proving infectious, I fell asleep to dream confusedly of 'Yankee Doodle,' pistols, and pickpockets.

In due time I awoke; we were stopping still, and there was a light on our right. "We're at Rock Island, I suppose?" I asked sleepily. A laugh from my friends and the hunters followed the question; after which they informed me in the most polite tones that we were where we had been for the last five hours, namely stationary on the prairie. The intense cold and heavy dew which accompany an American dawn made me yet more amazed at the characteristic patience with which the Americans submit to an unavoidable necessity, however disagreeable. It is true that there were complaints of cold, and heavy sighs, but no blame was imputed to anyone, and the quiescence of my companions made me quite ashamed of my English impatience. In England we should have had a perfect chorus of complaints, varied by "rowing" the conductor, abuse of the company, and resolutions to write to the *Times*, or bring up the subject of railway mismanagement in the House of Commons. These people sat quietly, ate, slept, and smoked, and were thankful when the cars at last moved off to their destination.

On we flew to the West, the land of Wild Indians and buffaloes, on the narrow rims of metal with which this "great people" is girdling the earth. Evening succeeded noon, and twilight to the blaze of a summer day; the yellow sun sank cloudless behind the waves of the rolling prairie, yet still we hurried on, only stopping our headlong course to take in wood and water at some nameless stations. When the sun set, it set behind the prairie waves. I was oblivious of any changes during the night, and at rosy dawn an ocean of long green grass encircled us round. Still on—belts of timber diversify the prospect—we rush into a thick wood, and, emerging from it, arrive at Rock Island, an unfinished-looking settlement, which might bear the name of the Desert City, situated at the confluence of the Rock River and Mississippi. We stop at a little wharf, where waits a little steamer of uncouth construction; we step in, a steam-whistle breaks the silence of that dewy dawn, and at a very rapid rate we run between high wooded bluffs, down a turbid stream, whirling in rapid eddies. We steam for three miles, and land at a clearing containing the small settlement of Davenport. We had come down the Mississippi, mightiest of rivers! half a mile wide seventeen hundred miles from its mouth, and were in the *far West*. Waggons with white tilts, thick-hided oxen with heavy yokes, mettlesome steeds with high peaked saddles, picketed to stumps of trees, lashing away the flies with their tails; emigrants on blue boxes, wondering if this were the El Dorado of their dreams; arms, accoutrements, and baggage surrounded the house or shed where we were to breakfast. Most of our companions were bound for Nebraska, Oregon, and Utah, the most distant districts of which they would scarcely reach with their slow-paced animals for four months; exposed in the mean time to the attacks of the Sioux, Comanches, and Blackfeet.

There, in a long wooden shed with blackened rafters and an earthen floor, we breakfasted, at seven o'clock, on johnny-cake, squirrels, buffalo-hump, dampers, and buckwheat, tea and corn spirit, with a crowd of emigrants, hunters, and adventurers; and soon after re-embarked for Rock Island, our little steamer with difficulty stemming the mighty tide of the

Father of Rivers. The machinery, such as it was, was very visible, the boiler patched in several places, and steam escaped in different directions. I asked the captain if he were not in the habit of "sitting upon the safety-valve," but he stoutly denied the charge. The vernacular of this neighbourhood was rather startling to an English ear. "Who's the alligator to hum?" asked a broad-shouldered Kentuckian of his neighbour, pointing to a frame shanty on the shore, which did not look to me like the abode of that amphibious and carnivorous creature. "Well, old alligator, what's the time o' day?" asked another man, bringing down a brawny paw, with a resounding thump, upon the Herculean shoulders of the first querist, thereby giving me the information that in the West *alligator* is a designation of the *genus homo*; in fact, that it is customary for a man to address his fellow-man as "old alligator," instead of "old fellow." At eight we left Rock Island, and, turning my unwilling steps eastward from the land of adventure and romance, we entered the cars for Chicago.

They were extremely crowded, and my friends, securing me the only comfortable seat in one of them, were obliged to go into the next, much to their indignation; but protestations were of no use. The engine-bell rang, a fearful rush followed, which resulted in the passage down the centre being filled with standing men; the conductor shouted "Go a-head," and we were off for Lake Michigan in the "Lightning Express," warranted to go sixty-seven miles an hour! I had found it necessary to study physiognomy since leaving England, and was horrified by the appearance of my next neighbour. His forehead was low, his deep-set and restless eyes significant of cunning, and I at once set him down as a swindler or pickpocket. My convictions of the truth of my inferences were so strong, that I removed my purse, in which, however, acting by advice, I never carried more than five dollars, from my pocket, leaving in it only my handkerchief and the checks for my baggage, knowing that I could not possibly keep awake the whole morning. In spite of my endeavours to the contrary, I soon sank into an oblivious state, from which I awoke to the consciousness that my companion was withdrawing his hand from my pocket. My first impulse was to make an exclamation, my second, which I carried into execution, to ascertain my loss; which I found to be the very alarming one of my baggage-checks; my whole property being thereby placed at this vagabond's disposal, for I knew perfectly well, that if I claimed my trunks without my checks, the acute baggage-master would have set me down as a bold swindler. The keen-eyed conductor was not in the car, and, had he been there, the necessity for habitual suspicion, incidental to his position, would so far have removed his original sentiments of generosity as to make him turn a deaf ear to my request, and there was not one of my fellow-travellers whose physiognomy would have warranted me in appealing to him. So, recollecting that my checks were marked Chicago, and seeing that the thief's ticket bore the same name, I resolved to wait the chapter of accidents, or the re-appearance of my friends. I was scarcely able to decide whether this proof of the reliance to be placed upon physiognomy was not an adequate compensation for the annoyance I was experiencing, at the probability of my hoarded treasures falling into the hands of an adventurer.

During the morning we crossed some prairie-country, and stopped at several stations, patches of successful cultivation showing that there must be cultivators, though I rarely saw their habitations. The cars still continued so full that my friends could not join me, and I began to be seriously anxious about the fate of my luggage. At midday, spires and trees, and lofty blocks of building, rising from a grass-prairie on one side, and from the blue waters of Lake Michigan on the other, showed that we were approaching Chicago. Along beaten tracks through the grass, waggons with white tilts drawn by oxen were proceeding west, sometimes accompanied by armed horsemen.

With a whoop like an Indian war-whoop the cars ran into a shed—they stopped—the pickpocket got up—I got up too—the baggage-master came to the door: "This gentleman has the checks for my baggage," said I, pointing to the thief. Bewildered, he took them from his waistcoat-pocket, gave them to the baggage-master, and went hastily away. I had no inclination to cry 'Stop thief!' and had barely time to congratulate myself on the fortunate impulse which had led me to say what I did, when my friends appeared from the next car. They were too highly amused with my recital to sympathise at all with my feelings of annoyance, and one of them, a gentleman filling a high situation in the East, laughed heartily, saying, in a thoroughly American tone, "The English ladies must be 'cute customers, if they can outwit Yankee pickpockets."

Meaning to stay all night at Chicago, we drove to the two best hotels, but, finding them full, were induced to betake ourselves to an advertising house, the name of which it is unnecessary to give, though it will never be effaced from my memory. The charge advertised was a dollar a day, and for this every comfort and advantage were promised.

The inn was a large brick building at the corner of a street, with nothing very unprepossessing in its external appearance. The wooden stairs were dirty enough, and, on ascending them to the so-called "ladies' parlour," I found a large, meanly-furnished apartment, garnished with six spittoons, which, however, to my disgust, did not prevent the floor from receiving a large quantity of tobacco-juice.

There were two rifles, a pistol, and a powder-flask on the table; two Irish emigrant women were seated on the floor (which swarmed with black beetles and ants), undressing a screaming child; a woman evidently in a fever was tossing restlessly on the sofa; two females in tarnished Bloomer habiliments were looking out of the window; and other extraordinary-looking human beings filled the room. I asked for accommodation for the night, hoping that I should find a room where I could sit quietly. A dirty chambermaid took me to a room or dormitory containing four beds. In one part of it three women were affectionately and assiduously nursing a sick child; in another, two were combing tangled hair; upon which I declared that I must have a room to myself.

The chambermaid then took me down a long, darkish passage, and showed me a small room without a fireplace, and only lighted by a pane of glass in the door; consequently, it was nearly dark. There was a small bed with a dirty buffalo-skin upon it; I took it up, and swarms of living creatures fell out of it, and the floor was literally alive with them. The sight of such a room made me feel quite ill, and it was with the greatest reluctance that I deposited my bonnet and shawl in it.

Outside the door were some medicine-bottles and other suspicious signs of illness, and, after making some cautious inquiries, we found that there was a case of typhus fever in the house, also one of Asiatic cholera, and three of ague! My friends were extremely shocked with the aspect of affairs. I believe that they were annoyed that I should see such a specimen of an hotel in their country, and they decided, that, as I could not possibly remain there for the night, I should go on to Detroit alone, as they were detained to Chicago on business. Though I certainly felt rather out of my element in this place, I was not at all sorry for the opportunity, thus accidentally given me, of seeing something of American society in its lowest grade.

We went down to dinner, and only the fact of not having tasted food for many hours could have made me touch it in such a room. We were in a long apartment, with one table down the middle, with plates laid for one hundred people. Every seat was occupied, these seats being benches of somewhat uncouth workmanship. The floor had recently been washed, and emitted a damp fetid odour. At one side was a large fireplace, where, in spite of the heat of the day, sundry manipulations were going on, coming under the general name of cookery. At the end of the room was a long leaden trough or sink, where three greasy scullery-boys without shoes, were perpetually engaged in washing plates, which they wiped upon their aprons. The plates, however, were not washed, only superficially rinsed. There were four brigand-looking waiters with prodigious beards and moustachios.

There was no great variety at table. There were eight boiled legs of mutton, nearly raw; six antiquated fowls, whose legs were of the consistence of guitar-strings; baked pork with "onion fixings," the meat swimming in grease; and for vegetable, yams, corn-cobs, and squash. A cup of stewed tea, sweetened with molasses, stood by each plate, and no fermented liquor of any description was consumed by the company. There were no carving-knives, so each person *hacked* the joints with his own, and some of those present carved them dexterously with bowie-knives taken out of their belts. Neither were there salt-spoons, so everybody dipped his greasy knife into the little pewter pot containing salt. Dinner began, and after satisfying my own hunger with the least objectionable dish, namely "pork with onion fixings," I had leisure to look round me.

Every quarter of the globe had contributed to swell that motley array, even China. Motives of interest or adventure had drawn them all together to this extraordinary outpost of civilisation, and soon would disperse them among lands where civilisation is unknown.

As far as I could judge, we were the only representatives of England. There were Scots, for Scots are always to be found where there is any hope of honest gain—there were Irish emigrants, speaking with a rich brogue—French traders from St. Louis—Mexicans fron Santa Fé—Californians fitting out, and Californians coming home with fortunes made—keen-eyed speculators from New England—packmen from Canada— "Prairie-men," trappers, hunters, and adventurers of all descriptions. Many of these wore bowie-knives or pistols in their belts. The costumes were very varied and picturesque. Two Bloomers in very poor green habiliments sat opposite to me, and did not appear to attract any attention, though Bloomerism is happily defunct in the States.

There had been three duels at Chicago in the morning, and one of the duellists, a swarthy, dark-browed villain, sat next but one to me. The quarrel originated in a gambling-house, and this Mexican's opponent was mortally wounded, and there he sat, with the guilt of human blood upon his hands, describing to his *vis-à-vis* the way in which he had taken aim at his adversary, and no one seemed to think anything about it. From what I heard, I fear duelling must have become very common in the West, and no wonder, from the number of lawless spirits who congregate where they can be comparatively unfettered.

The second course consisted exclusively of pumpkin-pies; but when the waiters changed the plates, their way of cleaning the knives and forks was so peculiarly disgusting, that I did not attempt to eat anything. But I must remark that in this motley assembly there was nothing of coarseness, and not a word of bad language—indeed, nothing which could offend the most fastidious ears. I must in this respect bear very favourable testimony to the Americans; for, in the course of my somewhat extensive travels in the United States, and mixing as I did very frequently with the lower classes, I never heard any of that language which so frequently offends the ear in England.[1]

I suppose that there is no country in the world where the presence of a lady is such a restraint upon manners and conversation. A female, whatever her age or rank may be, is invariably treated with deferential respect; and if this deference may occasionally trespass upon the limits of absurdity, or if the extinct chivalry of the past ages of Europe meets with a partial revival upon the shores of America, this extreme is vastly preferable to the *brusquerie*, if not incivility, which ladies, as I have heard, too often meet with in England.

The apparently temperate habits in the United States form another very pleasing feature to dwell upon. It is to be feared that there is a considerable amount of drunkenness among the

1 I must not be misunderstood here. Profane language is only too notoriously common in the States, but custom, which in America is frequently stronger than law, totally prohibits its use before ladies.

English, Irish, and Germans, who form a large portion of the American population; but the temperate, tea-drinking, water-drinking habits of the native Americans are most remarkable. In fact, I only saw one intoxicated person in the States, and he was a Scotch fiddler. At the hotels, even when sitting down to dinner in a room with four hundred persons, I never on any occasion saw more than two bottles of wine on the table, and I know from experience that in many private dwelling-houses there is no fermented liquor at all. In the West, more especially at the rude hotels where I stopped, I never saw wine, beer, or spirits upon the table; and the spectacle gratified me exceedingly, of seeing fierce-looking, armed, and bearded men, drinking frequently in the day of that cup "which cheers, but not inebriates." Water is a beverage which I never enjoyed in purity and perfection before I visited America. It is provided in abundance in the cars, the hotels, the waiting-rooms, the steamers, and even the stores, in crystal jugs or stone filters, and it is always iced. This may be either the result or the cause of the temperance of the people.

Ancient history tells us of a people who used to intoxicate their slaves, and, while they were in that condition, display them to their sons, to disgust them early with the degrading vice of drunkenness.

The emigrants who have left our shores, more particularly the Irish, have voluntarily enacted the part formerly assigned to the slaves of the Spartans. Certain it is that their intemperance, with the evils of which the Americans are only too well acquainted, has produced a beneficial result, by causing a strong reaction in favour of temperance principles.

The national oath of the English, which has earned for them abroad a horrible *sobriquet*, and the execrations which belong to the French, Italian, and Spanish nations, are unfortunately but too well known, because they are too often heard. Indeed, I have scarcely ever travelled in England by coach or railway—I have seldom driven through a crowded street, or ridden on horseback through quiet agricultural villages—without hearing language in direct defiance of the third commandment. Profanity and drunkenness are among the crying sins of the English lower orders. Much has been said upon the subject of swearing in the United States. I can only say that, travelling in them as I have travelled in England, and mixing with people of a much lower class than I ever was thrown among in England—mixing with these people too on terms of perfect equality—I never heard an oath till after I crossed the Canadian frontier. With regard to both these things, of course I only speak of what fell under my own observation.

After dinner, being only too glad to escape from a house where pestilence was rife, we went out into Chicago. It is a wonderful place, and tells more forcibly of the astonishing energy and progress of the Americans than anything I saw. Forty years ago the whole ground on which the town stands could have been bought for six hundred dollars; now, a person would give ten thousand for the site of a single store. It is built on a level prairie, only slightly elevated above the lake surface. It lies on both sides of the Chicago river, about a mile above its entrance into Lake Michigan. By the construction of piers, a large artificial harbour has been made at the mouth of this river.

The city has sprung up rapidly, and is supplied with all the accessories of a high state of civilisation. Chicago, in everything that contributes to *real use and comfort*, will compare favourably with any city in the world. In 1830 it was a mere trading-post, situated in the theatre of the Black Hawk war. In 1850 its population was only 28,000 people; it has now not less than 60,000.[1] It had not a mile of railway in 1850; now fourteen lines radiate from it, bringing to it the trade of an area of country equalling 150,000 square miles. One hundred heavy trains arrive and depart from it daily. It has a commerce commensurate with its magnitude. It employs about 70,000

1 By the last census, taken in June, 1855, the population of Chicago was given at 87,000 souls, thus showing the extraordinary increase of 27,000 within a year.

tons of shipping, nearly one-half being steamers and propellers. The lumber-trade, which is chiefly carried on with Buffalo, is becoming very profitable. The exports of Chicago, to the East, of bread-stuffs for the past year, exceeded 13,000,000 bushels; and a city which, in 1840, numbered only 4000 inhabitants, is now one of the largest exporting grain-markets in the world.

Chicago is connected with the western rivers by a sloop canal—one of the most magnificent works ever undertaken. It is also connected with the Mississippi at several points by railroad. It is regularly laid out with wide airy streets, much more cleanly than those of Cincinnati. The wooden houses are fast giving place to lofty substantial structures of brick, or a stone similar in appearance to white marble, and are often six stories high. These houses, as in all business streets in the American cities, are disfigured, up to the third story, by large glaring sign-boards containing the names and occupations of their residents. The side-walks are of wood, and, wherever they are made of this unsubstantial material, one frequently finds oneself stepping into a hole, or upon the end of a board which tilts up under one's feet. The houses are always let in flats, so that there are generally three stores one above another. These stores are very handsome, those of the outfitters particularly so, though the quantity of goods displayed in the streets gives them rather a barbaric appearance. The side-walks are literally encumbered with bales of scarlet flannel, and every other article of an emigrant's outfit. At the outfitters' stores you can buy anything, from a cart-nail to a revolver; from a suit of oilskin to a paper of needles. The streets present an extraordinary spectacle. Everything reminds that one is standing on the very verge of western civilisation.

The roads are crowded to an inconvenient extent with carriages of curious construction, waggons, carts, and men on horseback, and the side-walks with eager foot-passengers. By the side of a carriage drawn by two or three handsome horses, a creaking waggon with a white tilt, drawn by four heavy oxen, may be seen—Mexicans and hunters dash down the crowded streets at full gallop on mettlesome steeds, with bits so powerful as to throw their horses on their haunches when they meet with any obstacle. They ride animals that look too proud to touch the earth, on high-peaked saddles, with pistols in the holsters, short stirrups, and long, cruel-looking Spanish spurs. They wear scarlet caps or palmetto hats, and high jack-boots. Knives are stuck into their belts, and light rifles are slung behind them. These picturesque beings—the bullock-waggons setting out for the Far West—the medley of different nations and costumes in the streets—make the city a spectacle of great interest.

The deep hollow roar of the locomotive, and the shrill scream from the steamboat, are heard here all day; a continuous stream of life ever bustles through the city, and, standing as it does on the very verge of western civilisation, Chicago is a vast emporium of the trade of the districts east and west of the Mississippi.

At an office in one of the streets Mr. C—— took my ticket for Toronto by railway, steamer, railway, and steamer, only paying eight dollars and a half, or about thirty-four shillings, for a journey of seven hundred miles!

We returned to tea at the hotel, and found our viands and companions just the same as at dinner. It is impossible to give an idea of the "western men" to anyone who has not seen one at least as a specimen. They are the man before whom the Indians melt away as grass before the scythe. They shoot them down on the smallest provocation, and speak of "head of Indian," as we do in England of head of game. Their bearing is bold, reckless, and independent in the extreme; they are as ready to fight a foe as to wait upon women and children with tender assiduity; their very appearance says to you, "Stranger, I belong to the greatest, most enlightened, and most progressive nation on earth; I may be the President or a *millionaire* next year; I don't care a straw for you or anyone else."

Illinois is a State which has sprung up, as if by magic, to be one of the most fruitful in the West. It was settled by men from the New England States—men who carried with them those characteristics which have made the New Englander's career one of active enterprise, and successful progress, wherever he has been. Not many years ago the name of Illinois was nearly unknown, and on her soil the hardy settler battled with the forest-trees for space in which to sow his first crops. Her roads were merely rude and often impassable tracks through forest or prairie; now she has in operation and course of construction two thousand and seventy miles of those iron sinews of commercial progress—railroads, running like a network over the State.

At seven o'clock, with a feeling of great relief, mingled with thankfulness at having escaped untouched by the terrible pestilence which had ravaged Chicago, I left the hotel, more appropriately termed a "*caravanserai*," and my friends placed me in the "Lightning Express," warranted to go sixty-seven miles an hour.

Unless it may be St. Louis, I fancy that Chicago is more worth a visit than any other of the western cities. Even one day at it was worth a voyage across the Atlantic, and a land-journey of eighteen hundred miles.

CHAPTER IX

A vexatious incident—John Bull enraged—Woman's rights—
Alligators become hosses—A popular host—Military display—
A mirth-provoking gun—Grave reminiscences—Attractions
of the fair—Past and present—a floating palace—Black
companions—A black baby—Externals of Buffalo—
The flag of England.

The night-cars are always crowded both in Canada and the States, because people in business are anxious to save a day if they have any expedition to make, and, as many of the cars are fitted up with seats of a most comfortable kind for night-travelling, a person accustomed to them can sleep in them as well as on a sofa. After leaving Chicago, they seemed about to rush with a whoop into the moonlit waters of Lake Michigan, and in reality it was not much better. For four miles we ran along a plank-road supported only on piles. There was a single track, and the carriages projecting over the whole, there was no bridge to be seen, and we really seemed to be going along on the water. These insecure railways are not uncommon in the States; the dangers of the one on the Hudson river have been experienced by many travellers to their cost.

We ran three hundred miles through central Michigan in ten hours, including stoppages. We dashed through woods, across prairies, and over bridges without parapets, at a uniform rate of progress. A boy making continual peregrinations with iced water alleviated the thirst of the passengers, for the night was intensely hot, and I managed to sleep very comfortably till awoke by the intense cold of dawn. During the evening an incident most vexatious to me occurred.

The cars were very full, and were not able to seat all the passengers. Consequently, according to the usages of American etiquette, the gentlemen vacated the seats in favour of the ladies, who took possession of them in a very ungracious manner as I thought. The gentlemen stood in the passage down the centre. At last all but one had given up their seats, and while stopping at a station another lady entered.

"A seat for a lady," said the conductor, when he saw the crowded state of the car. The one gentleman did not stir. "A seat for a lady," repeated the man in a more imperious tone. Still no movement on the part of the gentleman appealed to. "A seat for a lady; don't you see there's a lady wanting one?" now vociferated several voices at once, but without producing any effect. "Get up for this lady," said one bolder than the rest, giving the stranger a sharp admonition on the shoulder. He pulled his travelling cap over his eyes, and doggedly refused to stir. There was now a regular hubbub in the car; American blood was up, and several gentlemen tried to induce the offender to move.

"I'm an Englishman, and I tell you I won't be brow-beat by you beastly Yankees. I've paid for my seat, and I mean to keep it," savagely shouted the offender, thus verifying my worst suspicions.

"I thought so!—I knew it!—A regular John Bull trick! just like them!" were some of the observations made, and very mild they were, considering the aggravated circumstances.

Two men took the culprit by his shoulders, and the others, pressing behind, impelled him to the door, amid a chorus of groans and hisses, disposing of him finally by placing him in the emigrant-car, installing the lady in the vacated seat. I could almost fancy that the shade of the departed Judge Lynch stood by with an approving smile.

I was so thoroughly ashamed of my countryman, and so afraid of my nationality being discovered, that, if anyone spoke to me, I adopted every Americanism which I could think of in reply. The country within fifty miles of Detroit is a pretty alternation of prairie, wood, corn-fields, peach and apple orchards. The maize is the staple of the country; you see it in the fields; you have corn-cobs for breakfast; corn-cobs, mush, and hominy for dinner; johnny-cake for tea; and the very bread contains a third part of Indian meal!

I thought the little I saw of Michigan very fertile and pretty. It is another of the newly constituted States, and was known until recently under the name of the "Michigan Territory." This State is a peninsula between the Huron and Michigan Lakes, and borders in one part closely on Canada. It has a salubrious climate and a fertile soil, and is rapidly becoming a very productive State. Of late years the influx of emigrants of a better class has been very great. The State has great capabilities for saw and flour mills; the Grand Rapids alone have a fall of fifteen feet in a mile, and afford immense water-power.

In Michigan, human beings have ceased to be "*alligators*," they are "*hosses*." Thus one man says to another, "How do you do, old hoss?" or, "What's the time o' day, old hoss?" When I reached Detroit I was amused when a conductor said to me, "One o' them 'ere hosses will take your trunks," pointing as he spoke to a group of porters.

On arriving at Detroit I met for the first time with tokens of British enterprise and energy, and of the growing importance of Canada West. Several persons in the cars were going to New York, and they took the ferry at Detroit, and went down to Niagara Bridge by the Canada Great Western Railway, as the most expeditious route. I drove through the very pleasant streets of Detroit to the National Hotel, where I was to join the Walrences. Having indulged the hope of rejoining my former travelling companions here, I was greatly disappointed at finding a note from them, containing the intelligence that they had been summoned by telegraph to Toronto, to a sick relative. They requested me to join them there, and hoped I should find no difficulty on the journey!

It was the time of the State fair, and every room in the inn was occupied; but Mr. Benjamin, the very popular host of the National, on hearing my circumstances, would on no account suffer me to seek another abode, and requested a gentleman to give up his room to me, which with true American politeness he instantly did. I cannot speak too highly of the National Hotel, or of its deservedly popular landlord. I found that I could not leave Detroit before the next night, and at most hotels a lady alone would have been very uncomfortably placed. Breakfast was over, but, as soon as I retired to my room, the waiter appeared with an abundant repast, for which no additional charge was made. I sat in my room the whole day, and Mr. Benjamin came twice to my door to know if I wanted anything. He introduced me to a widow lady, whose room I afterwards shared; and when I went down at night to the steamer, he sent one of his clerks with me, to save me any trouble about my luggage. He also gave me a note to an hotel-keeper at Buffalo, requesting him to pay me every attention, in case I should be detained for a night on the road. The hotel was a perfect pattern of cleanliness, elegance, and comfort; and the waiters, about fifty of whom were Dutch, attended scrupulously to every wish, actual or supposed, of the guests. If these pages should ever meet Mr. Benjamin's eye, it may be a slight gratification to him to know that his kindness to a stranger has been both remembered and appreciated.

I had some letters of introduction to residents at Detroit, and here, as in all other places which I visited, I had but to sow them to reap a rich harvest of kindness and hospitality. I spent two days most agreeably at Detroit, in a very refined and intellectual circle, perfectly free from those mannerisms which I had expected to find in a place so distant from the coast. The concurrent testimony of many impartial persons goes to prove that in every American town highly polished and intellectual society is to be met with.

My bedroom window at the National Hotel looked into one of the widest and most bustling streets of Detroit. It was the day of the State fair, consequently I saw the town under a very favourable aspect. The contents of several special trains, and hundreds of waggons, crowded the streets, the "waggons" frequently drawn by very handsome horses. The private carriages were of a superior class to any I had previously seen in the States; the harness was handsome and richly plated, and elegantly dressed ladies filled the interiors. But in amusing contrast, the coachmen all looked like wild Irishmen enlisted for the occasion, and drove in a standing posture. Young farmers, many of them dressed in the extreme of the fashion of Young America, were dashing about in their light waggons, driving tandem or span; heavily laden drays were proceeding at a slower speed; and all this traffic was carried on under the shade of fine trees.

Military bands playing 'The Star-spangled Banner,' and 'Hail Columbia,' were constantly passing and repassing, and the whole population seemed on the *qui vive*. Squadrons of cavalry continually passed my window, the men in gorgeous uniforms, with high waving plumes. Their horses were very handsome, but were not at all willing to display themselves by walking slowly, or in rank, and the riders would seem to have been selected for their corpulence, probably under the supposition that the weight of both men and horses would tell in a charge.

The air 'Hail Columbia' is a very fine one, and doubtless thrills American hearts, as ours are thrilled by the National Anthem. Two regiments of foot followed the cavalry, one with peaceful-looking green and white plumes, the other with horsetails dyed scarlet. The privates had a more independent air than our own regulars, and were principally the sons of respectable citizens. They appeared to have been well drilled, and were superior in appearance to our militia; but it must be remembered that the militia of America constitutes the real military force of the country, and is paid and cared for accordingly; the regular army only amounting to ten thousand men.

A gun of the artillery followed, and the spectacle made me laugh immoderately, though I had no one with whom to share my amusement. It was a new-looking gun of shining brass, perfectly innocent of the taste of gunpowder, and mounted on a carriage suspiciously like a timber-truck, which had *once* been painted. Six very respectable-looking artillerymen were clustering upon this vehicle, but they had to hold hard, for it

137

jolted unmercifully. It was drawn by four horses of different colours and sizes, and they appeared animated by the principle of mutual repulsion. One of these was ridden by a soldier, seated on a saddle placed so far upon the horse's neck, that it gave him the appearance of clinging to the mane. The harness was shabby and travel-soiled, and the traces were of rope, which seemed to require continual "fixing," to judge from the frequency with which the rider jumped off to adjust them. The artillery-men were also continually stopping the vehicle, to rearrange the limber of the gun.

While I was instituting an invidious comparison between this gun and our well-appointed, well-horsed, well-manned artillery at Woolwich, the thought suddenly flashed across my mind that the militia forces of America beat us at Lexington, Saratoga, and Ticonderoga. "A change came o'er the spirit of my dream,"—from the ridiculous to the sublime was but a step; and the grotesque gun-carriage was instantly invested with sublimity.

Various attractions were presented at the fair. There were horse-races and trotting-matches; a trotting bull warranted to beat the fastest horse in Michigan; and bands of music. Phineas Taylor Barnum presented the spectacle of his very superior menagerie; in one place a wizard offered to show the smallness of the difference between *meum* and *tuum*; the Siamese Twins in another displayed their monstrous and inseparable union; and vocalists were awaiting the commands of the lovers of song.

There was a large piece of ground devoted to an agricultural exhibition; and here, as at home, Cochin China fowls were "the observed of all observers," and realised fabulous prices. In a long range of booths, devoted to the products of manufacturing industry, some of the costliest productions of the looms of Europe were exhibited for sale. There were peep-shows, and swings, and merry-go-rounds, and hobby-horses, and, with so many inducements offered, it will not be supposed that holiday people were wanting.

Suddenly, while the diversions were at their height, and in the midst of the intense heat, a deluge burst over Detroit, like the breaking of a waterspout, in a few minutes turning the streets into rivers, deep enough in many places to cover the fetlocks of the horses. It rained as it only rains in a hot climate, and the storm was accompanied by thunder and lightning. Waggons and carriages hurried furiously along; stages intended to carry twelve persons at six cents were conveying twenty through the flood at a dollar each; and ladies drenched to the skin, with white dresses and silk stockings the colour of mud, were hurrying along over the slippery side-walks. An infantry regiment of militia took to their heels and ran off at full pelt,—and a large body of *heavy* cavalry dashed by in a perfect hurricane of moustaches, draggled plumes, cross-bands, gigantic white gloves, and clattering sabres, clearing the streets effectually.

A hundred years ago Detroit was a little French village of wooden houses, a mere post for carrying on the fur-trade with the Indians. Some of these houses still remain, dingy, many-windowed, many-gabled buildings, of antique construction. Canoes laden with peltry were perhaps the only craft which disturbed the waters of the Detroit river.

The old times are changed, and a thriving commercial town of 40,000 inhabitants stands on the site of the French trading-post. Handsome quays and extensive wharfs now line the shores of the Detroit river, and to look at the through of magnificent steamers and small sailing-vessels lying along them, sometimes two or three deep, one would suppose oneself at an English seaport. The streets, which contain very handsome stores, are planted with trees, and are alive with business; and hotels, banks, and offices appear in every direction. Altogether Detroit is a very pleasing place, and, from its position, bids fair to be a very important one.

I had to leave the friends whose acquaintance and kindness rendered Detroit so agreeable to me, in the middle of a very interesting conversation. Before ten at night I found myself on

139

an apparently interminable wharf, creeping between cart-wheels and over bales of wool to the *Mayflower* steamer, which was just leaving for Buffalo.

Passing through the hall of the *Mayflower*, which was rather a confused and dimly-lighted scene, I went up to the saloon by a very handsome staircase with elaborate bronze balustrades. My bewildered eyes surveyed a fairy scene, an eastern palace, a vision of the Arabian Nights. I could not have believed that such magnificence existed in a ship; it impressed me much more than anything I have seen in the palaces of England.

The *Mayflower* was a steam-ship of 2200 tons burthen, her length 336 feet, and her extreme breadth 60. She was of 1000 horse-power, with 81-inch cylinders, and a stroke of 12 feet. I speak of her in the past tense, because she has since been totally cast away in a storm on Lake Erie. This lake bears a very bad character, and persons are warned not to venture upon it at so stormy a season of the year as September, but, had the weather been very rough, I should not have regretted my voyage in so splendid a steamer.

The saloon was 300 feet long; it had an arched roof and Gothic cornice, with a moulding below of gilded grapes and vine-leaves. It was 10 feet high, and the projections of the ceiling, the mouldings, and the panels of the doors of the state-rooms were all richly gilded. About the middle there was an enclosure for the engine, scarcely obstructing the view. This enclosure was Gothic, to match the roof, and at each end had a window of plate-glass, 6 feet square, through which the mechanism of the engine could be seen. The engine itself, being a high-pressure one, and consequently without the incumbrances of condenser and air-pump, occupied much less room than one of ours in a ship of the same tonnage. Every stationary part of the machinery was of polished steel, or bronze, with elaborate castings; a crank indicator and a clock faced each other, and the whole was lighted by two large coloured lamps. These windows were a favourite lounge of the curious and scientific. The carpet was of rich velvet pile, in groups of brilliant flowers, and dotted over with chairs, sofas, and *tête-à-têtes* of carved walnut-wood, cushioned with the richest green velvet: the tables were of marble with gilded pedestals. There was a very handsome piano, and both it and the tables supported massive vases of beautiful Sèvres or Dresden china, filled with exotic flowers. On one table was a richly-chased silver tray, with a silver ewer of iced water upon it. The saloon was brilliantly lighted by eight chandeliers with dependent glass lustres; and at each end two mirrors, the height of the room, prolonged interminably the magnificent scene.

In such an apartment one would naturally expect to see elegantly-dressed gentlemen and ladies; but no—western men, in palmetto hats and great boots, lounged upon the superb sofas, and negroes and negresses chattered and promenaded. Porcelain spittoons in considerable numbers garnished the floor, and their office was by no means a sinecure one, even in the saloon exclusively devoted to ladies.

I saw only one person whom I liked to speak to, among my three hundred fellow-voyagers. This was a tall, pale, and very lady-like person in deep mourning, with a perfectly uninterested look, and such deep lines of sorrow on her face, that I saw at a glance that the world had no power to interest or please her. She sat on the same sofa with me, and was helplessly puzzling over the *route* from Buffalo to Albany with a gruff, uncouth son, who seemed by no means disposed to aid her in her difficulties. As I was able to give her the information she wanted, we entered into conversation for two hours. She soon told me her history, merely an ordinary one, of love, bereavement, and sorrow. She had been a widow for a year, and she said that her desolation was so great that her sole wish was to die. Her sons were taking her a tour, in the hope of raising her spirits, but she said she was just moved about and dressed like a doll, that she had not one ray of comfort, and that all shrunk from her hopeless and repining grief. She asked me to tell her if any widow of my acquaintance had been able to bear her loss with resignation; and when I told her of some instances among my own relation, she burst into tears and said, "I am ever arraigning the wisdom of God, and how can I hope for his consolations?" The task of a comforter is ever a hard one, and in her instance it was particularly so, to point to the "Balm of Gilead," as revealed in sacred Scripture; for a stranger to show her in all kindness that comfort could never be experienced while, as she herself owned, she was living in the neglect of every duty both to God and man.

She seemed roused for the moment, and thanked me for the sympathy which I most sincerely felt, hoping at the same time to renew the conversation in the morning. We had a stormy night, from which she suffered so much as to be unable to leave her berth the next day, and I saw nothing further of her beyond a brief glimpse which I caught of her at Buffalo, as she was carried ashore, looking more despairing even than the night before.

Below this saloon is the ladies' cabin, also very handsome, but disfigured by numerous spittoons, and beneath this again is a small cabin with berths two deep round the sides; and in this abode, as the ship was full, I took a berth for the night with a southern lady, her two female saves, four negresses, and a mulatto woman, who had just purchased their freedom in Tennessee. These blacks were really lady-like and intelligent, and so agreeable and *naïve* that, although they chattered to me till two in the morning, I was not the least tired of them.

They wanted me to bring them all home to England, to which they have been taught to look as to a land of liberty and happiness; and it was with much difficulty that I made them understand that I should not be able to find employment for them. I asked one of them, a very fine-looking mulatto, how long she had been married, and her age. She replied that she was thirty-four, and had been married twenty-one years!

Their black faces and woolly hair contrasted most ludicrously with the white pillow-case. After sleeping for a time, I was awoke by a dissonance of sounds—groaning, straining, creaking, and the crash of waves and roar of winds. I dressed with difficulty, and, crawling to the window, beheld a cloudless sky, a thin, blue, stormy-looking mist, and waves higher than I had ever seen those on the ocean; indeed, Lake Erie was one sheet of raging, furious billows, which dashed about our leviathan but top-heavy steamer as if she had been a plaything.

I saw two schooners scudding with only their foresails set, and shortly after a vessel making signals of distress, having lost her masts, bulwarks, and boats in the gale. We were enabled to render her very seasonable assistance. I was not now surprised at the caution given by the stewardess the previous night, namely, that the less I undressed the better, in case of an accident.

While the gale lasted, being too much inured to rough weather to feel alarmed, I amused myself with watching the different effects produced by it on the feelings of different persons. The Southern lady was frantic with terror. First she requested me, in no very gentle tones, to call the stewardess. I went to the abode of that functionary, and found her lying on the floor sea-sick; her beautiful auburn hair tangled and dishevelled. "Oh! madam, how could you sleep?" she said; "we've had such an awful night! I've never been so ill before."

I returned from my useless errand, and the lady then *commanded* me to go instantly to the captain and ask him to come. "He's attending to the ship," I urged. "Go, then, if you've any pity, and ask him if we shall be lost." "There's no danger, as far as I can judge; the engines work regularly, and the ship obeys her helm." The *Mayflower* gave a heavier roll than usual. "Oh my God! Oh Heaven!" shrieked the unhappy lady; "forgive me! Mercy! mercy!" A lull followed, in which she called to one of her slaves for a glass of water; but the poor creature was too ill to move, and, seeing that her mistress was about to grow angry, I went up to the saloon for it. On my way to the table I nearly tumbled over a prostrate man, whom I had noticed the night before as conspicuous for his audacious and hardy bearing.

g we're going to Davy Jones," he said; "I've been saying my Ps all night—little good, I guess. I've been a sinner too long. I've been many a"—a groan followed. I looked at the reckless spar. He was lying on the floor, with his hat and shoes off, and rifle beside him. His face was ghastly, but, I verily believe, more from the effects of sea-sickness than fear. He begged me, in idle tones, to get him some brandy; but I could not find any way to give it to him, and went down with the water.

Two slaves were as frightened as people almost stupified by illness could be; but when I asked one of the freed negroes if she were alarmed, she said, "Me no fear; if me die, me go Jesus Christ; if me live, me serve him here—*better to die!*"

It has been said that "poverty, sickness, all the ills of life, are Paradise to what we fear of death"—that "it is not that life is sweet but that death is bitter." Here the poet and the philosopher might have learned a lesson. This poor, untutored negress probably knew nothing more "than her Bible true;" but she had that knowledge of a future state which reason, unassisted by the light of revelation, could never have learned; she knew yet more—she knew God as revealed in Christ, and in that knowledge, under its highest and truest name of *Faith*, she feared not the summons which would call her into the presence of the Judge of all. The infidel may hug his heartless creed, which, by ignoring alike futurity and the Divine government, makes an aimless chaos of the past, and a gloomy obscurity of the future; but, in the "hour of death and in the day of judgment," the boldest atheist in existence would thankfully exchange his failing theories for the poor African's simple creed.

Providence, which has not endowed the negro with intellectual powers of the highest order, has given him an amount of *heart* and enthusiasm to which we are strangers. He is warm and ardent in his attachments, fierce in his resentfulness, terrible in his revenge. The black troops of our West Indian colonies, when let loose, fight with more fury and bloodthirstiness than those of any white race. This temperament is carried into religion, and nowhere on earth does our Lord find a more loving and zealous disciple than in the converted and Christianized negro. It is indeed true that, in America only, more than three million free-born Africans wear the chains of servitude; but it is no less true that in many instances the Gospel has penetrated the shades of their Egyptian darkness, giving them

> "A clear escape form tyrannizing lust,
> A full immunity from penal woe."

Many persons who have crossed the Atlantic without annoyance are discomposed by the short chopping surges of these inland seas, and the poor negresses suffered dreadfully from sea-sickness.

As the stewardess was upstairs, and too ill herself to attend upon anyone, I did what I could for them, getting them pillows, camphor, &c., only too happy that I was in a condition to be useful. One of them, a young married woman with a baby of three months old, was alarmingly ill, and, as the poor infant was in danger of being seriously injured by the rolling of the ship, I took it on my lap for an hour till the gale moderated, thereby gaining the lasting kindly remembrance of its poor mother. I am sure that a white infant would have screamed in a most appalling way, for, as I had never taken a baby in my arms before, I held it in a very awkward manner; but the poor little black thing, wearied with its struggles on the floor, lay very passively, every now and then turning its little monkey-face up to mine, with a look of understanding and confidence which quite conciliated my good will. It was so awfully ugly, so much like a black ape, and so little like the young of the human species, that I was obliged while I held it to avert my eyes from it, lest in a sudden fit of foolish prejudice and disgust I should let it fall. Meanwhile, the Southern lady was very ill, but not too ill, I am sorry to say, to box the ears of her slaves.

The gale moderated about nine in the morning, leaving a very rough, foamy sea, which reflected in a peculiarly dazzling and disagreeable way the cloudless and piercing blue of the sky. The saloon looked as magnificent as by candle-light, with the sunshine streaming through a running window of stained glass.

Dinner on a plentiful scale was served at one, but out of 300 passengers only about 30 were able to avail themselves of it. Large glass tubs of vanilla cream-ice were served. The voyage was peculiarly uninteresting, as we were out of sight of land nearly the whole day; my friend the widow did not appear, and, when I attempted to write, the inkstand rolled off the table. It was just sunset when we reached Buffalo, and moored at a wharf crowded with large steamers receiving and discharging cargo. Owing to the gale, we were two hours too late for the Niagara cars, and I slept at the Western Hotel, where I received every attention.

Buffalo is one of the best samples of American progress. It is a regularly laid-out and substantially built city of 65,000 inhabitants. It is still in the vigour of youth, for the present town only dates from 1813. It stands at the foot of Lake Erie, at the opening of the Hudson canal, where the commerce of the great chain of inland lakes is condensed. It is very "going ahead;" its inhabitants are ever changing; its population is composed of all nations, with a very large proportion of Germans, French, and Irish. But their national characteristics, though not lost, are seen through a medium of pure Americanism. They all rush about—the lethargic German keeps pace with the energetic Yankee; and the Irishman, no longer in rags, "guesses" and "spekilates" in the brogue of Erin. Western travellers pass through Buffalo; tourists bound for Canada pass through Buffalo; the traffic of lakes, canals, and several lines of rail centres at Buffalo; so engines scream, and steamers puff, all day long. It has a great shipbuilding trade, and to all appearance is one of the most progressive and go-ahead cities in the Union.

I left Buffalo on a clear, frosty morning, by a line which ran between lumber-yards[1] on a prodigious scale and the hard white beach of Lake Erie. Soon after leaving the city, the lake becomes narrow and rapid, and finally hurries along with fearful velocity. I knew that I was looking at the commencement of the rapids of Niagara, but the cars ran into some clearings, and presently stopped at a very bustling station, where a very officious man shouted, "Niagara Falls Station!" The name grated unpleasantly upon my ears. A man appeared at the door of the car in which I was the only passenger—"You for Lewiston, quick, this way!" and hurried me into a stage of uncouth construction, drawn by four horses. We jolted along the very worst road I ever travelled on—corduroy was Elysium to it. No level was observed; it seemed to be a mere track along waste land, running through holes, over hillocks and stumps of trees. We were one hour and three-quarters in going a short seven miles. If I had been better acquainted with the neighbourhood, I might, as I only found out when it was too late, have crossed the bridge at Niagara Falls, spent three hours in sight of Niagara, proceeding to Queenston in time for the steamer by the Canada cars!

On our way to Lewiston we met forty of these four-horse stages. I caught a distant view of the falls, and a nearer one of the yet incomplete suspension bridge, which, when finished, will be one of the greatest triumphs of engineering art.

Beyond this the scenery is very beautiful. The road runs among forest trees of luxuriant growth, and peach and apple orchards, upon the American bank of the Niagara river. This bank is a cliff 300 feet high, and from the edge of the road you may throw a stone into the boiling torrent below; yet the only parapet is a rotten fence, in many places completely destroyed. When you begin to descend the steep hill to Lewiston the drive is absolutely frightful. The cumbrous vehicle creaks, jolts, and swings, and, in spite of friction-breaks and other appliances,

1 Lumber is sawn timber.

gradually acquires an impetus which sends it at full speed down the tremendous hill, and round the sharp corner, to the hotel at Lewiston. While I was waiting there watching the stages, and buying peaches, of which I got six for a penny, a stage came at full speed down the hill, with only two men on the driving-seat. The back straps had evidently given way, and the whole machine had a tendency to jump forward, when, in coming down the steepest part of the declivity, it got a jolt, and in the most ridiculous way turned "topsy-turvy," the roof coming down upon the horses' backs. The men were thrown off unhurt, but the poor animals were very much cut and bruised.

I crossed Lake Ontario to Toronto in the *Peerless*, a very smart, safe, iron steamer, with the saloon and chief weight below. The fittings of this beautiful little vessel are in perfect taste. We stooped for two hours at the wharf at Niagara, a town on the British side, protected once by a now disused and dismantled fort. The cars at length came up, two hours after their time, and the excuse given for the delay was, that they had run over a cow!

In grim contrast to the dismantled English Fort Massassaqua, Fort Niagara stands on the American side, and is a place of considerable strength. There I saw sentinels in grey uniforms, and the flag of the stars and stripes.

Captain D—— of the *Peerless* brought his beautiful little vessel from the Clyde in 6000 pieces, and is justly proud of her. I sat next him at dinner, and found that we knew some of the same people in Scotland. Gaelic was a further introduction; and though so many thousand miles away, for a moment I felt myself at home when we spoke of the majestic Cuchullins and the heathery braes of Balquidder. In the *Peerless* everyone took wine or liqueurs. There was no bill of fare, but a long list of wines and spirits was placed by each plate. Instead of being disturbed in the middle of dinner by a poke on the shoulder, and the demand, "Dinner ticket, or fifty cents," I was allowed to remain as long as I pleased, and at the conclusion of the

148

voyage a gentlemanly Highland purser asked me for my passage and dinner money together.

We passed a number of brigs and schooners under full sail, their canvass remarkable for its whiteness; their hulls also were snowy white. They looked as though "they were drifting with the dead, to shores where all was dumb."

Late in the evening we entered the harbour of Toronto, which is a very capacious one, and is protected by a natural mole of sand some miles in extent. Though this breakwater has some houses and a few trees, it is the picture of dreary desolation.

The city of Toronto, the stronghold of Canadian learning and loyalty, presents an imposing appearance, as seen from the water. It stands on ground sloping upwards from the lake, and manufactories, colleges, asylums, church spires, and public buildings, the whole faced by a handsome line of quays, present themselves at once to the eye.

A soft and familiar sound came off from the shore; it was the well-known note of the British bugle, and the flag whose silken folds were rising and falling on the breeze was the meteor flag of England. Long may it brave "the battle and the breeze"! English uniforms were glancing among the crowd on the quay, English faces surrounded me, English voices rang in my ears; the *négligé* costumes which met my eyes were in the best style of England. A thrill of pleasure went through my heart on finding, more than 4000 miles from home, the characteristics of my own loved land.

But I must add that there were unpleasant characteristics peculiarly English also. I could never have landed, the confusion was so great, had not Captain D— assisted me. One porter ran off with one trunk, another with another, while three were fighting for the possession of my valise, till silenced by the cane of a custom-house officer. Then there was a clamorous demand for "wharfage," and the hackman charged half a dollar for taking me a quarter of a mile. All this somewhat damped my ecstacies, and contrasted unfavourably with the

149

orderly and easy way in which I landed on the shore of the United States.

At Russell's Hotel I rejoined Mr. and Mrs. Walrence, who said "they would have been extremely surprised if a lady in *their* country had met with the slightest difficulty or annoyance" in travelling alone for 700 miles!

My ecstacies were still further toned down when I woke the next morning with my neck, hands, and face stinging and swollen from the bites of innumerable mosquitoes.

CHAPTER X

The Place of Council—Its progress and its people—English hearts—"Sebastopol is taken"—Squibs and crackers—A ship on her beam-ends—Selfishness—A mongrel city—A Scot—Constancy rewarded—Monetary difficulties—Detention on a bridge—A Canadian homestead—Life in the clearings—The bush on fire— A word on farming—The "bee" and its produce—Eccentricities of Mr. Haldimands—A ride on a troop-horse—Scotch patriotism—An English church—The servant nuisance— Richard Cobden.

The people of Toronto informed me, immediately on my arrival in their city, that "Toronto is the most English place to be met with out of England." At first I was at a loss to understand their meaning. Wooden houses, long streets crossing each other at right angles, and wooden side-walks, looked very un-English to my eye. But when I had been for a few days at Toronto, and had become accustomed to the necessarily-unfinished appearance of a town which has only enjoyed sixty years of existence, I fully agreed with the laudatory remarks passed upon it. The wooden houses have altogether disappeared from the principal streets, and have been replaced by substantial erections of brick and stone. The churches are numerous, and of tasteful architecture. The public edifices are well situated and very handsome. King Street, the principal thoroughfare, is two miles in length, and the side-walks are lined with handsome shops. The outskirts of Toronto abound in villa residences, standing in gardens or shrubberies. The people do not run *"hurry skurry"* along the streets, but there are no idlers to be observed. Hirsute eccentricities have also disappeared; the beard is rarely seen, and the moustache is not considered a necessary ornament. The faded careworn look of the American ladies has given place to the bright complexion, the dimpled smile, and the active elastic tread, so peculiarly English. Indeed, in walking along the streets, there is

151

nothing to tell that one is not in England; and if anything were needed to complete the illusion, those sure tokens of British civilisation, a jail and a lunatic asylum, are not wanting.

Toronto possesses in a remarkable degree the appearances of stability and progress. No town on the Western Continent has progressed more rapidly; certainly none more surely. I conversed with an old gentleman who remembered its site when it was covered with a forest, when the smoke of Indian wigwams ascended through the trees, and when wild fowl crowded the waters of the harbour. The place then bore the name of Toronto—the Place of Council. The name was changed by the first settlers to Little York, but in 1814 its euphonious name of Toronto was again bestowed upon it. Its population in 1801 was 336; it is now nearly 50,000.

Toronto is not the fungus growth, staring and wooden, of a temporary necessity; it is the result of persevering industry, well-applied capital, and healthy and progressive commercial prosperity. Various railroads are in course of construction, which will make it the exporting market for the increasing produce of the interior; and as the migratory Canadian Legislature is now stationary at Toronto for four years, its future progress will probably be more rapid than its past. Its wharfs are always crowded with freight and passenger steamers, by which it communicates two or three times a day with the great cities of the United States, and Quebec and Montreal. It is the seat of Canadian learning, and, besides excellent schools, possesses a university, and several theological and general seminaries. The society is said to be highly superior. I give willing testimony in favour of this assertion, from the little which I saw of it, but an attack of ague prevented me from presenting my letters of introduction. It is a very musical place, and at Toronto Jenny Lind gave the only concerts with which she honoured Canada. A large number of the inhabitants are Scotch, which may account for the admirable way in which the Sabbath is observed.

If I was pleased to find that the streets, the stores, the accent, the manners were English, I was rejoiced to see that from the highest to the lowest the hearts of the people were English also. I was at Toronto when the false despatch was received announcing the capture of Sebastopol and of the Russian army. I was spending the evening at the house of a friend, when a gentleman ran in to say that the church bells were ringing for a great victory! It was but the work of a few minutes for us to jump into a hack, and drive at full speed to the office of the *Globe* newspaper, where the report was apparently confirmed. A great crowd in a state of eager excitement besieged the doors, and presently a man mounted on a lamp-post read the words, "*Sebastopol is taken! The Russian fleet burnt! Eighteen thousand killed and wounded. Loss of the Allies, two thousand five hundred.*" This news had been telegraphed from Boston, and surely the trembling tongue of steel had never before told such a bloody tale. One shout of "Hurrah for Old England" burst from the crowd, and hearty English cheers were given, which were caught up and repeated down the crowded streets of Toronto. The shout thrilled through my heart; it told that the flag of England waved over the loyal, true-hearted, and brave; it told of attachment to the constitution and the throne; it told that in our times of difficulty and danger "St. George and merry England" would prove a gathering cry even on the prosperous shores of Lake Ontario. Greater enthusiasm could not have been exhibited on the receipt of this false but glorious news in any city at home. The bells, which a few days before had tolled for the catastrophe of the *Arctic*, now pealed forth in triumph for the victory of the Alma. Toronto knew no rest on that night. Those who rejoiced over a victory gained over the northern despot were those who had successfully resisted the despotism of a band of rebels. The streets were almost impassable from the crowds who thronged them. Hand-rockets exploded almost into people's eyes—serpents and squibs were hissing and cracking over the pavements—and people were rushing in all directions for fuel for the different bonfires. The largest of

153

these was opposite the St. Lawrence Hall. It was a monster one of tar-barrels, and lighted up the whole street, paling the sickly flame of the gas-lamps. There was a large and accumulating crowd round it, shouting, "Hurrah for Old England! Down with the Rooshians! Three cheers for the Queen!" and the like. Sky-rockets were blazing high in air, men were rushing about firing muskets, the small swivels of the steamers at the wharfs were firing incessantly, and carts with combustibles were going at full speed along the streets, each fresh arrival being hailed with enthusiastic cheering. There were firemen, too, in their picturesque dresses, who had turned out at the first sound of the bells, and their services were soon put in requisition, for enthusiasm produced recklessness, and two or three shingle-roofs were set on fire by the descent of rockets upon them. This display of attachment to England was not confined to the loyal and aristocratic city of Toronto; at Hamilton, a thriving commercial place, of suspected American tendencies, the town-council was assembled at the time the despatch was received, and instantly voted a sum for an illumination.

From my praise of Toronto I must except the hotels, which are of a very inferior class. They are a poor imitation of those in the States. Russell's Hotel, at which I stayed for eight days, was a disagreeable contrast to the National Hotel at Detroit, and another of some pretensions, the North American, was said to be even more comfortless. The bedrooms at Russell's swarmed with mosquitoes; and the waiters, who were runaway slaves, were inattentive and uncivil.

After staying some little time with my friends at Toronto, I went to pay a visit to some friends at Hamilton. The afternoon was very windy and stormy. The lake looked very unpromising from the wharf; the island protected the harbour, but beyond this the waves were breaking with fury. Several persons who came down, intending to take their passage for Hamilton, were deterred by the threatening aspect of the weather, but, not having heard anything against the character of Lake Ontario, I had sufficient confidence in it to persevere in my intention. I said to the captain, "I suppose it won't be rough?" to which he replied that he could not flatter me by saying so, adding that he had never seen so many persons sick as in the morning. Dinner was served immediately on our leaving the harbour, but the number of those who sat down, at first about thirty, soon diminished to five, the others having rushed in a most mysterious manner to state rooms or windows. For my own part, I cannot say that the allowed excellence of the *cuisine* tempted me to make a very substantial meal, and I was glad of an excuse for retiring to a state-room, which I shared with a lady who had just taken leave of her three children. This cabin was very prettily arranged, but the movements of things were rather erratic, and my valise gave most disagreeable manifestations of spiritual agency.

The ship was making little way, and rolling and pitching fearfully, and, knowing how very top-heavy she was, I did not at all like the glimpses of raging water which I with difficulty obtained through the cabin windows. To understand what followed it will be necessary for the reader to recollect that the saloon and state-rooms in this vessel formed an erection or deck-house about eight feet high upon the deck, and that the part of the saloon where most of the passengers were congregated, as well as the state-room where I was sitting, were within a few feet of the bow of the ship, and consequently exposed to the fury of the waves. I had sat in my state-room for half an hour, feeling very apathetic, and wishing myself anywhere but where I was, when something struck the ship, and the wretched fabric fell over on her side. Another and another—then silence for a second, broken only by the crash and roar of winds and waters. The inner door burst open, letting in an inundation of water. My companion jumped up, shrieking, "Oh, my children! we're lost—we're lost!" and crawled, pale and trembling, into the saloon. The vessel was lying on her side, therefore locomotion was most difficult; but sea-sick people were emerging from their state-rooms, shrieking, some that they were lost—others for their children—

others for mercy; while a group of gentlemen, less noisy, but not less frightened, and drenched to the skin, were standing together, with pale and ashy faces. "What is the matter?" inquired my companion, taking hold of one of these men. "Say your prayers, for we are going down," was the brutal reply. For the first and only time during my American travels I was really petrified with fear. Suddenly a wave struck the hapless vessel, and with a stunning crash broke through the thin woodwork of the side of the saloon. I caught hold of a life-buoy which was near me—a gentleman clutched it from me, for fright makes some men selfish—and, breathless, I was thrown down into the gurgling water. I learned then how quickly thoughts can pass through the mind, for in those few seconds I thought less of the anticipated death-struggle amid the boiling surges of the lake, and of the quiet sleep beneath its gloomy waters, than of the unsatisfactory manner in which those at home would glean the terrible tidings from the accident columns of a newspaper. Another minute, and I was swept through the open door into a state-room—another one of suspense, and the ship righted as if by a superhuman effort. There seemed a respite—there was a silence, broken only by the roar of winds and waves, and with the respite came hope. Shortly after, the master of the ship appeared, with his hat off, and completely drenched. "Thank God, we're safe!" he said, and returned to his duty. We had all supposed that we had struck on a rock or wreck. I never knew the precise nature of our danger beyond this, that the vessel had been thrown on her beam-ends in a squall, and that, the wind immediately veering round, the fury of the waves had been spent upon her.

Many of the passengers now wished the captain to return, but he said that he should incur greater danger in an attempt to make the harbour of Toronto than by proceeding down the open lake. For some time nothing was to be seen but a dense fog, a storm of sleet which quite darkened the air, and raging waves, on which we mounted sometimes, while at others we were buried between them. In another hour the gale had completely subsided, and, after we had changed our drenched habiliments, no token remained of the previous storm but the drowned and dismantled appearance of the saloon, and the resolution on my own mind never to trust myself again on one of these fearful lakes. I was amused to observe that those people who had displayed the greatest symptoms of fear during the storm were the first to protest that, "as for them, they never thought there was any danger." The afternoon, though cold, was extremely beautiful, but, owing to the storm in the early part of our voyage, we did not reach Hamilton till nightfall, or three hours after our appointed time.

I do not like these inland lakes, or tideless fresh-water seas, as they may more appropriately be termed. I know Lake Ontario well; I have crossed it twice, and have been up and down it five times. I have sojourned upon its shores, and have seen them under the hot light of an autumn sun, and underneath a mantle of wintry snow; but there is to me something peculiarly oppressive about this vast expanse of water. If the lake is rough, there are no harbours of refuge in which to take shelter—if calm, the waters, though blue, pure, and clear, look monotonous and dead. The very ships look lonely things; their hulls and sails are white, and some of them have been known in time of cholera to drift over the lake from day to day, with none to guide the helm. The shores, too, are flat and uninteresting; my eyes wearied of following that interminable boundary of trees stretching away to the distant horizon.

Yet Lake Ontario affords great advantages to both Canada and the United States. The former has the large towns of Hamilton, Toronto, and Kingston on its shores, with the exporting places of Oakville, Credit, and Cobourg. The important towns of Oswego and Rochester, with smaller ones too numerous to name, are on the American side. This lake is five hundred miles round, and, owing to its very great depth, never freezes, except just along the shores. An immense trade is carried on upon it, both in steamers and sailing vessels. A ship-canal connects Lake Ontario with Lake Erie, thereby overcoming the obstacle to navigation produced by the Falls of Niagara. This stupendous work is called the Welland Canal.

At Hamilton I received a most cordial welcome from the friends whom I went to visit, and saw something of the surrounding country. It is, I think, the most bustling place in Canada. It is a very juvenile city, yet already has a population of twenty-five thousand people. The stores and hotels are handsome, and the streets are brilliantly lighted with gas. Hamilton has a peculiarly unfinished appearance. Indications of progress meet one on every side—there are houses being built, and housed being pulled down to make room for larger and more substantial ones—streets are being extended, and new ones are being staked out, and every external feature seems to be acquiring fresh and rapid development. People hurry about as if their lives depended on their speed. "I guess" and "I calculate" are frequently heard, together with "Well posted up," and "A long chalk;" and locomotives and steamers whistle all day long. Hamilton is a very Americanised place. I heard of "grievances, independence, and annexation," and, altogether, should have supposed it to be on the other side of the boundary-line.

It is situated on a little lake, called Burlington Bay, separated from Lake Ontario by a narrow strip of sandy shingle. This has been cut through, and, as two steamers leave the pier at Hamilton at the same hour every morning, there is a daily and very exciting race for the first entrance into the narrow passage. This racing is sometimes productive of very serious collisions. The town is built upon very low and aguish ground, at the foot of a peculiar and steep eminence, which the inhabitants dignify with the name of the Mountain. I ascended this mountain, which might better be called a molehill, by a flight of a hundred and thirty steps. The view from the top was very magnificent, but, as an elevated building offered us one still more extensive, we ascended to the roof by six flights of steps, to see a *camera obscura* which was ostentatiously advertised. A very good *camera obscura* might have been worth so long an ascent in a house redolent of spirits and onions; but after we had reached the top, with a great expenditure of toil and breath, a ragged, shoeless little boy very pompously opened the door of a small wooden erection, and introduced us to four panes of coloured glass, through which we viewed the town of Hamilton, under the different aspects of spring, summer, autumn, and winter!

Dundurn Castle, a handsome, castellated, baronial-looking building, the residence of the present Premier, Sir Allan M'Nab, is near Hamilton, and it has besides some very handsome stone villa residences. There I saw, for the first and only time in the New World, beautifully kept grass lawns, with flower-beds in the English style. One very fine morning, when the maple-leaves were tinted with the first scarlet of the fall, my friends took me to see Ancaster and Dundas; the former, an old place, very like some of our grey, quiet Lancashire villages—the latter a good type of the rapid development and enterprising spirit which are making Canada West to rival the States in rapidity of progress. There were bridges in course of construction—railway embankments swarming with labourers—macadamised roads succeeding those of corduroy and plank—snake-fences giving place to those of posts and rails, and stone walls—and saw and grist mills were springing up wherever a "water privilege" could be found. Laden waggons proceeded heavily along the roads, and the encouraging announcements of "Cash for wheat," and "Cash for wool," were frequently to be seen. The views were very fine as we skirted the Mountain, but Canadian scenery is monotonous and rather gloomy; though the glorious tints of the American fall give the leaves of some of the trees the appearance rather of tropical flowers than of foliage.

Ancaster is an old place, outstripped by towns of ten years' existence, as it has neither a port nor a river. There was an agricultural show, and monster pumpkins and overgrown cabbages were displayed to admiring crowds, under the shadow of a prodigious union jack.

Dundas, a near neighbour of Ancaster, has completely eclipsed it. This appears to be one of the busiest little places in Canada West. It is a collection of woollen-mills, grist-mills, and iron-foundries; and though, in my preformed notions of political economy, I had supposed manufactures suited exclusively to an old country, in which capital and labour are alike redundant, the aspect of this place was most thriving. In one of the flour-mills the machinery seemed as perfect as in the biscuit factory at Portsmouth—by some ingenious mechanism the flour was cooled, barrelled, and branded with great celerity. At an iron-foundry I was surprised to find that steam-engines and flour-mill machinery could not be manufactured fast enough to meet the demand. In this neighbourhood I heard rather an interesting anecdote of what steady perseverance can do, in the history of a Scot from the shores of the Forth.

This young man was a pauper boy, and was apprenticed to the master of an iron-foundry in Scotland, but ran away before the expiration of his apprenticeship, and, entering a ship at Glasgow, worked his passage across to Quebec. Here he gained employment for some months as a porter, and, having saved a little money, went up to the neighbourhood of Lake Simcoe, where he became a day labourer. Here he fell in love with his master's daughter, who returned his affection, but her father scornfully rejected the humble Scotchman's suit. Love but added an incentive to ambition; and obtaining work in a neighbouring township, he increased his income by teaching reading, writing, and arithmetic in the evenings. He lived penuriously, denied himself even necessaries, and carefully treasured his hoarded savings. Late one evening, clothed almost in rags, he sought the house of his lady-love, and told her that within two years he would come to claim her hand of her father, with a waggon and pair of horses.

Still in his ragged clothing, for it does not appear that he had any other, he trudged to Toronto, and sought employment, his accumulated savings sewn up in the lining of his waistcoat. He went about from person to person, but could not obtain employment, and his waggon and horses receded further and further in the dim perspective. One day, while walking along at the unfinished end of King Street West, he saw something glittering in the mud, and, on taking it up, found it to be the steel snap of a pocket-book. This pocket-book contained notes to the amount of one hundred and fifty dollars; and the next day a reward of five-and-twenty was offered to the finder of them. The Scotchman waited on the owner, who was a tool manufacturer, and, declining the reward, asked only for work, for "leave to toil," as Burns has expressed it. This was granted him; and in less than four months he became a clerk in the establishment. His salary was gradually raised—in the evenings he obtained employment in writing for a lawyer, and his savings, judiciously managed, increased to such an extent, that at the end of eighteen months he purchased a thriving farm in the neighbourhood of London, and, as there was water-power upon it, he built a grist-mill. His industry still continued successful, and just before the two years expired he drove in a light waggon, with two hardy Canadian horses, to the dwelling of his former master, to claim his daughter's hand; though, be it remembered, he had never held any communication with her since he parted from her in rags two years before. At first they did not recognise the vagrant, ragged Scotch labourer, in the well-dressed driver and possessor of the "knowing-looking" equipage. His altered circumstances removed all difficulty on the father's part—the maiden had been constant—and soon afterwards they were married. He still continued to prosper, and add land to land; and three years after his marriage sent twenty pounds to his former master in Scotland, as a compensation for the loss of his services. Strange to say, the son of that very master is now employed in the mill of the runaway apprentice. Such instances as this, while they afford encouragement to honest industry, show at the same time the great capabilities of Canada West.

At Hamilton, where the stores are excellent, I made several purchases, but I was extremely puzzled with the Canadian currency. The States money is very convenient. I soon understood dollars, cents, and dimes; but in the colonies I never knew what my money was worth. In Prince Edward Island the sovereign is worth thirty shillings; in New Brunswick and Nova Scotia twenty-five; while in Canada, at the time of my visit, it was worth twenty-four and fourpence. There your shilling is fifteenpence, or a quarter-dollar; while your quarter-dollar is a shilling. Your sixpence is sevenpence-half-penny, or a "York shilling;" while your penny is a "copper" of indeterminate value apparently. Comparatively speaking, very little metallic money is in circulation. You receive bills marked five shillings, when, to your surprise, you can only change them for four metallic shillings. Altogether in Canada I had to rely upon people's honesty, or probably on their ignorance of my ignorance; for any attempts at explanation only made "confusion worse confounded," and I seldom comprehended anything of a higher grade than a "York shilling." From my stupidity about the currency, and my frequent query, "How many dollars or cents is it?" together with my offering dirty crumpled pieces of paper bearing such names as Troy, Palmyra, and Geneva, which were in fact notes of American banks which might have suspended payment, I was constantly taken, not for an ignoramus from the "Old Country," but for a "genuine Down-Easter." Canadian credit is excellent; but the banking system of the States is on a very insecure footing; some bank or other "breaks" every day, and lists of the defaulters are posted up in the steamboats and hotels.

Within a few days after my resolution never again to trust myself on Lake Ontario, I sailed down it, on a very beautiful morning, to Toronto. The royal mail steamer *Arabian* raced with us for the narrow entrance to the canal which connects Burlington Bay with the main lake, and both captains "piled on" to their utmost ability, but the *Arabian* passed us in triumph. The morning was so very fine, that I half forgot my dislike to Lake Ontario. On the land side there was a succession of slightly elevated promontories, covered with forests abounding in recent clearings, their sombre colouring being relieved by the brilliant blue of the lake. I saw, for the only time, that beautiful phenomenon called the "water-mirage," by which trees, ships, and houses are placed in the most extraordinary and sometimes inverted positions. Yet still these endless promontories stretched away, till their distant outlines were lost in the soft blue haze of the Indian summer. Yet there was an oppressiveness about the tideless water and pestilential shore, and the white-hulled ships looked like deserted punished things, whose doom for ages was to be ceaseless sailing over these gloomy waters.

At Toronto my kind friend Mr. Forrest met me. He and his wife had invited me some months before to visit them in their distant home in the Canadian *bush*; therefore I was not a little surprised at the equipage which awaited me at the hotel, as I had expected to jolt for twenty-two miles, over corduroy roads, in a lumber-waggon. It was the most dashing vehicle which I saw in Canada. It was a most *unbush-like*, sporting-looking, high, mail phaëton, mounted by four steps; it had three seats, a hood in front, and a rack for luggage behind. It would hold eight persons. The body and wheels were painted bright scarlet and black; and it was drawn by a pair of very showy-looking horses, about sixteen "hands" high, with elegant and well-blacked harness. Mr. Forrest looked more like a sporting English squire than an emigrant.

We drove out of Toronto by the Lake shore road, and I could scarcely believe we were not by the sea, for a heavy surf was rolling and crashing upon the beach, and no land was in sight on the opposite side. After some time we came to a stream, with a most clumsy swing bridge, which was open for the passage of two huge rafts laden with flour. This proceeding had already occupied more than an hour, as we were informed by some unfortunate *détenus*. We waited for half an hour while the raftmen dawdled about it, but the rafts could not get through the surf, so they were obliged to desist. I now reasonably supposed that they would have shut the bridge as fast as possible, as about twenty vehicles, with numerous foot-passengers, were waiting on either side; but no, they moved it for a little distance, then smoked a bit, then moved it a few inches and smoked again, and so on for another half-hour, while we were exposed to a pitiless north-east wind. They evidently enjoyed our discomfiture, and were trying how much of annoyance we would bear patiently. Fiery tempers have to be curbed in Canada West, for the same spirit which at home leads men not to "touch their hats" to those above them in station, here would vent itself in open insolence and arrogance, if one requested them to be a little quicker in their motions. The fabric would hardly come together at all, and then only three joists appeared without anything to cover them. This the men seemed to consider *un fait accompli*, and sat down to smoke. At length, when it seemed impossible to bear a longer detention with any semblance of patience, they covered these joists with some planks, over which our horses, used to pick their way, passed in safety, not, however, without overturning one of the boards, and leaving a most dangerous gap. This was a favourable specimen of a Canadian bridge.

The manners of the emigrants who settle in Canada are far from prepossessing. Wherever I heard torrents of slang and abuse of England; wherever I noticed brutality of manner, unaccompanied by respect to ladies, I always found upon inquiry that the delinquent had newly arrived from the old country. Some time before I visited America, I saw a letter from a young man who had emigrated, containing these words: "Here I haven't to *bow and cringe* to gentlemen of the aristocracy—that is, to a man who has a better coat on than myself." I was not prepared to find this feeling so very prevalent among the lower classes in our own possessions. The children are an improvement on their parents, and develop loyal and constitutional sentiments. The Irish are the noisiest of the enemies of England, and carry with them to Canada the most inveterate enmity to "Sassenach" rule. The term "*slang-whangers*" must have been invented for these.

After some miles of very bad road, which once had been corduroy, we got upon a plank-road, upon which the draught is nearly as light as upon a railroad. When these roads are good, the driving upon them is very easy; when they are out of repair it is just the reverse. We came to an Indian village of clapboard houses, built some years ago by Government for some families of the Six Nations who resided here with their chief; but they disliked the advances of the white man, and their remnants have removed farther to the west. We drove for many miles through woods of the American oak, little more than brushwood, but gorgeous in all shades of colouring, from the scarlet of the geranium to deep crimson and Tyrian purple. Oh! our poor faded tints of autumn, about which we write sentimental poetry! Turning sharply round a bank of moss, and descending a long hill, we entered the bush. There all my dreams of Canadian scenery were more than realised. Trees grew in every variety of the picturesque. The forest was dark and oppressively still, and such a deadly chill came on, that I drew my cloak closer around me. A fragrant but heavy smell arose, and Mr. Forrest said that we were going down into a cedar swamp, where there was a chill even in the hottest weather. It was very beautiful. Emerging from this, we came upon a little whitewashed English church, standing upon a steep knoll, with its little spire rising through the trees; and leaving this behind, we turned off upon a road through very wild country. The ground had once been cleared, but no use had been made of it, and it was covered with charred stumps about two feet high. Beyond this appeared an interminable bush. Mr. Forrest told me that his house was near, and, from the appearance of the country, I expected to come upon a log cabin; but we turned into a field, and drove under some very fine apple-trees to a house the very perfection of elegance and comfort. It looked as if a pretty villa from Norwood or Hampstead had been transported to this Canadian clearing. The dwelling was a substantially built brick one-storied house, with a deep green verandah surrounding it, as a protection from the snow in winter and the heat in summer. Apple-trees, laden with richly-coloured fruit, were planted round, and sumach-trees, in all the glorious colouring of the fall, were opposite the front door. The very house seemed to smile a welcome; and seldom have I met a more cordial one than I received from Mrs. Forrest, the kindly and graceful hostess, who met me at the door, her pretty simple dress of pink and white muslin contrasting strangely with the charred stumps which were in sight, and the long lines of gloomy bush which stood out dark and sharp against the evening sky.

"Will you go into the drawing-room?" asked Mrs. Forrest. I was surprised, for I had not associated a *drawing-room* with emigrant life in Canada; but I followed her along a pretty entrance-lobby, floored with polished oak, into a lofty room furnished with all the elegances and luxuries of the mansion of an affluent Englishman at home, a beautiful piano not being wanting. It was in this house, containing every comfort, and welcomed with the kindest hospitality, that I received my first impressions of "life in the clearings." My hosts were only recovering from the fatigues of a "thrashing bee" of the day before, and, while we were playing at bagatelle, one of the *gentlemen* assistants came to the door, and asked if the "*Boss*" were at home. A lady told me that, when she first came out, a servant asked her "How the boss liked his shirts done?" As Mrs. Moodie had not then enlightened the world on the subject of settlers' slang, the lady did not understand her, and asked what she meant by the "boss,"—to which she replied, "Why, lawk, missus, your hubby, to be sure."

I spent some time with these kind and most agreeable friends, and returned to them after a visit to the Falls of Niagara. My sojourn with them is among my sunniest memories of Canada. Though my expectations were in one sense entirely disappointed on awaking to the pleasant consciousness of reposing on the softest of feathers, I did not feel romance enough to wish myself on a buffalo robe on the floor of a log-cabin. Nearly every day I saw some operation of

Canadian farming, with its difficulties and pleasures. Among the former is that of obtaining men to do the work. The wages given are five shillings per diem, and in many cases "rations" besides. While I was at Mr. Forrest's, two men were sinking a well, and one coolly took up his tools and walked away because *only* half a pound of butter had been allowed for breakfast. Mr. Forrest possesses sixty acres of land, fifteen of which are still in bush. The barns are very large and substantial, more so than at home; for no produce can be left out of doors in the winter. There were two hundred and fifty bushels of wheat, the produce of a "thrashing bee," and various other edibles. Oxen, huge and powerful, do all the draught-work on this farm, and their stable looked the very perfection of comfort. Round the house "snake-fences" had given place to those of post and rail; but a few hundred yards away was the uncleared bush. The land thus railed round had been cleared for some years; the grass is good, and the stumps few in number. Leaving this, we came to the stubble of last year, where the stumps were more numerous, and then to the land only cleared in the spring, covered thickly with charred stumps, the soil rich and black, and wheat springing up in all directions. Beyond this there was nothing but bush. A scramble through a bush, though very interesting in its way, produces disagreeable consequences.

When the excitement of the novelty was over, and I returned to the house, I contemplated with very woeful feelings the inroad which had been made upon my wardrobe—the garments torn in all directions beyond any possibility of repair, and the shoes reduced to the consistency of soaked brown paper with wading through a bog. It was a serious consideration to me, who at that time was travelling through the West with a very small and very wayworn portmanteau, with Glasgow, Torquay, Boston, Rock Island, and I know not what besides upon it. The bush, however, for the time being, was very enjoyable, in spite of numerous bruises and scratches. Huge pines raised their heads to heaven, others lay prostrate and rotting away, probably thrown down in some tornado. In the distance numbers of trees were lying on the ground, and men were cutting off their branches and burning them in heaps, which slowly smouldered away, and sent up clouds of curling blue smoke, which diffused itself as a thin blue veil over the dark pines.

This bush is in dangerous proximity to Mr. Forrest's house. The fire ran through it in the spring, and many of the trees, which are still standing, are blackened by its effects. One night in April, after a prolonged drought, just as the household were retiring to rest, Mr. Forrest looked out of the window, and saw a light in the bush scarcely bigger or brighter than a glow-worm. Presently it rushed up a tall pine, entwining its fiery arms round the very highest branches. The fire burned on for a fortnight; they knew it must burn till rain came, and Mr. Forrest and his man never left it day or night, all their food being carried to the bush. One night, during a breeze, it made a sudden rush towards the house. In a twinkling they got out the oxen and plough, and, some of the neighbours coming to their assistance, they ploughed up so much soil between the fire and the stubble round the house, that it stopped; but not before Mr. Forrest's straw hat was burnt, and the hair of the oxen singed. Mrs. Forrest meanwhile, though trembling for her husband's safety, was occupied in wetting blankets, and carrying them to the roof of the house, for the dry shingles would have been ignited by a spark. On our return, it was necessary to climb over some "snake" or zigzag fences about six feet high. These are fences peculiar to new countries, and though very cheap, requiring neither tools nor nails, have a peculiarly untidy appearance. It is not thought wise to buy a farm which has not enough bush or growing timber for both rails and firewood.

In clearing, of which I saw all the processes, the first is to cut down the trees, in which difficult operation axes of British manufacture are rendered useless after a few hours' work. The trees are cut about two feet above the root, and often bring others down with them in their fall. Sometimes these trees are split up at the time into rails or firewood; sometimes dragged to the saw-mills to be made into lumber; but are often piled into heaps and burnt—a necessary but prodigal waste of wood, to which I never became reconciled. When the wood has been cleared off, wheat is sown among the stumps, and then grass, which appears only to last about four years. Fire is put on the tops of these unsightly stumps to burn them down as much as possible, and when it is supposed, after two or three years, that the roots have rotted in the ground, several oxen are attached by a chain to each, and pull it out. Generally this is done by means of a "logging bee." I must explain this term, as it refers neither to the industrious insect nor the imperial bee of Napoleon. The very name reminds me of early rising, healthy activity, merriment, and a well-spread board.

A "bee" is a necessity arising from the great scarcity of labour in the New World. When a person wishes to thrash his corn, he gives notice to eight or ten of his neighbours, and a day is appointed on which they are to meet at his house. For two or three days before, grand culinary preparations are made by the hostess, and on the preceding evening a table is loaded with provisions. The morning comes, and eight or ten stalwart Saxons make their appearance, and work hard till noon, while the lady of the house is engaged in hotter work before the fire, in the preparation of hot meat, puddings, and pies; for well she knows that the good humour of her guests depends on the quantity and quality of her viands. They come in to dinner, black (from the dust of a peculiar Canadian weed), hot, tired, hungry, and thirsty. They eat as no other people eat, and set all our notions of the separability of different viands at defiance. At the end of the day they have a very substantial supper, with plenty of whisky, and, if everything has been satisfactory, the convivial proceedings are prolonged till past midnight. The giver of a "bee" is bound to attend the "bees" of all his neighbours. A "thrashing bee" is considered a very "slow affair" by the younger portion of the community. There are "quilting bees," where the thick quilts, so necessary in Canada, are fabricated; "apple bees," where this fruit is sliced and strung for the winter; "shelling bees," where peas in bushels are shelled and barrelled; and "logging bees," where the decayed stumps in the clearings are rooted up by oxen. At the quilting, apple, and shelling bees there are numbers of the fair sex, and games, dancing, and merry-making are invariably kept up till the morning.

In the winter, as in the eastern colonies, all outdoor employments are stopped, and dancing and evening parties of different kinds are continually given. The whole country is like one vast road, and the fine, cold, aurora-lighted nights are cheery with the lively sound of the sleigh-bells, as merry parties, enveloped in furs, drive briskly over the crisp surface of the snow.

The way of life at Mr. Forrest's was peculiarly agreeable. The breakfast-hour was nominally seven, and afterwards Mr. Forrest went out to his farm. The one Irish servant, who never seemed happy with her shoes on, was capable of little else than boiling potatoes, so all the preparations for dinner devolved upon Mrs. Forrest, who till she came to Canada had never attempted anything in the culinary line. I used to accompany her into the kitchen, and learned how to solve the problem which puzzled an English king, viz. "How apples get into a dumpling." We dined at the mediæval hour of twelve, and everything was of home raising. Fresh meat is a rarity; but a calf had been killed, and furnished dinners for seven days, and the most marvellous thing was, that each day it was dressed in a different manner, Mrs. Forrest's skill in this respect rivalling that of *Alexis Soyer*. A home-fed pig, one of eleven slaughtered on one fell day, produced the excellent ham; the squash and potatoes were from the garden; and the bread and beer were from home-grown wheat and hops. After dinner Mr. Forrest and I used to take lengthy rides, along wild roads, on horses of extraordinary capabilities, and in the evening we used to have bagatelle and reading aloud. Such was life in the clearings. On one or two evenings some very agreeable neighbours came in; and in addition to bagatelle we had puzzles, conundrums, and conjuring tricks. One of these "neighbours" was a young married lady, the prettiest person I had seen in America. She was a French Canadian, and added to the graces of person and manner for which they are famed a cleverness and sprightliness peculiarly her own. I was very much pleased with the friendly, agreeable society of the neighbourhood. There are a great many gentlemen residing there, with fixed incomes, who have adopted Canada as their home because of the comforts which they can enjoy in an untaxed country, and one in which it is not necessary to keep up appearances. For instance, a gentleman does not lose caste by grooming his own horse, or driving his own produce to market in a lumber-waggon; and a lady is not less a lady, though she may wear a dress and bonnet of a fashion three years old.

I was surprised one morning by the phenomenon of some morning-callers—yes, morning-callers in a Canadian clearing. I sighed to think that such a pest and accompaniment of civilisation should have crossed the Atlantic. The "callers" of that morning, the Haldimands, amused me very much. They give themselves great airs—Canada with them is a "wretched hole;" the society is composed of "boors." In a few minutes they had asked me who I was—where I came from—what I was doing there—how I got to know my friends—and if I had come to live with them. Mr. Haldimands, finding I came from England, asked me if I knew a certain beautiful young lady, and recounted his flirtations with her. Dukes, earls, and viscounts flowed from his nimble tongue—"When I was hunting with Lord this," or "When I was waltzing with Lady that." His regrets were after the Opera and Almack's, and his height of felicity seemed to be driving a four-in-hand drag. After expatiating to me in the most vociferous manner on the delights of titled society, he turned to Mrs. Forrest and said, "After the society in which we used to move, you may imagine how distasteful all

171

this is to us"—barely a civil speech, I thought. This eccentric individual was taking a lady, whom he considered a person of consequence, a drive in a carriage, when a man driving a lumber-waggon kept crossing the road in front of him, hindering his progress. Mr. Haldimands gradually got into a towering passion, which resulted in his springing out, throwing the reins to the lady, and rushing furiously at the teamster with his fists squared, shouting in a perfect scream, "Flesh and blood can't bear this. One of us must die!" The man whipped up his horses and made off, and Mr. Haldimands tried in vain to hush up a story which made him appear so superlatively ridiculous.

We actually paid some morning visits, and I thought the society very agreeable and free from gossip. One of our visits was paid to the family of one of the oldest settlers in Canada. His place was the very perfection of beauty; it was built in a park formed out of a civilised wood, the grounds extending to the verge of a precipice, looking from which I saw the river, sometimes glittering in the sunshine, sometimes foaming along in a wood—just realising Mrs. Moodie's charming description of the Otonabee. Far below, the water glittered like diamond sparks among the dark woods; pines had fallen into and across it, in the way in which trees only fall in America, and no two trees were of the same tint; the wild vine hung over the precipice, and smothered the trees with its clusters and tendrils, and hurriedly in some places, gently in others, the cold rivulet flowed down to the lake,—no bold speculator having as yet dared to turn the water privilege to account.

My first ride was an amusing one, for various reasons. My riding-habit was left at Toronto, but this seemed not to be a difficulty. Mrs. Forrest's fashionable habit and white gauntlet-gloves fitted me beautifully; and the difficulty about a hat was at once overcome by sending to an obliging neighbour, who politely sent a very stylish-looking plumed riding-hat. There was a side-saddle and a most elegant bridle; indeed, the whole equipment would not have disgraced *Rotten Row*. But, the horse! My courage had to be "screwed to the sticking point" before I could mount him. He was a very fine animal—a magnificent coal-black charger sixteen hands high, with a most determined will of his own, not broken for the saddle. Mr. Forrest rode a splendid bay, which seldom went over six consecutive yards of ground without performing some erratic movement. My horse's paces were, a tremendous trot, breaking sometimes into a furious gallop, in both which he acted in a perfectly independent manner, any attempts of mine to control him with my whole strength and weight being alike useless. We came to the top of a precipice overlooking the river, where his gyrations were so fearful that I turned him into the bush. It appeared to me a ride of imminent dangers and hair-breadth escapes. By this beauteous river we came to a place where rain and flood had worn the precipice into a steep declivity, shelving towards another precipice, and my horse, accustomed to it, took me down where an English donkey would scarcely have ventured. Beauty might be written upon everything in this dell. I never saw a fairer compound of rock, wood, and water. Above was flat and comparatively un-interesting country; then these precipices, with trees growing out wherever they could find a footing, arrayed in all the gorgeous colouring of the American fall. At the foot of these was a narrow, brightgreen savannah, with fine trees growing upon it, as though planted by someone anxious to produce a park-like effect. Above this, the dell contracted to the width of Dovedale, and through it all, the river, sometimes a foaming, brawling stream, at others fringed with flowers, and quiescent in deep, clear pools, pours down to the lake. After galloping upon this savannah we plunged into the river, and, after our horses had broken through a plank-bridge at the great risk of their legs, we rode for many miles through bush and clearing, down sandy tracks and scratching thickets, to the pebbly beach of Lake Ontario.

The contrast between the horses and their equipments, and the country we rode through, was somewhat singular. The former were suitable for Hyde Park; the latter was mere bush-riding—climbing down precipices, fording rapid rivers, scrambling through fences and over timber, floundering in mud, going through the bush with hands before us to push the branches from our faces, and, finally, watering our horses in the blue, deep waters of Lake Ontario—yet I never enjoyed a ride along the green lanes of England so much as this one in the wild scenery of Canada.

The Sundays that I spent at Mr. Forrest's were very enjoyable, though the heat of the first was nearly insupportable, and the cold of the last like that of an English Christmas in bygone years. There are multitudes of Presbyterians in Western Canada, who worship in their pure and simple faith with as much fervency and sincerity as did their covenanting forefathers in the days of the persecuting Dundee; and the quaint old Psalms, to which they are so much attached, sung to the strange old tunes, sound to them as sweet among the backwoods of Canada as in the peaceful villages of the Lowlands, or in the remote Highland glens, where I have often listened to their slow and plaintive strains borne upon the mountain breezes. "Are ye frae the braes of Gleneffar?" said an old Scotchwoman to me; "were ye at our kirk o' Sabbath last, ye would na' ken the difference."

The Irishman declaims against the land he has forsaken—the Englishman too often suffers the remembrance of his poverty to sever the tie which binds him to the land of his birth—but where shall we find the Scotchman in whose breast love of his country is not a prominent feeling? Whether it be the light-haired Saxon from the South, or the dark-haired, sallow-visaged Celt from the Highlands, driven forth by the gaunt hand of famine, all look back to Scotland as to *their country*"—the mention of its name kindles animation in the dim eye of age, and causes the bounding heart of youth to leap with enthusiasm. It may be that the Scotch emigrant's only remembrance is of the cold hut on the lone hill-side, where years wore away in poverty and hunger, but to him it is the dearest spot of earth. It may be that he has attained a competence in Canada, and that its fertile soil produces crops which the heathery braes of Scotland would never yield—no matter, it is yet his *home!*—it is the land where his fathers sleep—it is the land of his birth; his dreams are of the "mountain and the flood"—of lonely lochs and mountain-girded firths; and when the purple light on a summer evening streams over the forest, he fancies that the same beams are falling on Morven and the Cuchullins, and that the soft sound pervading the air is the echo of the shepherd's pipe. To the latest hour of his life he cherishes the idea of returning to some homestead by a tumbling burnie. He never can bring himself to utter to his mountain land, from the depths of his heart, the melancholy words, *"Che til na tuille."*[1]

The Episcopal church was only two miles from us, but we were most mercilessly jolted over a plank-road, where many of the planks had made a descent into a sea of mud, on the depth of which I did not attempt to speculate. Even in beautiful England I never saw a prettier sight than the assembling of the congregation. The church is built upon a very steep little knoll, the base of which is nearly encircled by a river. Close to it is a long shed, in which the horses are tethered during service, and little belligerent sounds, such as screaming and kicking, occasionally find their way into church. The building is light and pretty inside, very simple, but in excellent taste; and though there is no organ, the singing and chanting, conducted by the younger portion of the congregation, is on a par with some of the best in our town churches at home. There were no persons poorly clad, and all looked happy, sturdy, and independent. The bright scarlet leaves of the oak and maple pressed against the windows, giving them in the sunlight something of the appearance of stained glass; the rippling of the river was heard below, and round us, far, far away, stretched the forest. Here, where the great Manitou was once

1 "We return no more."

worshipped, a purer faith now reigns, and the allegiance of the people is more firmly established by "the sound of the church-going bells" than by the bayonets of our troops. These heaven-pointing spires are links between Canada and England; they remind the emigrant of the ivy-mantled church in which he was first taught to bend his knees to his Creator, and of the hallowed dust around its walls, where the sacred ashes of his fathers sleep.

There is great attachment to England among those who are protected by her laws, and live under the shadow of her standard of freedom. In many instances, no remembrances of wrongs received, of injuries sustained, of hopeless poverty and ill-requited toil, can sever that holiest, most sacred of ties, which binds, until his latest breath, the heart of the exile to his native land.

The great annoyance of which people complain in this pleasant land is the difficulty of obtaining domestic servants, and the extraordinary specimens of humanity who go out in this capacity. It is difficult to obtain any, and those that are procured are solely Irish Roman Catholics, who think it a great hardship to wear shoes, and speak of their master as the "*boss*." At one house where I visited, the servant or "help," after condescending to bring in the dinner, took a book from the *chiffonier*, and sat down on the sofa to read it. On being remonstrated with for her conduct, she replied that she "would not remain an hour in a house where those she *helped* had an objection to a young lady's improving her mind!" At an hotel at Toronto, one chambermaid, pointing to another, said, "That *young lady* will show you your room." I left Mr. Forrest's even for three days with great regret, and after a nine miles drive on a very wet morning, and a water transit of two hours, found myself at Toronto, where as usual on the wharf I was greeted by the clamorous demand for "wharfage." I found the Walrences and other agreeable acquaintances at Russell's hotel, but was surprised with what I thought rather a want of discrimination on the part of all; I was showing a valuable collection of autographs, beginning with Cromwell, and containing, in addition to those of several deceased and living royal personages, valuable letters of Scott, Byron, Wellington, Russell, Palmerston, Wilberforce, Dickens, &c. The shades of kings, statesmen, and poets, might almost have been incited to appear, when the signature of Richard Cobden was preferred before all.

CHAPTER XI

"Have you seen the Falls?"—"No." "Then you've seen nothing of America." I might have seen Trenton Falls, Gennessee Falls, the Falls of Montmorenci and Lorette; but I had seen nothing if I had not seen the Falls (*par excellence*) of Niagara. There were divers reasons why my friends in the States were anxious that I should see Niagara. One was, as I was frequently told, that all I had seen, even to the "*Prayer Eyes*," would go for nothing on my return; for in England, America was supposed to be a vast tract of country containing *one* town—New York; and one astonishing natural phenomenon, called Niagara. "See New York, Quebec, and Niagara," was the direction I received when I started upon my travels. I never could make out how, but somehow or other, from my earliest infancy, I had been familiar with the name of Niagara, and, from the numerous pictures I had seen of it, I could, I suppose, have sketched a very accurate likeness of the Horse-shoe Fall. Since I landed at Portland, I had continually met with people who went into ecstatic raptures with Niagara; and after passing within sight of its spray, and within hearing of its roar—after seeing it the great centre of attraction to all persons of every class—my desire to see it for myself became absorbing. Numerous difficulties had arisen, and at one time I had reluctantly given up all hope of seeing it, when Mr. and Mrs. Walrence kindly said, that, if I would go with them, they would return to the east by way of Niagara.

Between the anticipation of this event, and the din of the rejoicings for the "capture of Sebastopol," I slept very little on the night before leaving Toronto, and was by no means sorry when the cold grey of dawn quenched the light of tar-barrels and gas-lamps. I crossed Lake Ontario in the iron steamer *Peerless*; the lake was rough as usual, and, after a promenade of two hours on the spray-drenched deck, I retired to the cabin, and spent some time in dreamily wondering whether Niagara itself would compensate for the discomforts of the journey thither. Captain D—— gravely informed me that there were "a good many cases" below, and I never saw people so deplorably sea-sick as in this steamer. An Indian officer who had crossed the Line seventeen times was sea-sick for the first time on Lake Ontario. The short, cross, chopping seas affect most people. The only persons in the saloon who were not discomposed by them were two tall school-girls, who seemed to have innumerable whispered confidences and secrets to confide to each other.

We touched the wharf at Niagara, a town on the British side of the Niagara river—"cars for Buffalo, all aboard,"—and just crossing a platform, we entered the Canada cars, and on the top of some frightful precipices, and round some terrific curves, we were whirled to the Clifton House at Niagara. I left the cars, and walked down the slope to the verge of the cliff; I forgot my friends, who had called me to the hotel to lunch—I forgot everything—for I was looking at the Falls of Niagara.

> "No more than this!—what seem'd it now
>   By that far flood to stand?
> A thousand streams of lovelier flow
>   Bathe my own mountain land,
> And thence o'er waste and ocean track
> Their wild sweet voices call'd me back.
>
> They call'd me back to many a glade,
>   My childhood's haunt of play,

> Where brightly 'mid the birchen shade
>   Their waters glanced away:
> They call'd me with their thousand waves
> Back to my fathers' hills and graves."

The feelings which Mrs. Hemans had attributed to Bruce at the source of the Nile, were mine as I took my first view of Niagara. The Horse-shoe Fall at some distance to my right was partially hidden, but directly in front of me were the American and Crescent Falls. The former is perfectly straight, and looked like a gigantic mill-weir. This resemblance is further heightened by an enormous wooden many-windowed fabric, said to be the largest paper-mill in the United States. A whole collection of mills disfigures this romantic spot, which has received the name of Manchester, and bids fair to become a thriving manufacturing town! Even on the British side, where one would have hoped for a better state of things, there is a great fungus growth of museums, curiosity-shops, taverns, and pagodas with shining tin cupolas. Not far from where I stood, the members of a picnic party were flirting and laughing hilariously, throwing chicken-bones and peach-stones over the cliff, drinking champagne and soda-water. Just as I had succeeded in attaining the proper degree of mental abstraction with which it is necessary to contemplate Niagara, a ragged drosky-driver came up, "Yer honour, may be ye're in want of a carriage? I'll take ye the whole round—Goat Island, Whirlpool, and Deil's Hole—for the matter of four dollars." Niagara made a matter of "a round," dollars, and cents, was too much for my equanimity; and in the hope of losing my feelings of disappointment, I went into the Clifton House, enduring a whole volley of requests from the half-tipsy drosky-drivers who thronged the doorway.

This celebrated hotel, which is kept on the American plan, is a huge white block of building, with three green verandahs round it, and can accommodate about four hundred people. In the summer season it is the abode of almost unparalleled gaiety. Here congregate tourists, merchants, lawyers, officers, senators, wealthy southerners, and sallow down-easters, all flying alike from business and heat. Here meet all ranks, those of the highest character, and those who have no character to lose; those who by some fortunate accident have become possessed of a few dollars, and those whose mine of wealth lies in the gambling-house—all for the time being on terms of perfect equality. Balls, in doors and out of doors, nightly succeed to parties and picnics; the most novel of which are those in the beautiful garden in front of the hotel. This garden has spacious lawns lighted by lamps; and here, as in the 'Midsummer Night's Dream,' the visitors dance on summer evenings to the strains of invisible music. But at the time of my second visit to the Falls all the gaiety was over; the men of business had returned to the cities, the southerners had fled to their sunny homes—part of the house was shut up, and in the great dining-room, with tables for three hundred, we sat down to lunch with about twenty-five persons, most of them Americans and Germans of the most repulsive description. After this meal, eaten in the "five minutes all aboard" style, we started on a sight-seeing expedition. Instead of being allowed to sit quietly on Table Rock, gazing upon the cataract, the visitor, yielding to the demands of a supposed necessity, is dragged a weary round—he must see the Falls from the front, from above, and from below; he must go behind them, and be drenched by them; he must descend spiral staircases at the risk of his limbs, and cross ferries at that of his life; he must visit Bloody Run, the Burning Springs, and Indian curiosity-shops, which have nothing to do with them at all; and when the poor wretch is thoroughly bewildered and wearied by "doing Niagara," he is allowed to steal quietly off to what he really came to see—the mighty Horse-shoe Fall, with all its accompaniments of majesty, sublimity, and terror.

Round the door of the Clifton House were about twenty ragged, vociferous drosky-drivers, of most demoralised appearance, all clamorous for "a fare." "We want to go to Goat

Island; how much is it?" "Five dollars." "I'll take you for four dollars and a half." "No, sir, he's a cheat and a blackguard; I'll take you for four." "I'll take you as cheap as anyone," shouts a man in rags; "I'll take you for three." "Very well." "I'll take you as cheap as he; he's drunk, and his carriage isn't fit for a lady to step into," shouted the man who at first asked five dollars. After this they commenced a regular *mêlée*, when blows were given and received, and frequent allusions were made to "the bones of St. Patrick." At last our friend in rags succeeded in driving up to the door, and we found his carriage really unfit for ladies, as the stuffing in most places was quite bare, and the step and splash-boards were only kept in their places by pieces of rope. The shouting and squabbling were accompanied by Niagara, whose deep awful thundering bass drowns all other sounds.

We drove for two miles along the precipice bank of the Niagara river: this precipice is 250 feet high, without a parapet, and the green, deep flood rages below. At the Suspension Bridge they demanded a toll of sixty cents, and contempt-uously refused two five-dollar notes offered them by Mr. Walrence, saying they were only waste paper. This extra-ordinary bridge, over which a train of cars weighing 440 tons has recently passed, has a span of 800 feet, and a double roadway, the upper one being used by the railway. The floor of the bridge is 230 feet above the river, and the depth of the river immediately under it is 250 feet! The view from it is magnificent; to the left the furious river, confined in a narrow space, rushes in rapids to the Whirlpool; and to the right the Horse-shoe Fall pours its torrent of waters into the dark and ever invisible abyss. When we reached the American side we had to declare to a custom-house officer that we were no smugglers; and then by an *awful* road, partly covered with stumps, and partly full of holes, over the one, and through the other, our half-tipsy driver jolted us, till we wished ourselves a thousand miles from Niagara Falls. "There now, faith, and wasn't I nearly done for myself?" he exclaimed, as a jolt threw him from his seat, nearly over the dash-board.

We passed through the town bearing the names of Niagara Falls and Manchester, an agglomeration of tea-gardens, curiosity-shops, and monster hotels, with domes of shining tin. We drove down a steep hill, and crossed a very insecure-looking wooden bridge to a small wooded island, where a man with a strong nasal twang demanded a toll of twenty-five cents, and anon we crossed a long bridge over the lesser rapids.

The cloudy morning had given place to a glorious day, abounding in varieties of light and shade; a slight shower had fallen, and the sparkling rain-drops hung from every leaf and twig; a rainbow spanned the Niagara river, and the leaves wore the glorious scarlet and crimson tints of the American autumn. Sun and sky were propitious; it was the season and the day in which to see Niagara. Quarrelsome drosky drivers, incongruous mills, and the thousand trumperies of the place, were all forgotten in the perfect beauty of the scene—in the full, the joyous realisation of my ideas of Niagara. Beauty and terror here formed a perfect combination. Around islets covered with fair foliage of trees and vines, and carpeted with moss untrodden by the foot of man, the waters, in wild turmoil, rage and foam: rushing on recklessly beneath the trembling bridge on which we stood to their doomed fall. This place is called "The Hell of Waters," and has been the scene of more than one terrible tragedy.

This bridge took us to Iris Island, so named from the rainbows which perpetually hover round its base. Everything of terrestrial beauty may be found in Iris Island. It stands amid the eternal din of the waters, a barrier between the Canadian and American Falls. It is not more than sixty-two acres in extent, yet it has groves of huge forest trees, and secluded roads underneath them in the deepest shade, far apparently from the busy world, yet thousands from every part of the globe yearly tread its walks of beauty. We stopped at the top of a dizzy pathway, and, leaving the Walrences to purchase some curiosities, I descended it, crossed a trembling foot-bridge, and stood alone on Luna Island, between the Crescent and

American Falls. This beauteous and richly-embowered little spot, which is said to tremble, and looks as if any wave might sweep it away, has a view of matchless magnificence. From it can be seen the whole expanse of the American rapids, rolling and struggling down, chafing the sunny islets, as if jealous of their beauty. The Canadian Fall was on my left; away in front stretched the scarlet woods; the incongruities of the place were out of sight; and at my feet the broad sheet of the American Fall tumbled down in terrible majesty. The violence of the rapids cannot be imagined by one who has not seen their resistless force. The turbulent waters are flung upwards, as if infuriated against the sky. The rocks, whose jagged points are seen among them, fling off the hurried and foamy waves, as if with supernatural strength. Nearer and nearer they come to the Fall, becoming every instant more agitated; they seem to recoil as they approach its verge; a momentary calm follows, and then, like all their predecessors, they go down the abyss together. There is something very exciting in this view; one cannot help investing Niagara with feelings of human agony and apprehension; one feels a new sensation, something neither terror, wonder, nor admiration, as one looks at the phenomena which it displays. I have been surprised to see how a visit to the Falls galvanises the most matter-of-fact person into a brief exercise of the imaginative powers.

As the sound of the muffled drum too often accompanies the trumpet, so the beauty of Luna Island must ever remain associated in my mind with a terrible catastrophe which recently occurred there. Niagara was at its gayest, and the summer at its hottest, when a joyous party went to spend the day on Luna Island. It consisted of a Mr. and Mrs. De Forest, their beautiful child "Nettie," a young man of great talent and promise, Mr. Addington, and a few other persons. It was a fair evening in June, when moonlight was struggling for ascendancy with the declining beams of the setting sun. The elders of the party, being tired, repaired to the seats on Iris Island to rest, Mr. De Forest calling to Nettie, "Come here, my child; don't go near the water."

"Never mind—let her alone—I'll watch her," said Mr. Addington, for the child was very beautiful and a great favourite, and the youthful members of the party started for Luna Island. Nettie pulled Addington's coat in her glee. "Ah! you rogue, you're caught," said he, catching hold of her; "shall I throw you in?" She sprang forward from his arms, one step too far, and fell into the roaring rapid. "Oh, mercy! save—she's gone!" the young man cried, and sprang into the water. He caught hold of Nettie, and, by one or two vigorous strokes, aided by an eddy, was brought close to the Island; one instant more, and his terrified companions would have been able to lay hold of him; but no—the hour of both was come; the waves of the rapid hurried them past; one piercing cry came from Mr. Addington's lips, "For Jesus' sake, O save our souls!" and, locked in each other's arms, both were carried over the fatal Falls. The dashing torrent rolled onward, unheeding that bitter despairing cry of human agony, and the bodies of these two, hurried into eternity in the bloom of youth, were not found for some days. Mrs. De Forest did not long survive the fate of her child.

The guide related to me another story in which my readers may be interested, as it is one of the poetical legends of the Indians. It took place in years now long gone by, when the Indians worshipped the Great Spirit where they beheld such a manifestation of his power. Here, where the presence of Deity made the forest ring, and the ground tremble, the Indians offered a living sacrifice once a year, to be conveyed by the water spirit to the unknown gulf. Annually, in the month of August, the sachem gave the word, and fruits and flowers were stowed in a white canoe, to be paddled by the fairest maiden among the tribes.

The tribe thought itself highly honoured when its turn came to float the blooming offering to the shrine of the Great Spirit, and still more honoured was the maid who was a fitting sacrifice.

Oronto, the proudest chief of the Senecas, had an only child named Lena. This chief was a noted and dreaded warrior; over many a bloody fight his single eagle plume had waved, and ever in battle he left the red track of his hatchet and tomahawk. Years rolled by, and every one sent its summer offering to the thunder god of the then unexplored Niagara. Oronto danced at many a feast which followed the sacrificial gift, which his tribe had rejoicingly given in their turn. He felt not for the fathers whose children were thus taken from their wigwams, and committed to the grave of the roaring waters. Calma, his wife, had fallen by a foeman's arrow, and in the blood of his enemies he had terribly avenged his bereavement. Fifteen years had passed since then, and the infant which Calma left had matured into a beautiful maiden. The day of sacrifice came; it was the year of the Senecas, and Lena was acknowledged to be the fairest maiden of the tribe. The moonlit hour has come, the rejoicing dance goes on; Oronto has, without a tear, parted from his child, to meet her in the happy hunting-grounds where the Great Spirit reigns. The yell of triumph rises from the assembled Indians. The white canoe, loosed by the sachems, has shot from the bank, but ere it has sped from the shore another dancing craft has gone forth upon the whirling water, and both have set out on a voyage to eternity.

The first bears the offering, Lena, seated amidst fruits and flowers; the second contains Oronto, the proud chief of the Senecas. Both seem to pause on the verge of the descent, then together rise on the whirling rapids. One mingled look of apprehension and affection is exchanged, and, while the woods ring with the yells of the savages, Oronto and Lena plunge into the abyss in their white canoes.[1]

This wild legend was told me by the guide in full view of the cataract, and seemed so real and life-like that I was somewhat startled by being accosted thus, by a voice speaking in a sharp nasal down-east twang: "Well, stranger, I guess that's the finest water-power you've ever set eyes on." My thoughts were

---

1 I have given both these anecdotes, as nearly as possible, in the bombastic language in which they were related to me by the guide.

likewise recalled to the fact that it was necessary to put on an oilskin dress, and scramble down a very dilapidated staircase to the Cave of the Winds, in order to "do" Niagara in the "regulation manner." This cave is partly behind the American Fall, and is the abode of howling winds and ceaseless eddies of spray. It is an extremely good shower-bath, but the day was rather too cold to make that luxury enjoyable. I went down another steep path, and, after crossing a shaky foot-bridge over part of the Grand Rapids, ascended Prospect Tower, a stone erection 45 feet high, built on the very verge of the Horse-shoe Fall. It is said that people feel involuntary suicidal intentions while standing on the balcony round this tower. I did not experience them myself, possibly because my only companion was the half-tipsy Irish drosky-driver. The view from this tower is awful: the edifice has been twice swept away, and probably no strength of masonry could permanently endure the wear of the rushing water at its base.

Down come those beauteous billows, as if eager for their terrible leap. Along the ledge over which they fall they are still for one moment in a sheet of clear, brilliant green; another, and down they fall like cataracts of driven snow, chasing each other, till, roaring and hissing, they reach the abyss, sending up a column of spray 100 feet in height. No existing words can describe it, no painter can give the remotest idea of it; it is the voice of the Great Creator, its name signifying, in the beautiful language of the Iroquois, "The Thunder of Waters." Looking from this tower, above you see the Grand Rapids, one dizzy sheet of leaping foamy billows, and below you look, *if you can*, into the very caldron itself, and see how the bright-green waves are lost in foam and mist; and behind you look to shore, and shudder to think how the frail bridge by which you came in another moment may be washed away. I felt as I came down the trembling staircase that one wish of my life had been gratified in seeing Niagara.

Some graves were recently discovered in Iris Island, with skeletons in a sitting posture inside them, probably the remains of those aboriginal races who here in their ignorance worshipped the Great Spirit, within the sound of his almighty voice. We paused on the bridge, and looked once more at the islets in the rapids, and stopped on Bath Island, lovely in itself, but desecrated by the presence of a remarkably hirsute American, who keeps a toll-house, with the words "Ice-creams" and "Indian Curiosities" painted in large letters upon it. Again another bridge, by which we crossed to the main land; and while overwhelmed at once by the beauty and the sublimity of the scene, all at once the idea struck me that the Yankee who called Niagara "an almighty fine water privilege" was tolerably correct in his definition, for the water is led off in several directions for the use of large saw and paper mills.

We made several purchases at an Indian curiosity-shop, where we paid for the articles about six times their value, and meanwhile our driver took the opportunity of getting "summat warm," which very nearly resulted in our getting something *cold*, for twice, in driving over a stump, he all but upset us into ponds. Crossing the suspension-bridge we arrived at the *V. R.* custom-house, where a tiresome detention usually occurs; but a few words spoken in Gaelic to the Scotch officer produced a magical effect, which might have been the same had we possessed anything contraband. A drive of three miles brought us to the whirlpool. The giant cliffs, which rise to the height of nearly 300 feet, wall in the waters and confine their impetuous rush, so that their force raises them in the middle, and hurls them up some feet in the air. Their fury is resistless, and the bodies of those who are carried over the falls are whirled round here in a horrible dance, frequently till decomposition takes place. There is nothing to excite admiration about the whirlpool; the impression which it leaves on the mind is highly unpleasing.

Another disagreeable necessity was to visit a dark, deep chasm in the bank, a very gloomy spot. This demon-titled cavity has never felt the influence of a ray of light. A massive cliff rises above it, and a narrow stream, bearing the horrible name of Bloody Run, pours over this cliff into the chasm. To most minds there is a strange fascination about the terrible and mysterious, and, in spite of warning looks and beseeching gestures on the part of Mr. Walrence, who feared the effect of the story on the weak nerves of his wife, I sat down by the chasm and asked the origin of the name Bloody Run. I will confess that, as I looked down into the yawning hole, imagination lent an added horror to the tale, which was bad enough in itself.

In 1759, while the French, who had in their pay the Seneca Indians, hovered round the British, a large supply of provisions was forwarded from Fort Niagara to Fort Schlosser by the latter, under the escort of a hundred regulars. The savage chief of the Senecas, anxious to obtain the promised reward for scalps, formed an ambuscade of chosen warriors, several hundred in number. The Devil's Hole was the spot chosen—it seemed made on purpose for the bloody project. It was a hot, sultry day in August, and the British, scattered and sauntered on their toilsome way, till, overcome by fatigue or curiosity, they sat down near the margin of the precipice. A fearful yell arose, accompanied by a volley of bullets, and the Indians, breaking from their cover, under the combined influences of ferocity and "fire-water," rushed upon their unhappy victims before they had time to stand to their arms, and tomahawked them on the spot. Waggons, horses, soldiers, and drivers were then hurled over the precipice, and the little stream ran into the Niagara river a torrent purple with human gore. Only two escaped to tell the terrible tale. Some years ago, bones, arms, and broken wheels were found among the rocks, mementos of the barbarity which has given the little streamlet the terror-inspiring name of Bloody Run.

After depositing our purchases at the Clifton House, where the waiter warned us to put them under lock and key, I hoped that sight-seeing was over, and that at last I should be able to gaze upon what I had really come to visit—the Falls of Niagara. But no; I was to be victimised still further; I must "go behind the great sheet." Mr. and Mrs. Walrence would not go; they said their heads would not stand it, but that, as an Englishwoman, go I must. In America the capabilities of English ladies are very much overrated. It is supposed that they go out in all weathers, invariably walk ten miles a day, and leap five-barred fences on horseback. Yielding to "the inexorable law of a stern necessity," I went to the Rock House, and a very pleasing girl produced a suit of oiled calico. I took off my cloak, bonnet, and dress. "Oh," she said, "you must change everything, *it's so very wet.*" As, to save time, I kept demurring to taking off various articles of apparel, I always received the same reply, and finally abandoned myself to a complete change of attire. I looked in the mirror, and beheld as complete a tatterdemallion as one could see begging upon an Irish highway, though there was nothing about the dress which the most lively imagination could have tortured into the picturesque. The externals of this strange equipment consisted of an oiled calico hood, a garment like a carter's frock, a pair of blue worsted stockings, and a pair of India-rubber shoes much too large for me. My appearance was so comic as to excite the laughter of my grave friends, and I had to reflect that numbers of persons had gone out in the same attire before I could make up my mind to run the gauntlet of the loiterers round the door. Here a negro guide of most repulsive appearance awaited me, and I waded through a perfect sea of mud to the shaft by which people go under Table Rock. My friends were evidently ashamed of my appearance, but they met me here to wish me a safe return, and, following the guide, I dived down a spiral staircase, very dark and very much out of repair.

Leaving this staircase, I followed the guide along a narrow path covered with fragments of shale, with Table Rock above and the deep abyss below. A cold, damp wind blew against me, succeeded by a sharp pelting rain, and the path became more slippery and difficult. Still I was not near the sheet of water, and felt not the slightest dizziness. I speedily arrived at the difficult point of my progress: heavy gusts almost blew me away; showers of spray nearly blinded me; I was quite deafened and half-drowned; I wished to retreat, and essayed to use my voice to stop the progress of my guide. I raised it to a scream, but it was lost in the thunder of the cataract. The negro saw my incertitude and extended his hand. I shuddered even there as I took hold of it, not quite free from the juvenile idea that "the black comes off." He seemed at that moment to wear the aspect of a black imp leading me to destruction.

The path is a narrow, slippery ledge of rock. I am blinded with spray, the darkening sheet of water is before me. Shall I go on? The spray beats against my face, driven by the contending gusts of wind which rush into the eyes, nostrils, and mouth, and almost prevent my progress; the narrowing ledge is not more than a foot wide, and the boiling gulf is seventy feet below. Yet thousands have pursued this way before, so why should not I? I grasp tighter hold of the guide's hand, and proceed step by step holding down my head. The water beats against me, the path narrows, and will only hold my two feet abreast. I ask the guide to stop, but my voice is drowned by the "Thunder of Waters." He guesses what I would say, and shrieks in my ear, "*It's worse going back.*" I make a desperate attempt: four steps more and I am at the end of the ledge; my breath is taken away, and I can only just stand against the gusts of wind which are driving the water against me. The gulf is but a few inches from me, and, gasping for breath, and drenched to the skin, I become conscious that I have reached *Termination Rock*.

Once arrived at this place, the clouds of driving spray are a little thinner, and, though it is still very difficult either to see or breathe, the magnificence of the temple, which is here formed by the natural bend of the cataract and the backward shelve of the precipice, makes a lasting impression on the mind. The temple seems a fit and awful shrine for Him who "rides on the wings of mighty winds," and, completely shut out from man's puny works, the mind rises naturally in adoring contemplation to Him whose voice is heard in the "thunder of waters." The path was so very narrow that I had to shuffle backwards for a few feet, and then, drenched, shivering, and breathless, my goloshes full of water and slipping off at every step, I fought my way through the blinding clouds of spray, and, climbing up the darkened staircase, again stood on Table Rock, with water dripping from my hair and garments. It is usual for those persons who survive the expedition to take hot brandy and water after changing their dresses; and it was probably from neglecting this precaution that I took such a severe chill as afterwards produced the ague. On the whole, this achievement is pleasanter in the remembrance than in the act. There is nothing whatever to boast of in having accomplished it, and nothing to regret in leaving it undone. I knew the danger and disagreeableness of the exploit before I went, and, had I known that "going behind the sheet" was synonymous with "going to Termination Rock," I should never have gone. No person who has not a very strong head ought to go at all, and it is by everyone far better omitted, as the remaining portion of Table Rock may fall at any moment, for which reason some of the most respectable guides decline to take visitors underneath it. I believe that no amateur ever thinks of going a second time. After all, the front view is the only one for Niagara—going behind the sheet is like going behind a picture-frame.

After this we went to the top of a tower, where I had a very good bird's-eye view of the Falls, the Rapids, and the general aspect of the country, and then, refusing to be victimised by burning springs, museums, prisoned eagles, and mangy buffaloes, I left the Walrences, who were tired, to go to the hotel, and walked down to the ferry, and, scrambling out to the rock farthest in the water and nearest to the cataract, I sat down completely undisturbed in view of the mighty fall. I was not distracted by parasitic guides or sandwich-eating visitors; the vile museums, pagodas, and tea-gardens were out of sight: the sublimity of the Falls far exceeded my expectations, and I appreciated them the more perhaps from having been disappointed with the first view. As I sat watching them, a complete oblivion of everything but the falls themselves stole over me. A person may be very learned in statistics—he may tell you that the falls are 160 feet high—that their whole width is nearly four-fifths of a mile—that, according to estimate, ninety million tons of water pass over them every hour—that they are the outlet of several bodies of water covering one hundred and fifty thousand square miles; but unless he has seen Niagara, he cannot form the faintest conception of it. It was so very like what I had expected, and yet so totally different. I sat there watching that sea-green curve against the sky till sunset, and then the crimson rays just fell upon the column of spray above the Canadian Fall, turning it a most beautiful rose-colour. The sun set; a young moon arose, and brilliant stars shone through the light veil of mist, and in the darkness the cataract looked like drifted snow. I rose at length, perfectly unconscious that I had been watching the Falls for nearly four hours, and that my clothes were saturated with the damp and mist. It would be out of place to enter upon the numerous geological speculations which have arisen upon the structure and recession of Niagara. It seems as if the faint light which science has shed upon the abyss of bygone ages were but to show that its depths must remain for ever unlighted by human reason and research.

There was such an air of gloom about the Clifton House that we sat in the balcony till the cold became intense; and as it was too dark to see anything but a white object in front, I could not help regretting the waste (as it seems) of this wonderful display going on, when no eyes can feast upon its sublimity. In the saloon there was a little fair-haired boy of seven years old, with the intellectual faculties largely developed—indeed, so much so as to be painfully suggestive of water on the brain. His father called him into the middle of the room, and he repeated a long oration of Daniel Webster's without once halting for a word, giving to it the action and emphasis of the orator. This was a fair specimen of the frequent undue development of the minds of American children.

At Niagara I finally took leave of the Walrences, as I had many visits to pay, and near midnight left for Hamilton, under the escort of a very kind, but very Grandisonian Scotch gentleman. I was intensely tired and sleepy, and it was a very cheerless thing to leave a warm room at midnight for an omnibus-drive of two miles along a bad, unlighted road. There did not appear to be any waiting-room at the bustling station at the suspension bridge, for, alas! the hollow scream of the locomotive is heard even above the thunder of Niagara. I slept in the cars for an hour before we started, and never woke till the conductor demanded payment of my fare in no very gentle tones. We reached Hamilton shortly after two in the morning, in the midst of a high wind and pouring rain; and in company with a dozen very dirty emigrants we entered a lumber waggon with a canvas top, drawn by one miserable horse. The curtains very imperfectly kept out the rain, and we were in continual fear of an upset. At last the vehicle went down on one side, and all the Irish emigrants tumbled over each other and us, with a profusion of "Ochs," "murders," and "spalpeens." The driver composedly shouted to us to alight; the hole was only deep enough to sink the vehicle to the axletree. We got out into a very capacious lake of mud, and in again, in very ill humour. At last the horse fell down in a hole, and my Scotch friend and I got out and walked in the rain for some distance to a very comfortable hotel, the City Arms. The sun had scarcely warmed the world into waking life before I was startled from my sleep by the cry, "Six o'clock; all aboard for the 'bus at half-past, them as goes by the *Passport* and *Highlander*:" but it was half-past, and I had barely time to dress before the disagreeable shout of "All aboard!" echoed through the house, and I hurried downstairs into an omnibus, which held twenty-two persons inside, commodiously seated in arm-chairs. I went down Lake Ontario in the *Highlander*; Mr. Forrest met me on the wharf, and in a few hours I was again warmly welcomed at his hospitable house.

My relics of my visit to Niagara consisted of a few Indian curiosities, and a printed certificate filled up with my name,[1] stating that I had walked for 230 feet behind the great fall, which statement, I was assured by an American fellow-traveller, was "a sell right entirely, an almighty all-fired big flam."

---

1 "Niagara Falls, C. W.: Register Office, Table Rock.—This is to certify, that Miss —— has passed behind the Great Falling Sheet of Water to Termination Rock, being 230 feet behind the Great Horse-shoe Fall.—Given under my hand this 13th day of ——, 1854.—Thomas Barnett."

CHAPTER XII

The *Arabian*, by which I left Toronto, was inferior to any American steamer I had travelled in. It was crowded with both saloon and steerage passengers, bound for Cobourg, Port Hope, and Montreal. It was very bustling and dirty, and the carpet was plentifully sprinkled with tobacco-juice. The captain was very much flustered with his unusually large living cargo, but he was a good-hearted man, and very careful, having, to use his own phrase, "climbed in at the hawse-holes, and worked his way aft, instead of creeping in at the cabin window with his gloves on." The stewards were dirty, and the stewardess too smart to attend to the comforts of the passengers.

As passengers, crates, and boxes poured in at both the fore and aft entrances, I went out on the little slip of deck to look at the prevalent confusion, having previously ascertained that all my effects were secure. The scene was a very amusing one, for, acting out the maxim that "time is money," comparatively few of the passengers came down to the wharf more than five minutes before the hour of sailing. People, among whom were a number of "unprotected females," and juveniles who would not *move on*, were entangled among trucks and carts discharging cargo—hacks, horses, crates, and barrels. These passengers, who would find it difficult to elbow their way unencumbered, find it next to impossible when their hands are burdened with uncut books, baskets of provender, and diminutive carpet-bags. Horses back carts against helpless females, barrels roll upon people's toes, newspaper hawkers puff their wares, bonbon venders push their plaster of Paris abominations almost at people's eyes, yet, strange to say, it is very seldom that any accident occurs. Family groups invariably are separated, and distracted mammas are running after children whom everybody wishes out of the way, giving utterance to hopes that they are not on shore. Then the obedient papa is sent on shore to look after "that dear little Harry," who is probably all the time in the ladies' saloon on some child-fancier's lap eating bonbons. The board is drawn in—the moorings are cast off—the wheels revolve—the bell rings—the engine squeals, and away speeds the steamer down the calm waters of Lake Ontario. Little children and inquisitive young ladies are knocked down or blackened in coiling the hawser, by "hands" who, being nothing but *hands*, evidently cannot say, "I beg your pardon, miss." There were children, who always will go where they ought not to go, running against people, and taking hold of their clothes with sticky, smeared hands, asking commercial gentlemen to spin their tops, and corpulent ladies to play at hide and seek. I saw one stern-visaged gentleman tormented in this way till he looked ready to give the child its "final quietus."[1] There were angry people who had lost their portmanteaus, and were ransacking the state-rooms in quest of them, and indolent people who lay on the sofas reading novels and chewing tobacco. Some gentleman, taking no heed of a printed notice, goes to the ladies' cabin to see if his wife is safe on board, and meets with a rebuff from the stewardess, who tells him that "gentlemen are not admitted," and, knowing that the *sense*, or, as he would say, the *nonsense* of the community is against him, he beats a reluctant retreat. Everybody seems to have lost somebody or something, but in an hour or two the ladies are deep in novels, the gentlemen in the morning papers, the children have

1 American juveniles are, generally speaking, completely destitute of that agreeable shyness which prevents English and Scotch children from annoying strangers.

quarrelled themselves to sleep, and the captain has gone to smoke by the funnel.

I sat on the slip of deck with a lady from Lake Superior, niece of the accomplished poetess Mrs. Hemans, and she tried to arouse me into admiration of the shore of Lake Ontario; but I confess that I was too much occupied with a race which we were running with the American steamer *Maple-leaf*, to look at the flat, gloomy, forest-fringed coast. There is an inherent love of the excitement of a race in all human beings—even old ladies are not exempt from it, if we may believe a story which I heard on the Mississippi. An old lady was going down the river for the first time, and expressed to the captain her earnest hope that there would be no racing. Presently another boat neared them, and half the passengers urged the captain to "*pile on.*" The old lady shrieked and protested, but to no purpose; the skipper "piled on;" and as the race was a very long and doubtful one, she soon became excited. The rival boat shot ahead; the old lady gave a side of bacon, her sole possession, to feed the boiler fires—the boat was left behind—she clapped her hands—it ran ahead again, and, frantic, she seated herself upon the safety-valve! It was again doubtful, but, lo! the antagonist boat was *snagged*, and the lady gave a yell of perfect delight when she saw it discomfited, and a hundred human beings struggling in the water. Our race, however, was destitute of excitement, for the *Maple-leaf* was a much better sailer than ourselves.

Dinner constituted an important event in the day, and was despatched very voraciously, though some things were raw, others overdone, and all greasy. But the three hundred people who sat down to dinner were, as someone observed, three hundred reasons against eating anything. I had to endure a severe attack of ague, and about nine o'clock the stewardess gave up her room to me, and, as she faithfully promised to call me half an hour before we changed the boats, I slept very soundly. At five she came in—"Get up, miss, we're at Guana-noque; you've only five minutes to dress." I did dress in five minutes, and, leaving my watch, with some very valuable lockets, under my pillow, hastened across a narrow plank, half blinded by snow, into the clean, light, handsome steamer *New Era*. I did not allow myself to fall asleep in the very comfortable state-room which was provided for me by the friend with whom I was travelling, but hurried upstairs with the first grey of the chilly wintry dawn of the morning of the 18th of October. The saloon-windows were dimmed with snow, so I went out on deck and braved the driving wind and snow on that inhospitable morning, for we were in the Lake of the Thousand Islands. Travellers have written and spoken so much of the beauty of this celebrated piece of water, that I expected to be disappointed; but, *au contraire*, I am almost inclined to write a rhapsody myself.

For three hours we were sailing among these beautiful irregularly-formed islands. There are 1692 of them, and they vary in size from mere rocks to several acres in extent. Some of them are perfect paradises of beauty. They form a complete labyrinth, through which the pilot finds his way, guided by numerous beacons. Sometimes it appeared as if there were no egress, and as if we were running straight upon a rock, and the water is everywhere so deep, that from the deck of the steamer people can pull the leaves from the trees. A hundred varieties of trees and shrubs grow out of the grey lichen-covered rocks—it seems barbarous that the paddles of a steamer should disturb their delicate shadows. If I found this lake so beautiful on a day in the middle of October, when the bright autumn tints had changed into a russet brown, and when a chill north-east wind was blowing about the withered leaves, and the snow against the ship—and when, more than all, I was only just recovering from ague—what would it be on a bright summer-day, when the blue of heaven would be reflected in the clear waters of the St. Lawrence!

By nine a furious snow-storm rendered all objects indistinct, and the fog had thickened to such an extent that we could not see five feet ahead, so we came to anchor for an hour. A very excellent breakfast was despatched during this time, and at ten we steamed off again, steering by compass on a river barely a mile wide! The *New Era* was a boat of a remarkably light draught of water. The saloon, or deck-house, came to within fifteen feet of the bow, and on the hurricane-deck above there was a tower containing a double wheel, with which the ship is steered by chains one hundred feet long. There is a look-out place in front of this tower, generally occupied by the pilot, a handsome, ruffian-looking French *voyageur*, with earrings in his ears. Captain Chrysler, whose caution, urbanity, and kindness render him deservedly popular, seldom leaves this post of observation, and personally pays very great attention to his ship; for the river St. Lawrence has as bad a reputation for destroying the vessels which navigate it as the Mississippi.

The snow was now several inches deep on deck, and, melting near the deck-house, trickled under the doors into the saloon. The moisture inside, also, condensed upon the ceiling, and produced a constant shower-bath for the whole day. Sofas and carpets were alike wet, everybody sat in goloshes—the ladies in cloaks, the gentlemen in oilskins; the smell of the latter, and of so many wet woollen clothes, in an apartment heated by stove-heat, being almost unbearable. At twelve the fog and snow cleared away, and revealed to view the mighty St. Lawrence—a rapid stream whirling along in small eddies between slightly elevated banks dotted with white homesteads. We passed a gigantic raft, with five log shanties upon it, near Prescott. These rafts go slowly and safely down the St. Lawrence and the Ottawa, till they come to La Chine, where frequent catastrophes happen, if one may judge from the timber which strews the rocks. A gentleman read from a newspaper these terrible statistics, "horrible if true,"—"Forty-four murders and seven hundred murderous assaults have been committed at New York within the last six months." (*Sensation.*) We stopped at Prescott, one of the oldest towns in Canada, and shortly afterwards passed the blackened ruins of a windmill, and some houses held by a band of American "sympathisers" during the rebellion in 1838, but from which they were dislodged by the cannon of the royal troops. Five hundred American sympathisers, with several pieces of cannon, under cover of darkness, on a lovely night in May, landed at this place. Soon after, they were attacked by a party of English regulars and militiamen, who drove them into a windmill and two strong stone houses, which they loopholed, and defended themselves with a pertinacity which one would have called heroism, had it been in a better cause. They finally surrendered, and were carried prisoners to Kingston, where six of them were hanged. Their leader, a military adventurer, a Pole of the name of Von Schoultz, was the first to be executed. He fought with a skill and bravery worthy of the nation from whence he sprung, and died without complaint, except of those who had enticed him to fight for a godless cause, under the name of liberty.

Brighter days have since dawned upon Canada, and at this time the most discontented can scarcely find the shadow of a grievance to lay hold of.

As an instance of the way in which the utilitarian essentials of a high state of civilisation are diffused throughout Canada, I may mention that when we arrived at Cornwall I was able to telegraph to Kingston for my lost watch, and received a satisfactory answer in half an hour.

After sailing down this mighty river at a rapid rate for some hours, we ran the Galouse Rapids. Running the rapids is a favourite, and, I must add, a charming diversion of adventurous travellers. There is just that slight sense of danger which lends a zest to novelty, and it is furnished by the facts that some timid persons land before coming to the rapids, and that many vessels have come to an untimely end in descending them. There is a favourite story of General Amherst, who during the war was sent down by the river to attack Montreal, with three hundred and fifty men, and the first intimation which the inhabitants received of the intended surprise was through the bodies of the ill-fated detachment, clothed in the well-known scarlet, floating by their city, the victims of the ignorance or treachery of the pilot.

One of the great pleasures which I promised myself in my visit to Canada was from running these rapids, and I was not disappointed. At the Galouse, the river expands into a wide shallow stream, containing beautiful islands, among which the water rushes furiously, being broken into large waves, boiling, foaming, and whirling round. The steamer neared the rapids—half her steam was shut off—six men appeared at the wheel—we glided noiselessly along in smooth, green, deep water—the furious waves were before us—the steamer gave one perceptible downward plunge—the spray dashed over the bows—and at a speed of twenty-five miles an hour we hurried down the turbulent hill of waters, running so near the islands often that escape seemed hopeless—then guided safely away by the skill of the pilot.

The next rapid was the Longue Sault, above a mile in length. The St. Lawrence is here divided into two channels. The one we took is called the Lost Passage; the Indian pilot who knew it died, and it has only been recovered within the last five years. It is a very fine rapid, the islands being extremely picturesque. We went down it at dizzy speed, with all our steam on. I suppose that soon after this we entered the Lower Province, for the aspect of things totally changed. The villages bore French names; there were high wooden crosses by the water-side; the houses were many-gabled and many-windowed, with tiers of balconies; and the setting sun flashed upon Romish churches with spires of glittering tin. Everything was marked by stagnation and retrogression: the people are *habitans*, the clergy *curés*.

We ran the Cedars, a magnificent rapid, superior in beauty to the Grand Rapids at Niagara, and afterwards those of the Côteau du Lac and the Split Rock, but were obliged to anchor at La Chine, as its celebrated cataract can only be shot by daylight. It was cold and dark, and nearly all the passengers left La Chine by the cars for Montreal, to avoid what some people consider the perilous descent of this rapid. As both means of reaching Montreal were probably equally safe, I decided on remaining on board, having secured a state-room. My companions in the saloon were the captain's wife and a lady who seemed decidedly *flighty*, and totally occupied in waiting upon a poodle lapdog. After the captain left, the stokers and pokers, and stewards and cooks, extemporised a ball, with the assistance of a blind Scotch fiddler, and invited numerous lassies, who appeared as if by magic from a wharf to which we were moored. I cannot say that they tripped it "on the *light* fantastic toe," for brogues and highlows stumped heavily on the floor; but what was wanting in elegance was amply compensated for by merriment and vivacity. The conversation was rather of a polyglot character, being carried on in French, Gaelic, and English.

Throughout the night I was occupied in incessant attempts to keep up vital warmth, and when the steward called me at five o'clock, I found that I had been sleeping with the window open, and that the water in the jug was frozen. Wintry-looking stars were twinkling through a frosty fog; the wet hawsers were frozen stiff on deck; six came, the hour of starting, but still there were no signs of moving. Railroads have not yet taught punctuality to the Canadians, but better things are in store for them. Cold to the very bone, I walked up and down the saloon to warm myself. The floor was wet, and covered with saturated rugs; there were no fires in the stoves, and my only resource was to lean against the engine-enclosure, and warm my frozen hands on the hot wood. I was joined by a very old gentleman, who, amid many complaints, informed me that he had had an attack of apoplexy during the night, and someone, finding him insensible, had opened the jugular vein. His lank white hair flowed over his shoulders, and his neckcloth and shirt-front were smeared with blood. He said he had cut his wife's throat, and that her ghost was after him. "There, there!" he said, pointing to a corner. I looked at his eyes, and saw at once that I was in the company of a madman. He then said that he was king of the island of Montreal, and that he had murdered his wife because she was going to betray him to the Queen of England. He was now, he declared, going down to make a public entrance into Montreal. After this avowal I treated him with the respect due to his fancied rank, till I could call the stewards without exciting his suspicions. They said that he was a confirmed lunatic, and had several times attempted to lay violent hands upon himself. They thought he must have escaped from his keeper at Brockville, and, with true madman's cunning, he had secreted himself in the steamer. They kept him under strict surveillance till we arrived at Montreal, and frustrated an attempt which he made to throw himself into the rapid as we were descending it.

At seven we unmoored from the pier at La Chine, and steamed over the calm waters of the Lac St. Louis, under the care of a Canadian *voyageur*, who acted as a subordinate to an Indian pilot, who is said to be the only person acquainted with the passage, and whom the boats are obliged under penalty to take. The lake narrows at La Chine, and becomes again the St. Lawrence, which presents a most extraordinary appearance, being a hill of shallow rushing water about a mile wide, chafing a few islands which look ready to be carried away by it. The large river Ottawa joins the St. Lawrence a short distance from this, and mingles its turbid waters with that mighty flood. The river became more and more rapid till we entered what might be termed a *sea* of large, cross, leaping waves, and raging waters, enough to engulf a small boat. The idea of descending it in a steamer was an extraordinary one. It is said that from the shore a vessel looks as if it were hurrying to certain destruction. Still we hurry on, with eight men at the wheel—rocks appear like snags in the middle of the stream—we dash straight down upon rocky islets, strewn with the wrecks of rafts; but a turn of the wheel, and we rush by them in safety at a speed ('tis said) of thirty miles an hour, till a ragged ledge of rock stretches across the whirling stream. Still on we go—louder roars the flood—steeper appears the descent—earth, sky, and water seem mingled together. I involuntarily took hold of the rail—the madman attempted to jump over—the *flighty* lady screamed and embraced more closely her poodle-dog; we reached the ledge—one narrow space free from rocks appeared—down with one plunge went the bow into a turmoil of foam—and we had "shot the cataract" of La Chine.

The exploit is one of the most agreeable which the traveller can perform, and the thick morning mist added to the apparent danger. We steamed for four or five miles farther down the river, when suddenly the great curtain of mist was rolled up as by an invisible hand, and the scene which it revealed was *Montreal*.

I never saw a city which looked so magnificent from the water. It covers a very large extent of ground, which gently slopes upwards from the lake-like river, and is backed by the Mountain, a precipitous hill, 700 feet in height. It is decidedly foreign in appearance, even from a distance. When the fog cleared away it revealed this mountain, with the forest which covers it, all scarlet and purple; the blue waters of the river hurried joyously along; the Green and Belleisle mountains wore the rosy tints of dawn; the distances were bathed in a purple glow; and the tin roofs, lofty spires, and cupolas of Montreal flashed back the beams of the rising sun.

A lofty Gothic edifice, something from a distance like Westminster Abbey, and handsome public buildings, with a superb wharf a mile long, of hewn stone, present a very imposing appearance from the water. We landed from the first lock of a ship-canal, and I immediately drove to the residence of the Bishop of Montreal, a house near the mountain, in a very elevated situation, and commanding a magnificent view. From the Bishop and his family I received the greatest kindness, and have very agreeable recollections of Montreal.

It was a most curious and startling change from the wooden erections, wide streets, and the impress of novelty which pervaded everything I had seen in the New World, to the old stone edifices, lofty houses, narrow streets, and tin roofs of the city of Montreal. There are iron window-shutters, convents with grated windows and long dead walls; there are narrow thoroughfares, crowded with strangely-dressed *habitans,* and long processions of priests. Then the French origin of the town contrasts everywhere with the English occupation of it. There are streets—the Rue St. Geneviève, the Rue St. Antoine, and the Rue St. François Xavier; there are ancient customs and feudal privileges; Jesuit seminaries, and convents of the *Sœurs Gris* and the Sulpicians; priests in long black dresses; native carters in coats with hoods, woollen nightcaps, and coloured sashes; and barristers pleading in the French language. Then there are Manchester goods, in stores kept by bustling Yankees; soldiers lounge about in the scarlet and rifle uniforms of England; Presbyterian tunes sound from plain bald churches; the institutions are drawn alike from Paris and Westminster; and the public vehicles partake of the fashions of Lisbon and Long Acre. You hear "*Place aux dames*" on one side of the street, and "*g'lang*" on the other; and the United States have contributed their hotel system and their slang.

Montreal is an extraordinary place. It is alive with business and enterprising traders, with soldiers, carters, and equipages. Through the kindness of the Bishop, I saw everything of any interest in the town. The first thing which attracted my attention was the magnificent view from the windows of the See-house, over the wide St. Lawrence and the green mountains of Vermont; the next, an immense pair of elaborately-worked bronze gates, at a villa opposite, large enough for a royal residence. The side-walks in the outskirts of the town were still of the villanous wood, but in the streets they were very substantial, and, like the massive stone houses, look as if they had lasted for two hundred years, and might last for a thousand more. We visited, among other things, some schools—one, the Normal School, an extremely interesting one, where it is intended to train teachers, on Church-of-England principles. I was very much surprised and pleased with the amount of solid information and high attainments of the children, as evidenced by their composition, and answers to the Bishop of Montreal's very difficult questions. They looked sallow and emaciated, and, contrary to what I have observed in England, the girls seemed the most intelligent. The Bishop has also established a library, where, for the small sum of four shillings a year, people can regale themselves upon a variety of works, from the volumes of Alison, not more ponderous in appearance than matter, to the newspaper literature of the day.

The furriers' shops are by no means to be overlooked. There were sleigh-robes of buffalo, bear, fox, wolf, and racoon, varying in price from six to thirty guineas; and coats, leggings, gloves, and caps, rendered necessary by the severity of a winter in which the thermometer often stands at thirty degrees below zero. People vie with each other in the costliness of their furs and sleigh equipments; a complete set sometimes costing as much as a hundred guineas.

I went into the Romish cathedral, which is the largest Gothic building in the New World. It was intended to be very imposing—it has succeeded in being very extravagant; and if the architects intended that their work should live in the admiration of succeeding generations, like York Minster, Cologne, or Rouen, they have signally failed.

Internally, the effect of its vast size is totally destroyed by pews and galleries which accommodate ten thousand people. There are some very large and very hideous paintings in it, in a very inferior style of sign-painting. The ceiling is painted bright blue, and the high altar was one mass of gaudy tinsel decoration. In one corner there was a picture of babies being devoured by pigs, and trampled upon by horses, and underneath it was a box for offerings, with "This is the fate of the children of China" upon it. By it was a wooden box, hung with faded pink calico, containing small wooden re-presentations, in the Noah's-ark style, of dogs, horses, and pigs, and a tall man holding up a little dog by its hind legs. This peep-show (for I can call it nothing else) was at the same time so inexplicable and so ludicrous, that, to avoid shocking the feelings of a devout-looking woman who was praying near it by an "*éclat de rire*," we hurried from the church.

I met with many sincere and devout Romanists among the upper classes in Canada; I know that there are thousands among the simple *habitans*; and though, in a thoughtless moment, the fooleries and puerilities of their churches may excite a smile, it is a matter for the deepest regret that so many of our fellow-subjects should be the dupes of a despotic priesthood, and of a religion which cannot save.

Close to the cathedral is the convent of the Grey Sisters, who, with the most untiring zeal and kindness, fulfil the vocations of the Sisters of Charity. There are several other convents, some of them very strict; and their high walls and grated windows give Montreal a very Continental appearance. On a lady remarking to a sister in one of these, that the view from the windows was very beautiful, she replied, with a suppressed sigh, that she had never seen it. There are some very fine public buildings and banks; but as I am not writing a guidebook, I will not dilate upon their merits.

We walked round *Le Champ de Mars*, formerly the great resort of the Montreal young ladies, and along the Rue Notre Dame, to the market-place, which is said to be the second finest in the world, and, with its handsome *façade* and bright tin dome, forms one of the most prominent objects from the water. As those disgusting disfigurements of our English streets, butchers' shops, are not to be seen in the Canadian towns, nor, I believe I may say, in those in the States, there is an enormous display of meat in the Montreal market, of an appearance by no means tempting. The scene outside was extremely picturesque; there were hundreds of carts with shaggy, patient little horses in rows, with very miscellaneous tents—cabbages and butter jostling pork and hides. You may see here hundreds of *habitans*, who look as if they ought to have lived a century ago—shaggy men in fur caps and loose blue frieze coats with hoods, and with bright sashes of coloured wool round their waists; women also, with hard features and bronzed complexions, in large straw hats, high white caps, and noisy *sabots*. On all sides a jargon of Irish, English, and French is to be heard, the latter generally the broadest patois.

We went into the Council Chamber, the richly cushioned seats of which looked more fitted for sleep than deliberation; and I caught a glimpse of the ex-mayor, whose timidity during a time of popular ferment occasioned a great loss of human life. That popular Italian orator, "*Father Gavazzi,*" was engaged in denouncing the superstitions and impositions of Rome; and on a mob evincing symptoms of turbulence, this mayor gave the order to fire to the troops who were drawn up in the streets. Scarcely had the words passed his lips, when by one volley seventeen peaceful citizens (if I recollect rightly), coming out of the Unitarian chapel, were laid low.

Montreal is a turbulent place. It is not very many years since a mob assembled and burned down the Parliament House, for which exercise of the popular will the city is disqualified from being the seat of government. I saw something of Montreal society, which seemed to me to be quite on a par with that in our English provincial towns.

I left this ancient city at seven o'clock on a very dark, foggy evening for Quebec, the boats between the two cities running by night, in order that the merchants, by a happy combination of travelling with sleep, may not lose that time which to them is money. This mode of proceeding is very annoying to tourists, who thereby lose the far-famed beauties of the St. Lawrence. It is very obnoxious likewise to timid travellers, of whom there are a large number both male and female: for collisions and striking on rocks or shoals are accidents of such frequent occurrence, that, out of eight steamers which began the season, two only concluded it, two being disabled during my visit to Quebec.

Scarcely had we left the wharf at Montreal when we came into collision with a brig, and hooked her anchor into our woodwork, which event caused a chorus of screams from some ladies whose voices were rather stronger than their nerves, and its remedy a great deal of bad language in French, German, and English, from the crews of both vessels. After this we ran down to Quebec at the rate of seventeen miles an hour, and the *contretemps* did not prevent even those who had screamed the loudest from partaking of a most substantial supper, which was served at eight o'clock in the lowest story of the ship. The *John Munn* was a very fine boat, not at all the worse for having sunk in the river in the summer.

I considered Quebec quite the goal of my journey, for books, tongues, and poetry alike celebrate its beauty. Indeed, there seems to be only one opinion about it. From the lavish praise bestowed upon it by the eloquent and gifted author of 'Hochelaga' down to the homely encomiums pronounced by bluff sea captains, there seems a unanimity of admiration which is rarely met with. Even commercial travellers, absorbed in intricate calculations of dollars and cents, have been known to look up from their books to give it an enthusiastic expression of approval. I expected to be more pleased with it than with anything I had seen or was to see, and was insensate enough to rise at five o'clock and proceed into the saloon, when of course it was too dark for another hour to see anything. Daylight came, and from my corner by the fire I asked the stewardess when we should be in sight of Quebec? She replied that we were close to it. I went to the window, expecting that a vision of beauty would burst upon my eyes. All that I saw might be summed up in very few words—a few sticks placed vertically, which might be masts, and some tin spires looming through a very yellow, opaque medium. This was my *first* view of Quebec; happily, on my *last* the elements did full justice to its beauty. Other objects developed themselves as we steamed down to the wharf. There were huge rafts, some three or four acres in extent, which, having survived the perils which had beset them on their journey from the forests of the Ottawa, were now moored along the base of the lofty cliffs which, under the name of the Heights of

Abraham, have a world-wide celebrity. There were huge, square-sided, bluff-bowed, low-masted ships, lying at anchor in interminable lines, and little, dirty, vicious-looking steam-tugs twirling in and out among them; and there were grim-looking muzzles of guns protruding through embrasures, and peripatetic fur caps and bayonets behind parapets of very solid masonry.

Above all, shadowing all, and steeping all, was the thickest fog ever seen beyond the sound of Bow-bells. It lay thick and heavy on Point Diamond, dimming the lustre of the bayonets of the sentinels as they paced the lofty bastions, and looked down into the abyss of fog below. It lay yet heavier on the rapid St. Lawrence, and dripped from the spars and rigging of ships. It hung over and enveloped the town, where, combined with smoke, it formed a yellow canopy; and damp and chill it penetrated the flag of England, weighing it down in heavy folds, as though ominous of impending calamity.

Slowly winding our tortuous way among multitudinous ships, all vamped in drizzling mist, we were warped to the wharf, which was covered with a mixture of mud and coal-dust, permeated by the universal fog. Here vehicles of a most extraordinary nature awaited us, and, to my great surprise, they were all *open*. They were called *calashes*, and looked something like very high gigs with hoods and C springs. Where the dash-board was not, there was a little seat or perch for the driver, who with a foot on each shaft looked in a very precarious position. These conveyances have the most absurd appearance; there are, however, a few closed vehicles, both at Montreal and Quebec, which I believe are not to be found in the civilized world elsewhere, except in a few back streets of Lisbon. These consist of a square box on two wheels. This box has a top, back, and front, but where the sides ought to be there are curtains of deer-hide, which are a very imperfect protection from wind and rain. The driver sits on the roof, and the conveyance has a constant tendency backwards, which is partially counteracted by a band under the horse's body, but *only* partially, and the inexperienced denizen of the box fancies himself in a state of constant jeopardy.

In an open calash I drove to Russell's Hotel, along streets steeper, narrower, and dirtier than any I had ever seen. Arrived within two hundred yards of the hotel, we were set down in the mud. On alighting, a gentleman who had been my fellow-traveller politely offered to guide me, and soon after addressed me by name. "Who can you possibly be?" I asked—so completely had a beard metamorphosed an acquaintance of five years' standing.

Once within the hotel, I had the greatest difficulty in finding my way about. It is composed of three of the oldest houses in Quebec, and has no end of long passages, dark winding staircases, and queer little rooms. It is haunted to a fearful extent by rats; and direful stories, "horrible, if true," were related in the parlour of personal mutilations sustained by visitors. My room was by no means in the oldest part of the house, yet I used to hear nightly sorties made in a very systematic manner by these quadruped intruders. The waiters at Russell's are complained of for their incivility, but we thought them most profuse both in their civility and attentions. Nevertheless, with all its disagreeables, Russell's is the best hotel in Quebec; and, as a number of the members of the Legislative Assembly live there while Parliament meets in that city, it is very lively and amusing.

When my English friends Mr. and Mrs. Alderson arrived, we saw a good deal of the town; but it has been so often described, that I may as well pass on to other subjects. The glowing descriptions given of it by the author of 'Hochelaga' must be familiar to many of my readers. They leave nothing to be desired, except the genial glow of enthusiasm and kindliness of heart which threw a *couleur de rose* over everything he saw.

There are some notions which must be unlearned in Canada, or temporarily laid aside. At the beginning of winter, which is the gay season in this Paris of the New World, every unmarried gentleman, who chooses to do so, selects a young lady to be his companion in the numerous amusements of the time. It does not seem that anything more is needed than the consent of the maiden, who, when she acquiesces in the arrangement, is called a "*muffin*,"—for the mammas were "muffins" themselves in their day, and cannot refuse their daughters the same privilege. The gentleman is privileged to take the young lady about in his sleigh, to ride with her, to walk with her, to dance with her a whole evening without any remark, to escort her to parties, and be her attendant on all occasions. When the spring arrives, the arrangement is at an end, and I did not hear that an engagement is frequently the result, or that the same couple enter into this agreement for two successive winters. Probably the reason may be, that they see too much of each other.

This practice is almost universal at Montreal and Quebec. On the fine, frosty, moonlight nights, when the sleigh-bells ring merrily and the crisp snow crackles under the horse's feet, the gentlemen call to take their "muffins" to meetings of the sleighing-clubs, or to snowshoe picnics, or to champagne-suppers on the ice, from which they do not return till two in the morning; yet, with all this apparent freedom of manner, the Canadian ladies are perfectly modest, feminine, and ladylike; their simplicity of manners is great, and probably there is no country in the world where there is a larger amount of domestic felicity.

The beauty of the young ladies of Canada is celebrated, and, though on going into a large party one may not see more than two or three who are strikingly or regularly beautiful, the *tout ensemble* is most attractive; the eyes are invariably large and lustrous, dark and pensive, or blue and sparkling with vivacity. Their manners and movements are unaffected and elegant; they dress in exquisite taste; and with a grace peculiarly their own, their manners have a fascination and witchery which is perfectly irresistible. They generally receive their education at the convents, and go into society at a very early age, very frequently before they have seen sixteen summers, and after

213

this time the whirl of amusement precludes them from giving much time to literary employments. They are by no means deeply read, and few of them play anything more than modern dance music. They dance beautifully, and so great is their passion for this amusement, probably derived from their French ancestors, that married ladies frequently attend the same dancing classes with their children, in order to keep themselves in constant practice.

At the time of my visit to Quebec there were large parties every night, most of which were honoured with the presence of Lord Elgin and his suite. One of his *aides-de-camp* was Lord Bury, Lord Albemarle's son, who, on a tour through North America, became enamoured of Quebec. Lord Elgin's secretary was Mr. Oliphant, the talented author of the 'Russian Shores of the Black Sea,' who had also yielded to the fascinations of this northern capital. And no wonder! for there is not a friendlier place in the whole world. I went armed with but two letters of introduction, and received hospitality and kindness for which I can never be sufficiently grateful.

The cholera, which in America assumes nearly the fatality and rapidity of the plague, had during the summer ravaged Quebec. It had entered and desolated happy homes, and, not confining itself to the abodes of the poor and miserable, had attacked the rich, the gifted, and the beautiful. For long the Destroying Angel hovered over the devoted city—neither age nor infancy was spared, and numbers were daily hurried from the vigour of living manhood into the silence and oblivion of the grave. Vigorous people, walking along the streets, were suddenly seized with shiverings and cramp, and sank down on the pavement to rise no more, sometimes actually expiring on the cold, hard stones. Pleasure was forgotten, business was partially suspended; all who could, fled; the gloom upon the souls of the inhabitants was heavier than the brown cloud which was supposed to brood over the city; and the steamers which conveyed those who fled from the terrible pestilence arrived at Toronto freighted with the living and the *dead*.

214

Among the terror-stricken, the dying, and the dead, the ministers of religion pursued their holy calling, undaunted by the terrible sights which met them everywhere—the clergy of the different denominations vied with each other in their kindness and devotedness. The priests of Rome then gained a double influence. Armed with what appeared in the eyes of the people supernatural powers, they knew no rest either by night or day; they held the cross before many a darkening eye, and spoke to the bereaved, in the plenitude of their anguish, of a world where sorrow and separation are alike unknown. The heavy clang of tolling bells was hourly heard, as the pestilence-stricken were carried to their last homes. Medical skill availed nothing; the "pestilence which walketh in darkness" was only removed by Him in whose hand are the issues of life and death.

Quebec had been free from disease for about six weeks before I visited it; the victims of the pestilence were cold in their untimely graves; the sun of prosperity smiled upon the fortress-city, and it light-hearted inhabitants had just begun their nightly round of pleasure and gaiety. The viceroyalty of Lord Elgin was drawing rapidly to a close, and two parties, given every week at Government House, afforded an example which the good people of Quebec were not slow to follow. There were musical parties, *conversaziones*, and picnics to the Chaudière and Lorette; and people who were dancing till four or five o'clock in the morning were vigorous enough after ten for a gallop to Montmorenci.

The absolute restlessness of the city astonished me very much. The morning seemed to begin, with fashionable people, with a desultory breakfast at nine o'clock, after which some received callers, others paid visits, or walked into the town to make trifling purchases at the stores; while not a few of the young ladies promenaded St. Louis Street or the ramparts, where they were generally joined by the officers. Several officers said to me that no quarters in the world were so delightful as those at Quebec. A scarlet coat finds great favour with the fair sex at Quebec—civilians, however great their mental qualifications, are decidedly in the background; and I was amused to see young ensigns, with budding moustaches, who had just joined their regiments, preferred before men of high literary attainments. With balls, and moose-hunting, and sleigh-driving, and "tarboggining," and, last but not least, "muffins," the time passes rapidly by to them. A gentleman, who had just arrived from England, declared that "Quebec was a horrid place, not fit to live in." A few days after he met the same individual to whom he had made this uncomplimentary observation, and confided to him that he thought Quebec "the most delightful place in the whole world; for, do you know," he said, "I have got a muffin."

With the afternoon numerous riding parties are formed, for you cannot go three miles out of Quebec without coming to something beautiful; and calls of a more formal nature are paid; a military band performs on Durham Terrace or the Garden, which then assume the appearance of most fashionable promenades. The evening is spent in the ball-room, or at small social dancing parties, or during the winter, before ten at night, in the galleries of the House of Assembly; and the morning is well advanced before the world of Quebec is hushed in sleep.

Society is contained in very small limits at Quebec. Its *élite* are grouped round the ramparts and in the suburb of St. Louis. The city until recently has occupied a very isolated position, and has depended upon itself for society. It is therefore sociable, friendly, and hospitable; and though there is gossip— for where is it not to be found?—I never knew any in which there was so little of ill-nature. The little world in the upper part of the city is probably the most brilliant to be found anywhere in so small a compass. But there is a world below, another nation, seldom mentioned in the aristocratic quarter of St. Louis, where vice, crime, poverty, and misery jostle each other, as pleasure and politics do in the upper town. This is the suburb of St. Roch, in whose tall dark houses and fetid alleys those are to be found whose birthright is toil, who spend life in supplying the necessities of today, while indulging in gloomy apprehensions for tomorrow—who have not one comfort in the past to cling to, or one hope for the future to cheer.

St. Roch is as crowded as the upper town, but with a very different population—the poor, the degraded, and the vicious. Here fever destroys its tens, and cholera its hundreds. Here people stab each other, and think little of it. Here are narrow alleys, with high, black-looking, stone houses, with broken windows pasted over with paper in the lower stories, and stuffed with rags in the upper—gradations of wretchedness which I have observed in the Cowgate and West Port at Edinburgh. Here are shoeless women, who quiet their children with ardent spirits, and brutal men, who would kill both wives and children if they dared. Here are dust-heaps in which pigs with long snouts are ever routing—here are lean curs, wrangling with each other for leaner bones—here are ditches and puddles, and heaps of oyster-shells, and broken crockery, and cabbage-stalks, and fragments of hats and shoes. Here are torn notices on the walls offering rewards for the apprehension of thieves and murderers, painfully suggestive of dark deeds. A little further are lumber-yards and wharfs, and mud and sawdust, and dealers in old nails and rags and bones, and rotten posts and rails, and attempts at grass. Here are old barrel-hoops, and patches of old sails, and dead bushes and dead dogs, and old saucepans, and little plots of ground where cabbages and pumpkins drag on a pining existence. And then there is the river Charles, no longer clear and bright, as when trees and hills and flowers were mirrored on its surface, but foul, turbid, and polluted, with ship-yards and steam-engines and cranes and windlasses on its margin; and here Quebec ends.

From the rich, the fashionable, and the pleasure-seeking suburb of St. Louis few venture down into the quarter of St. Roch, save those who, at the risk of drawing in pestilence with every breath, mindful of their duty to God and man, enter those hideous dwellings, ministering to minds and bodies alike diseased. My first visit to St. Roch was on a Sunday afternoon. I had attended our own simple and beautiful service in the morning, and had seen the celebration of vespers in the Romish cathedral in the afternoon. Each church was thronged with well-dressed persons. It was a glorious day. The fashionable promenades were all crowded; gay uniforms and brilliant parasols thronged the ramparts; horsemen were cantering along St. Louis Street; priestly processions passed to and from the different churches; numbers of calashes containing pleasure-parties were dashing about; picnic parties were returning from Montmorenci and Lake Charles; groups of vivacious talkers, speaking in the language of France, were at every street-corner; Quebec had all the appearance, so painful to an English or Scottish eye, of a Continental sabbath.

Mr. and Mrs. Alderson and myself left this gay scene, and the constant toll of Romish bells, for St. Roch. They had lived peacefully in a rural part of Devonshire, and more recently in one of the prettiest and most thriving of the American cities; and when they first breathed the polluted air, they were desirous to return from what promised to be so peculiarly unpleasant, but kindly yielded to my desire to see something of the shady as well as the sunny side of Quebec.

No Sabbath-day with its hallowed accompaniments seemed to have dawned upon the inhabitants of St. Roch. We saw women with tangled hair standing in the streets, and men with pallid countenances and bloodshot eyes were reeling about, or sitting with their heads resting on their hands, looking out from windows stuffed with rags. There were children too, children in nothing but the name and stature—infancy without innocence, learning to take God's name in vain with its first lisping accents, preparing for a maturity of suffering and shame. I looked at these hideous houses, and hideous men and women too, and at their still more repulsive progeny, with sallow faces, dwarfed forms, and countenances precocious in the intelligence of villany; and contrasted them with the blue-eyed, rosy-cheeked infants of my English home, who chase butterflies and weave May garlands, and gather cowslips and buttercups; or the sallow children of a Highland shantie, who devour instruction in mud-floored huts, and con their tasks on the heathery sides of hills.

Yet, when you breathe the poisoned air, laden with everything noxious to health, and have the physical and moral senses alike met with everything that can disgust and offend, it ceases to be a matter of wonder that the fair tender plant of beautiful childhood refuses to grow in such a vitiated atmosphere. Here all distinctions between good and evil are speedily lost, if they were ever known; and men, women, and children become unnatural in vice, in irreligion, in manners and appearance. Such spots as these act like cankers, yearly spreading further and further their vitiating influences, preparing for all those fearful retributions in the shape of fever and pestilence which continually come down. Yet, lamentable as the state of such a population is, considered merely with regard to this world, it becomes fearful when we recollect that the wheels of Time are ceaselessly rolling on, bearing how few, alas! to heaven—what myriads to hell; and that, when "this trembling consciousness of being, which clings enamoured to its anguish," not because life is sweet, but because death is bitter, is over, there remains, for those who have known nothing on earth but misery and vice, "a fearful looking for of judgment and fiery indignation," when they that have done evil "shall rise to the resurrection of damnation."

It was not that the miserable degraded appearance of St. Roch was anything new to me; unfortunately the same state of things exists in a far greater degree in our large towns at home; what did surprise me was, to find it in the New World, and that such a gigantic evil should have required only two hundred years for its growth. It seemed to me also that at Quebec the gulf which separates the two worlds is greater even than that which lies between Belgravia and Bethnal Green or St. Giles's. The people who live in the lower town are principally employed on the wharfs, and in the lumber trade. But my readers will not thank me for detaining them in a pestiferous atmosphere, among such unpleasing scenes; we will therefore ascend into the High-street of the city, resplendent with gorgeous mercers' stores, and articles of luxury of every description. This street and several others were at this period impassable for carriages, the roadways being tunnelled, and heaped, and barricaded; which curious and highly disagreeable state of things was stated to arise from the laying down of water-pipes. At night, when fires were lighted in the narrow streets, and groups of roughly dressed Frenchmen were standing round them, Quebec presented the appearance of the Faubourg St. Antoine after a revolution.

Quebec is a most picturesque city externally and internally. From the citadel, which stands on a rock more than three hundred feet high, down to the crowded water-side, bustling with merchants, porters, and lumbermen, all is novel and original. Massive fortifications, with guns grinning from the embrasures, form a very prominent feature; a broad glacis looks peaceful in its greenness; ramparts line the Plains of Abraham; guards and sentries appear in all directions; nightfall brings with it the challenge—"*Who goes there?*" and narrow gateways form inconvenient entrances to street so steep that I wondered how mortal horses could ever toil up them. The streets are ever thronged with vehicles, particularly with rude carts drawn by rough horses, driven by French peasants, who move stolidly along, indifferent to the continual cry "*Place aux dames.*" The stores generally have French designations above them, the shopmen often speak very imperfect English; the names of the streets are French; Romish churches and convents abound, and Sisters of Charity, unwearied in their bene-volence, are to be seen visiting the afflicted.

Notices and cautions are posted up both in French and English; the light vivacious tones of the French Canadians are everywhere heard, and from the pillar sacred to the memory of Wolfe upon the Plains of Abraham, down to the red-coated sentry who challenges you upon the ramparts, everything tells of a conquered province, and of the time, not so very far distant either, when the lilies of France occupied the place from which the flag of England now so proudly waves.

I spent a few days at Russell's Hotel, which was very full, in spite of the rats. In Canadian hotels people are very sociable, and, as many during the season make Russell's their abode, the conversation was tolerably general at dinner. Many of the members of parliament lived there, and they used to tell very racy and amusing stories against each other. I heard one which was considered a proof of the truth of the saying, that "the tailor makes the gentleman." A gentleman called on a Mr. M——, who had been appointed to a place in the government, and in due time he went to return the visit. Meeting an Irishman in the street, he asked, "Where does Mr. 'Smith' live?"—"It's no use your going there." "I want to know where he lives, do you know?"—"Faith, I do; but it's no use your going there." Mr. M——, now getting angry, said, "I don't ask you for your advice, I simply want to know where Mr. 'Smith' lives."—"Well, spalpeen, he lives down that court; but I tell ye it's no use your going there, for I've just been there myself, and *he's got a man.*" It is said that the discomfited senator returned home and bought a *new hat!*

Passing out by the citadel, the Plains of Abraham, now a race-course, are entered upon; the battle-field being denoted by a simple monument bearing the inscription *"Here died Wolfe victorious."* Beyond this, three miles from the city, is Spencer-Wood, the residence of the Governor-General. It is beautifully situated, though the house is not spacious, and is rather old-fashioned. The ball-room, however, built by Lord Elgin, is a beautiful room, very large, admirably proportioned, and chastely decorated. Here a kind of vice-regal court is held; and during the latter months of Lord Elgin's tenure of office, Spencer-Wood was the scene of a continued round of gaiety and hospitality. Lord Elgin was considered extremely popular; the Reciprocity Treaty, supposed to confer great benefits on the country, was passed during his administration, and the resources of Canada were prodigiously developed, and its revenue greatly increased. Of his popularity at Quebec there could be no question. He was attached to the Canadians, with whom he mixed with the greatest kindness and affability. Far from his presence being considered a restraint at an evening party, the entrance of the Governor and his suite was always the signal for increased animation and liveliness.

The stiffness which was said to pervade in former times the parties at Spencer-Wood was entirely removed by him; and in addition to large balls and dinner-parties, at the time I was at Quebec he gave evening parties to eighty or a hundred persons twice a-week, when the greatest sociability prevailed; and in addition to dancing, which was kept up on these occasions till two or three in the morning, games such as French blindman's-buff were introduced, to the great delight of both old and young. The pleasure with which this innovation was received by the lively and mirth-loving Canadians showed the difference in character between themselves and the American ladies. I was afterwards at a party at New York, where a gentleman who had been at Spencer-Wood attempted to introduce one of these games, but it was received with gravity, and proved a signal failure. Lord Elgin certainly attained that end which is too frequently lost sight of in society—making people enjoy themselves. Personally, I may speak with much gratitude of his kindness during a short but very severe illness with which I was attacked while at Spencer-Wood. Glittering epaulettes, scarlet uniforms, and muslin dresses whirled before my dizzy eyes—I lost for a moment the power to articulate—a deathly chill came over me—I shivered, staggered, and would have fallen had I not been supported. I was carried upstairs, feeling sure that the terrible pestilence which I had so carefully avoided had at length seized me. The medical man arrived at two in the morning, and ordered the remedies which were usually employed at Quebec, a complete envelope of mustard plasters, a profusion of blankets, and as

222

much ice as I could possibly eat. The physician told me that cholera had again appeared in St. Roch, where I, strangely enough, had been on two successive afternoons. So great was the panic caused by the cholera, that, wherever it was necessary to account for my disappearance, Lord Elgin did so by saying that I was attacked with ague. The means used were blessed by a kind Providence to the removal of the malady, and in two or three days I was able to go about again, though I suffered severely for several subsequent weeks.

From Spencer-Wood I went to the house of the Hon. John Ross, from whom and from Mrs. Ross I received the greatest kindness—kindness which should make my recollections of Quebec lastingly agreeable. Mr. Ross's public situation as President of the Legislative Council gave me an opportunity of seeing many persons whose acquaintance I should not have made under other circumstances; and as parties were given every evening but one while I was at Quebec, to which I was invited with my hosts, I saw as much of its society as under ordinary circumstances I should have seen in a year. No position is pleasanter than that of an English stranger in Canada, with good introductions.

I received much kindness also from Dr. Mountain, the venerable Protestant Bishop of Quebec. He is well known as having, when Bishop of Montreal, undertaken an adventurous journey to the Red River settlements, for the purposes of ordination and confirmation. He performed the journey in an open canoe managed by French *voyageurs* and Indians. They went up the Ottawa, then by wild lakes and rivers into Lake Huron, through the labyrinth of islands in the Georgian Bay, and by the Sault Sainte Marie into Lake Superior, then an almost untraversed sheet of deep, dreary water. Thence they went up the Rainy River, and by almost unknown streams and lakes to their journey's end. They generally rested at night, lighting large fires by their tents, and were tormented by venomous insects. At the Mission settlements on the Red River the Bishop was received with great delight by the Christianized

Indians, who, in neat clothing and with books in their hands, assembled at the little church. The number of persons confirmed was 846, and there were likewise two ordinations. The stay of the Bishop at the Red River was only three weeks, and he accomplished his enterprising journey of two thousand miles in six weeks. He is one of the most unostentatious persons possible; it was not until he presented me with a volume containing an account of his visitation that I was aware that he was the prelate with the account of whose zeal and Christian devotedness I had long been familiar. He is now an aged man, and his countenance tells of the "love which looks kindly, and the wisdom which looks soberly, on all things."

CHAPTER XIII

The House of Commons—Canadian gallantry—
The constitution—Mr. Hincks—The ex-rebel—Parties and
leaders—A street-row—Repeated disappointments—The
"habitans"—Their houses and their virtues—A stationary
people—Progress and its effects—Montmorenci—The natural
staircase—The Indian summer—Lorette—The old people—
Beauties of Quebec—The John Munn—Fear and its
consequences—A gloomy journey.

One of the sights of Quebec—to me decidedly the most interesting one—was the House of Assembly. The Legislature were burned out of their house at Montreal, and more recently out of a very handsome one at Quebec—it is to be hoped this august body will be more fortunate at Toronto, the present place of meeting. The temporary place of sitting at Quebec seemed to me perfectly adapted for the purposes of hearing, seeing, and speaking.

It is a spacious apartment, with deep galleries, which hold about five hundred, round it, which were to Quebec what the Opera and the club-houses are to London. In fact, these galleries were crowded every night; and certainly, when I was there, fully one half of their occupants were ladies, who could see and be seen. The presence of ladies may have an effect in preventing the use of very intemperate language; and though it is maliciously said that some of the younger members speak more for the galleries than the house, and though some gallant individual may occasionally step upstairs to restore a truant handkerchief or boa to the fair owner, the distractions caused by their presence are very inconsiderable, and the arrangements for their comfort are a great reflection upon the miserable latticed hole to which lady listeners are condemned in the English House of Commons. I must remark, also, that the house was well warmed and ventilated, without the aid of alternating siroccos and north winds. The Speaker's chair, on a dais and covered with a canopy, was facing us, in which reclined the Speaker in his robes. In front of him was a table, at which sat two black-robed clerks, and on which a huge mace reposed; and behind him was the reporters' gallery, where the gentlemen of the press seemed to be most comfortably accommodated. There was a large open space in front of this table, extending to the bar, at which were seated the messengers of the house, and the Sergeant-at-arms with his sword. On either side of this open space were four rows of handsome desks, and morocco seats, to accommodate two members each, who sat as most amiable Gemini. The floor was richly carpeted, and the desks covered with crimson cloth, and, with the well-managed flood of light, the room was very complete.

The Canadian Constitution is as nearly a transcript of our own as anything colonial can be. The Governor can do no wrong—he must have a responsible cabinet taken from the members of the Legislature—his administration must have a working majority, as in England—and he must bow to public opinion by changing his advisers, when the representatives of the people lose confidence in the Government. The Legislative Council represents our House of Peers, and the Legislative Assembly, or Provincial Parliament, our House of Commons. The Upper House is appointed by the Crown, under the advice of the ministry of the day; but as a clamour has been raised against it as yielding too readily to the demands of the Lower House, a measure has been brought in for making its members elective for a term of years. If this change were carried, coupled with others on which it would not interest the English reader to dwell, it would bring about an approximation of the Canadian Constitution to that of the United States.

On one night on which I had the pleasure of attending the House, the subject under discussion was the Romish holidays, as connected with certain mercantile transactions. It sounds dry enough, but, as the debate was turned into an extremely interesting religious discussion, it was well worth hearing, and the crowded galleries remained in a state of quiescence.

Mr. Hincks, the late Premier, was speaking when we went in. He is by no means eloquent, but very pointed in his observations, and there is an amount of logical sequence in his speaking which is worthy of imitation elsewhere. He is a remarkable man, and will probably play a prominent part in the future political history of Canada.[1] He is the son of a Presbyterian minister at Cork, and emigrated to Toronto in 1832. During Lord Durham's administration he became editor of the *Examiner* newspaper, and entered the Parliament of the United Provinces in 1841. He afterwards filled the important position of Inspector-General of Finances, and finally became Prime Minister. His administration was, however, overturned early in 1854, and sundry grave charges were brought against him. He spoke in favour of the abolition of the privileges conceded to Romish holidays, and was followed by several French Canadians, two of them of the Rouge party, who spoke against the measure, one of them so eloquently as to remind me of the historical days of the Girondists.

Mr. Lyon Mackenzie, who led the rebellion which was so happily checked at Toronto, and narrowly escaped condign punishment, followed, and diverged from the question of promissory notes to the Russian war and other subjects; and when loud cries of "Question, question, order, order!" arose, he tore up his notes, and sat down abruptly in a most theatrical manner, amid bursts of laughter from both floor and galleries; for he appears to be the privileged buffoon of the House.

The appearance of the House is rather imposing; the members behave with extraordinary decorum; and to people accustomed to the noises and unseemly interruptions which characterise the British House of Commons, the silence and

1 This prognostication is not likely to be realised, as the late Sir W. Molesworth has appointed Mr. Hincks to the governorship of Barbadoes. If the new governor possesses *principle* as well as *talent*, this acknowledgment of colonial merit is a step in the right direction.

order of the Canadian House are very agreeable.[1] The members seemed to give full attention to the debate; very few were writing, and none were reading anything except Parliamentary papers, and no speaker was interrupted except on one occasion. There was extremely little walking about; but I observed one gentleman, a notorious exquisite, cross the floor several times, apparently with no other object than that of displaying his fine person in bowing profoundly to the Speaker. The gentlemanly appearance of the members, taken altogether, did not escape my notice.

Sir Allan M'Nab, the present Premier, is the head of a coalition ministry; fortunately, it is not necessary to offer any remarks upon its policy; and Canada, following the example of the mother-country, submits quietly to a coalition. The opposition, which is formed of the Liberal party, is seated opposite the Government, fronted by Mr. Lyon Mackenzie, who gives a wavering adherence to every party in succession, and is often indignantly disavowed by all. The Liberals of Upper Canada are ably led by Mr. George Brown, who excels in a highly lucid, powerful, and perspicuous course of reasoning, which cannot fail to produce an effect.

Then there is the Rouge party, led by the member for Montreal, which is principally composed of very versatile and enthusiastic Frenchmen of rather indefinite opinions and aims, professing a creed which appears a curious compound of Republicanism and Rationalism. The word Latitudinarianism defines it best. There are 130 members, divided into numerous "ists" and "ites." Most of the members for Lower Canada are French, and, consequently, the Romish party is a very powerful one in the House. Taken as a whole, the

1 In *justice* to the Canadian Parliament, I must insert the following extract from the '*Toronto Globe*,' from which it will appear that there are very disgraceful exceptions to this ordinarily decorous conduct:—
"Mr. Mackenzie attempted to speak, and held the floor for two or three minutes, although his voice was inaudible from the kicking of desks, caterwaulings, and snatches of songs from various parts of the house."

members are loyal, and have proved their attachment to England by a vote of £20,000 for the Patriotic Fund.

I think that all who are in the habit of reading the debates will allow that the speaking in the House will bear comparison with that in our House of Commons; and if some of the younger members in attempting the sublime occasionally attain the ridiculous, and mistake extravagance of expression for greatness of thought, these are faults which time and criticism will remedy. Canada is a great and prosperous country, and its Legislative Assembly is very creditable to so young a community. Bribery, corruption, and place-hunting are alleged against this body; but as these vices are largely developed in England, it would be bad taste to remark upon them, particularly as the most ardent correctors of abuses now reluctantly allow that they are inseparable from popular assemblies. It is needless to speak of the Upper House, which, as has been sarcastically remarked of our House of Peers, is merely a *"High Court of Registry"*—it remains to be seen whether an elective chamber would possess greater vitality and independence.

The Speaker of the Legislative Assembly is a Frenchman, and French and English are used indiscriminately in debate. Parliamentary notices and papers are also printed in both languages.

It was a cold, gloomy October morning, a cold east wind rustled the russet leaves, and a heavy, dry fog enveloped Point Diamond, when I left the bustle of Quebec for a quiet drive to Montmorenci in a light waggon with a very spirited little horse, a young lady acting as charioteer. The little animal was very impetuous, and rattled down the steep, crowded streets of Quebec at a pace which threatened to entangle our wheels with those of numerous carts driven by apathetic *habitans*, who were perfectly indifferent to the admonitions *"Prenez garde"* and *"Place aux dames,"* delivered in beseeching tones. We passed down a steep street, and through Palace-gate, into the district of St. Roch, teeming with Irish and dirt, for I fear it is a fact that, wherever you have the first, you invariably have the last. Beyond this there was a space covered with mud and sawdust, where two *habitans* were furiously quarrelling. One sprang upon the other like a hyena, knocked him down, and then attempted to bite and strangle him, amid the applause of numerous spectators.

Leaving Quebec behind, we drove for seven miles along a road in sight of the lesser branch of the St. Lawrence, which has on the other side the green and fertile island of Orleans. The houses along this road are so numerous as to present the appearance of a village the whole way. Frenchmen who arrive here in summer can scarcely believe that they are not in their own sunny land; the external characteristics of the country are so exactly similar. These dwellings are large, whitewashed, and many-windowed, and are always surrounded with balconies. The doors are reached by flights of steps, in order that they may be above the level of the snow in winter. The rooms are clean, but large and desolate-looking, and are generally ornamented with caricatures of the Virgin and uncouth representations of miracles. The women dress in the French style, and wear large straw hats out of doors, which were the source of constant disappointments to me, for I always expected to see a young, if not a pretty, face under a broad brim, and these females were remarkably ill-favoured; their complexions hardened, wrinkled, and bronzed, from the effects of hard toil, and the extremes of heat and cold. I heard the hum of spinning-wheels from many of the houses, for these industrious women spin their household linen, and the gray homespun in which the men are clothed. The furniture is antique, and made of oak, and looks as if it had been handed down from generation to generation. The men, largely assisted by the females, cultivate small plots of ground, and totally disregard all modern improvements. These French towns and villages improve but little. Popery, that great antidote to social progress, is the creed universally professed, and generally the only building of any pretensions is a large Romish church with

230

two lofty spires of polished tin. Education is not much prized; the desires of the simple *habitans* are limited to the attainment of a competence for life, and this their rudely-tilled farms supply them with. Few emigrants make this part of Canada even a temporary resting-place; the severity of the climate, the language, the religion, and the laws, are all against them; hence, though a professor of a purer faith may well blush to confess it, the vices which emigrants bring with them are unknown. These peasants are among the most harmless people under the sun; they are moral, sober, and contented, and zealous in the observances of their erroneous creed. Their children divide the land, and, as each prefers a piece of soil adjoining the road or river, strips of soil may occasionally be seen only a few yards in width. They strive after happiness rather than advancement, and who shall say that they are unsuccessful in their aim? As their fathers lived, so they live; each generation has the simplicity and superstition of the preceding one. In the autumn they gather in their scanty harvest, and in the long winter they spin and dance round their stove-sides. On Sundays and saints' days they assemble in crowds in their churches, dressed in the style of a hundred years since. Their wants and wishes are few, their manners are courteous and unsuspicious, they hold their faith with a blind and implicit credulity, and on summer evenings sing the songs of France as their fathers sang them in bygone days on the smiling banks of the rushing Rhone.

The road along which the dwellings of these small farmers lie is macadamised, and occasionally a cross stands by the roadside, at which devotees may be seen to prostrate themselves. There is a quiet, lethargic, old-world air about the country, contrasting strangely with the bustling, hurrying, restless progress of Upper Canada. Though the condition of the *habitans* is extremely unprofitable to themselves, it affords a short rest to the thinking and observing faculties of the stranger, over-strained as they are with taking in and contemplating the railroad progress of things in the New World.

While we admire and wonder at the vast material progress of Western Canada and the North-western States of the Union, considerations fraught with alarm will force themselves upon us. We think that great progress is being made in England, but, without having travelled in America, it is scarcely possible to believe what the Anglo-Saxon race is performing upon a new soil. In America we do not meet with factory operatives, seamstresses, or clerks overworked and underpaid, toiling their lives away in order to keep body and soul together; but we have people of all classes who could obtain competence and often affluence by moderate exertions, working harder than slaves—sacrificing home enjoyments, pleasure, and health itself to the one desire of the acquisition of wealth. Daring speculations fail; the struggle in unnatural competition with men of large capital, or dishonourable dealings, wears out at last the overtasked frame—life is spent in a whirl—death summons them, and finds them unprepared. Everybody who has any settled business is overworked. Voices of men crying for relaxation are heard from every quarter, yet none dare to pause in this race which they so madly run, in which happiness and mental and bodily health are among the least of their considerations. All are spurred on by the real or imaginary necessities of their position, driven along their headlong course by avarice, ambition, or eager competition.

The Falls of Montmorenci, which we reached after a drive of eight miles, are beautiful in the extreme, and, as the day was too cold for picnic parties, we had them all to ourselves. There is no great body of water, but the river takes an unbroken leap of 280 feet from a black narrow gorge. The scathed black cliffs descend in one sweep to the St. Lawrence, in fine contrast to the snowy whiteness of the fall. Montmorenci gave me greater sensations of pleasure than Niagara. There are no mills, museums, guides, or curiosity-shops. Whatever there is of beauty bears the fair impress of its Creator's hand; and if these Falls are beautiful on a late October day, when a chill east wind was howling through leafless trees looming through a cold, grey fog, what must they be in the burst of spring or the glowing luxuriance of summer?

We drove back for some distance, and entered a small *cabaret*, where some women were diligently engaged in spinning, and some men were superintending with intense interest the preparation of some *soupe maigre*. Their *patois* was scarcely intelligible, and a boy whom we took as our guide spoke no English. After encountering some high fences and swampy ground, we came to a narrow rocky pathway in a wood, with bright green, moss-covered trees, stones, and earth. On descending a rocky bank we came to the "natural staircase," where the rapid Montmorenci forces its way through a bed of limestone, the broken but extremely regular appearance of the layers being very much like wide steps. The scene at this place is wildly beautiful. The river, frequently only a few feet in width, sometimes foams furiously along between precipices covered with trees, and bearing the marks of years of attrition; then buries itself in dark gulfs, or rests quiescent for a moment in still black pools, before it reaches its final leap.

The day before I left Quebec I went to the romantic falls of Lorette, about thirteen miles from the city. It was a beauteous day. I should have called it oppressively warm, but that the air was fanned by a cool west wind. The Indian summer had come at last; "the Sagamores of the tribes had lighted their council-fires" on the western prairies. What would we not give for such a season! It is the rekindling of summer, but without its heat— it is autumn in its glories, but without its gloom. The air is soft like the breath of May; everything is veiled in a soft pure haze, and the sky is of a faint and misty blue.

A mysterious fascination seemed to bind us to St. Roch, for we kept missing our way and getting into "streams as black as Styx." But at length the city of Quebec, with its green glacis and frowning battlements, was left behind, and we drove through flat country abounding in old stone dwelling-houses, old farms, and large fields of stubble. We neared the blue hills, and put up our horses in the Indian village of Lorette. Beautiful

Lorette! I *must* not describe, for I *cannot*, how its river escapes from under the romantic bridge in a broad sheet of milk-white foam, and then, contracted between sullen barriers of rock, seeks the deep shade of the pine-clad precipices, and hastens to lose itself there. It is perfection, and beauty, and peace; and the rocky walks upon its forest-covered crags might be in Switzerland.

Being deserted by the gentlemen of the party, my fair young companion and I found our way to Lorette, which is a large village built by government for the Indians; but by inter-marrying with the French they have lost nearly all their distinctive characteristics, and the next generation will not even speak the Indian language. Here, as in every village in Lower Canada, there is a large Romish church, ornamented with gaudy paintings. We visited some of the squaws, who wear the Indian dress, and we made a few purchases. We were afterwards beset by Indian boys with bows and arrows of clumsy construction; but they took excellent aim, incited by the reward of coppers which we offered to them. It is grievous to see the remnants of an ancient race in such a degraded state; the more so as I believe that there is no intellectual inferiority as an obstacle to their improvement. I saw some drawings by an Indian youth which evinced considerable talent; one in particular, a likeness of Lord Elgin, was admirably executed.

I have understood that there is scarcely a greater difference between these half-breeds and the warlike tribes of Central America, than between them and the Christian Indians of the Red River settlements. There are about fourteen thousand Indians in Canada, few of them in a state of great poverty, for they possess annuities arising from the sale of their lands. They have no incentives to exertion, and spend their time in shooting, fishing, and drinking spirits in taverns, where they speedily acquire the vices of the white men without their habits of industry and enterprise. They have no idols, and seldom enter into hostile opposition to Christianity, readily exchanging the worship of the Great Spirit for its tenets, as far as convenient. It is very difficult, however, to arouse them to a sense of sin, or to any idea of the importance of the world to come; but at the same time, in no part of the world have missionary labours been more blessed than at the Red River settlements. Great changes have passed before their eyes. Year, as it succeeds year, sees them driven farther west, as their hunting-grounds are absorbed by the insatiate white races. The twang of the Indian bow, and the sharp report of the Indian rifle, are exchanged for the clink of the lumberer's axe and the "g'lang" of the sturdy settler. The corn waves in luxuriant crops over land once covered with the forest haunts of the moose, and the waters of the lakes over which the red man paddled in his bark canoe are now ploughed by crowded steamers. Where the bark dwellings of his fathers stood, the locomotive darts away on its iron road, and the helpless Indian looks on aghast at the power and resources of the pale-faced invaders of his soil

The boat by which I was to leave Quebec was to sail on the afternoon of the day on which I visited Lorette, but was detained till the evening by the postmaster-general, when a heavy fog came on, which prevented its departure till the next morning. The small-pox had broken out in the city, and rumours of cholera had reached and alarmed the gay inhabitants of St. Louis. I never saw terror so unrestrainedly developed as among some ladies on hearing of the return of the pestilence. One of them went into hysterics, and became so seriously ill that it was considered necessary for her to leave Quebec the same evening. In consequence of the delay of the boat, it was on a Sunday morning that I bade adieu to Quebec. I had never travelled on a Sunday before, and should not have done so on this occasion had it not been a matter of necessity. I am happy to state that no boats run on the St. Lawrence on the Sabbath, and the enforced sailing of the *John Munn* caused a great deal of grumbling among the stewards and crew. The streets were thronged with people going to early mass, and to a special service held to avert the heavy judgments which it was feared were impending over the city. The boat was full, and many persons who were flying from the cholera had slept on board.

I took a regretful farewell of my friends, and with them of beautiful Quebec. I had met with much of kindness and hospitality, but still I must confess that the excessive gaiety and bustle of the city exercise a depressing influence. People appear absorbed by the fleeting pleasures of the hour; the attractions of this life seem to overbalance the importance of the life to come; and among the poor there is a large amount of sin and sorrow—too many who enter the world without a blessing, and depart from it without a hope. The bright sun of the Indian summer poured down its flood of light upon the castled steep, and a faint blue mist was diffused over the scene of beauty. Long undulating lines showed where the blue hills rose above the green island of Orleans, and slept in the haze of that gorgeous season. Not a breath of wind stirred the heavy folds of the flag of England on the citadel, or ruffled the sleeping St. Lawrence, or the shadows of the countless ships on its surface; and the chimes of the bells of the Romish churches floated gently over the water. Such a morning I have seldom seen, and Quebec lay basking in beauty. Surely that morning's sun shone upon no fairer city! The genial rays of that autumn sun were typical of the warm kind hearts I was leaving behind, who had welcomed a stranger to their hospitable homes; and, as the bell rang, and the paddles revolved in the still deep water, a feeling of sorrow came over my heart when I reflected that the friendly voices might never again sound in my ear, and that the sunshine which was then glittering upon the fortress-city might, to my eyes, glitter upon it no more.

The *John Munn* was a very handsome boat, fitted up with that prodigality which I have elsewhere described as characteristic of the American steamers; but in the course of investigation I came upon the steerage, or that part of the middle floor which is devoted to the poorer class of emigrants, of whom five hundred had landed at Quebec only the day before. The spectacle here was extremely annoying, for men, women, and children were crowded together in an ill-ventilated space, with kettles, saucepans, blankets, bedding, and large blue boxes. There was a bar for the sale of spirits, which, I fear, was very much frequented, for towards night there were sounds of swearing, fighting, and scuffing, proceeding from this objectionable locality.

A day-boat was such a rare occurrence that some of the citizens of Quebec took the journey merely to make acquaintance with the beauties of their own river. We passed the Heights of Abraham, and Wolfe's Cove, famous in history; wooded slopes and beautiful villas; the Chaudière river, and its pine-hung banks; but I was so ill that even the beauty of the St. Lawrence could not detain me in the saloon, and I went down into the ladies' cabin, where I spent the rest of the day on a sofa wrapped in blankets. A good many of the ladies came downstairs to avoid some quadrilles which a French Canadian lady was playing, and a friend of mine, Colonel P——, having told someone that I had had the cholera, there was a good deal of mysterious buzzing in consequence, of which I only heard a few observations, such as—"How very imprudent!" "How very wrong to come into a public conveyance!" "Just as we were trying to leave it behind too!" But I was too ill to be amused, even when one lady went so far as to remove the blanket to look at my face. There was a very pale and nervous-looking young lady lying on a sofa opposite, staring fixedly at me. Suddenly she got up, and asked me if I were very ill? I replied that I had been so. "She's had the cholera, poor thing!" the stewardess unfortunately observed. "The cholera!" she said, with an affrighted look; and, hastily putting on her bonnet, vanished from the cabin, and never came down again. She had left Quebec because of the cholera, having previously made inquiries as to whether anyone had died of it in the *John Munn*; and now, being brought, as she fancied, into contact with it, her imagination was so strongly affected that she was soon taken seriously ill, and brandy and laudanum were in requisition. So great was the fear of contagion, that, though the boat was so full that many people had to sleep on sofas, no one would share a state-room with me.

We were delayed by fog, and did not reach Montreal till one in the morning. I found Montreal as warm and damp as it had been cold and bracing on my first visit; but the air was not warmer than the welcome which I received. Kind and tempting was the invitation to prolong my stay at the See House; enticing was the prospect offered me of a visit to a seigneurie on the Ottawa; and it was with very great reluctance that, after a sojourn of only one day, I left this abode of refinement and hospitality, and the valued friends who had received me with so much kindness, for a tedious journey to New York. I left the See House at five o'clock on the last day of October, so ill that I could scarcely speak or stand. It was pitch-dark, and the rain was pouring in torrents. The high wind blew out the lamp which was held at the door; an unpropitious commencement of a journey. Something was wrong with the harness; the uncouth vehicle was nearly upset backwards; the steam ferryboat was the height of gloom, heated to a stifling extent, and full of people with oil-skin coats and dripping umbrellas. We crossed the rushing St. Lawrence just as the yellow gas-lights of Montreal were struggling with the pale, murky dawn of an autumn morning, and reached the cars on the other side before it was light enough to see objects distinctly. Here the servant who had been kindly sent with me left me, and the few hours which were to elapse before I should join my friends seemed to present insurmountable difficulties. The people in the cars were French, the names of the stations were French, and "*Prenez-garde de la locomotive!*" denoted the crossings. How the *laissez-faire* habits of the *habitans* must be outraged by the clatter of a steam-engine passing their dwellings at a speed of thirty-five miles an hour! Yet these very *habitans* were talking in the most unconcerned manner in French about a railway accident in Upper Canada, by which forty-eight persons were killed! After a journey of two hours I reached Rouse's Point, and, entering a handsome steamer on Lake Champlain, took leave of the British dominions.

Before re-entering the territory of the stars and stripes, I will offer a few concluding remarks on Canada.

CHAPTER XIV

Concluding remarks on Canada–Territory–Climate–
Capabilities–Railways and canals–Advantages for
emigrants–Notices of emigration–Government–
The franchise–Revenue–Population–Religion–Education–
The press–Literature–Observations in conclusion.

The increasing interest which attaches to this noble colony fully justifies me in devoting a chapter to a fuller account of its state and capabilities than has yet been given here.

Canada extends from Gaspe, on the Gulf of St. Lawrence, to Lake Superior. Its shores are washed by the lakes Huron, Erie, and Ontario, and by the river St. Lawrence as far as the 45th parallel of latitude; from thence the river flows through the centre of the province to the sea. Canada is bounded on the west and south by the Great Lakes and the United States; to the east by New Brunswick and the ocean; and to the north by the Hudson's Bay territory, though its limits in this direction are by no means accurately defined. Canada is but a small portion of the vast tract of country known under the name of British America, the area of which is a ninth part of the globe, and is considerably larger than that of the United States, being 2,630,163,200 acres.

Canada contains 17,939,000 occupied acres of land, only 7,300,000 of which are cultivated; and about 137,000,000 acres are still unoccupied. Nearly the whole of this vast territory was originally covered with forests, and from the more distant districts timber still forms a most profitable article of export; but wherever the land is cleared it is found to be fertile in an uncommon degree. It is very deficient in coal, but in the neighbourhood of Lake Superior mineral treasures of great value have been discovered to abound.

Very erroneous ideas prevail in England on the subject of the Canadian climate. By many persons it is supposed that the country is for ever "locked in regions of thick-ribbed ice," and that skating and sleighing are favourite summer diversions of the inhabitants. Yet, on the contrary, Lower Canada, or that part of the country nearest to the mouth of the St. Lawrence, has a summer nearly equalling in heat those of tropical climates. Its winter is long and severe, frequently lasting from the beginning of December until April; but, if the thermometer stands at 35° below zero in January, it marks 90° in the shade in June. In the neighbourhood of Quebec the cold is not much exceeded by that within the polar circle, but the dryness of the air is so great that it is now strongly recommended for those of consumptive tendencies. I have seen a wonderful effect produced in the early stages of pulmonary disorders by a removal from the damp, variable climate of Europe to the dry, bracing atmosphere of Lower Canada. Spring is scarcely known, the transition from winter to summer is very rapid; but the autumn or *fall* is a long and very delightful season. It is not necessary to dwell further upon the Lower Canadian climate, as, owing to circumstances hereafter to be explained, few emigrants in any class of life make the Lower Province more than a temporary resting-place.

From the eastern coast to the western boundary the variations in climate are very considerable. The peninsula of Canada West enjoys a climate as mild as that of the state of New York. The mean temperature, taken from ten years' observation, was 44°, and the thermometer rarely falls lower than 11° below zero, while the heat in summer is not oppressive. The peach and vine mature their fruit in the neighbourhood of Lake Ontario, and tobacco is very successfully cultivated on the peninsula between Lake Erie and Lake Huron. It seems that Upper Canada, free from the extremes of heat and cold, is intended to receive a European population. Emigrants require to become acclimatised, which they generally are by an attack of ague, more or less severe; but the country is extraordinarily healthy; with the exception of occasional visitations of cholera, epidemic diseases are unknown, and the climate is very favourable to the duration of human life.

The capabilities of Canada are only now beginning to be appreciated. It has been principally known for its vast exports of timber, but these constitute a very small part of its wealth. Both by soil and climate Upper Canada is calculated to afford a vast and annually-increasing field for agricultural and pastoral pursuits. Wheat, barley, potatoes, turnips, maize, hops, and tobacco, can all be grown in perfection. Canada already exports large quantities of wheat and flour of a very superior description; and it is stated that in no country of the world is there so much wheat grown, in proportion to the population and the area under cultivation, as in that part of the country west of Kingston. The grain-growing district is almost without limit, extending as it does along the St. Lawrence, Lake Erie, and Lake Ontario, to Windsor, with a vast expanse of country to the north and west. The hops, which are an article of recent cultivation, are of very superior quality, and have hitherto been perfectly free from blight.

Vast as are the capabilities of Canada for agricultural pursuits, she also offers great facilities for the employment of capital in manufacturing industry, though it is questionable whether it is desirable to divert labour into these channels in a young country where it is dear and scarce. The streams which intersect the land afford an unlimited and very economical source of power, and have already been used to a considerable extent. Lower Canada and the shores of the Ottawa afford enormous supplies of white pine, and the districts about Lake Superior contain apparently inexhaustible quantities of ore, which yields a very large percentage of copper. We have thus in Canada about 1400 miles of territory, perhaps the most fertile and productive ever brought under the hands of the cultivator; and as though Providence had especially marked out this portion of the New World as a field for the enterprise of the European races, its natural facilities for transit and communication are nearly unequalled. The Upper Lakes, the St. Lawrence, the Ottawa, and the Saguenay, besides many rivers of lesser note, are so many natural highways for the conveyance of produce of every description from the most distant parts of the interior to the Atlantic Ocean. Without these natural facilities Canada could never have progressed to the extraordinary extent which she has already done.

Great as these adventitious advantages are, they have been further increased by British energy and enterprise. By means of ship-canals, formed to avoid the obstructions to navigation caused by the rapids of the St. Lawrence, Niagara, and the Sault Sainte Marie, small vessels can load at Liverpool and discharge their cargoes on the most distant shores of Lake Superior. On the Welland canal alone, which connects Lake Erie with Lake Ontario, the tolls taken in 1853 amounted to more than £65,000. In the same year 19,631 passengers and 1,075,218 tons of shipping passed through it: the traffic on the other canals is in like proportion, and is monthly on the increase. But an extensive railway system, to facilitate direct communication with the Atlantic at all seasons of the year, is paving the way for a further and rapid development of the resources of Canada, and for a vast increase in her material prosperity. Already the Great Western Company has formed a line from Windsor, opposite Detroit, U.S., to Toronto, passing through the important towns of Hamilton, London, and Woodstock: a branch also connects Toronto with Lake Simcoe, opening up the very fertile tract of land in that direction. Another railway extends from Fort Erie, opposite Buffalo, to Goderich on Lake Huron, a distance of 158 miles. A portion of the Grand Trunk Railway has recently been opened, and trains now regularly run between Quebec and Montreal, a distance of 186 miles. When this magnificent railway is completed it will connect the cities of Quebec, Montreal, and Toronto, where, joining the Great Western scheme, the whole of Upper and Lower Canada will be connected with the great lakes and the western States of the neighbouring republic. The main line will cross the St. Lawrence at Montreal by a tubular bridge two miles in length. The Grand Trunk Railway will have its eastern terminus at Portland, in the State of Maine, between which city and

Liverpool there will be regular weekly communication. This railway is, however, embarrassed by certain financial difficulties, which may retard for a time the completion of the gigantic undertaking.

Another railway connects the important city of Ottawa with Prescott, on the river St. Lawrence, and has its terminus opposite to the Ogdensburgh station of the Boston railway. Besides these there are numerous branches, completed or in course of construction, which will open up the industry of the whole of the interior. Some of these lines, particularly the Great Western, have a large traffic already, and promise to be very successful speculations.

The facilities for communication, and for the transit of produce, are among the most important of the advantages which Canada holds out to emigrants, but there are others which must not be overlooked. The healthiness of the climate has been already remarked upon, but it is an important consideration, as the bracing atmosphere and freedom from diseases allow to the hardy adventurer the free exercise of his vigour and strength.

Communication with England is becoming increasingly regular. During the summer months screw-steamers and sailing vessels ply between Liverpool and Quebec, from whence there is cheap and easy water communication with the districts bordering on the great lakes. From Quebec to Windsor, a distance of nearly 1000 miles, passengers are conveyed for the sum of 31s., and have the advantage of having their baggage under their eyes during the whole journey. The demand for labour in all parts of Canada West is great and increasing. The wages of farm-servants are £4 per month with board: day-labourers earn from 4s. to 5s. per diem, and in harvest 10s., without board. The wages of carpenters and other skilled workmen vary according to their abilities; but they range between 7s. and 12s. 6d. per diem, taking these as the highest and lowest prices.

The cost of living is considerably below that in this country;

for crockery, cutlery, &c., 50 per cent. advance on home retail prices is paid, and for clothing 50 to 75 per cent. addition on old country prices, if the articles are not of Canadian manufacture. The cost of a comfortable log-house with two floors, 16 feet by 24, is about £18; but it must be borne in mind that very little expenditure is needed on the part of the settler; his house and barns are generally built by himself, with the assistance of his neighbours; and a man with the slightest ingenuity or powers of imitation can also fabricate at a most trifling expense the few articles of household furniture needed at first. I have been in several log-houses where the bedsteads, tables, and chairs were all the work of the settlers themselves, at a cost probably of a few shillings; and though the workmanship was rough, yet the articles answer perfectly well for all practical purposes. Persons of sober, industrious habits, going out as workmen to Canada, speedily acquire comfort and independence. I have seen settlers who went out within the last eight years as day-labourers, now the owners of substantial homesteads, with the requisite quantity of farming-stock.

Canada West is also a most desirable locality for persons of intelligence who are possessed of a small capital. Along the great lakes and in the interior there are large tracts of land yet unoccupied. The price of wild land varies from 10s. to £10 per acre, according to the locality. Cleared farms, with good buildings, in the best townships, are worth from £10 to £15 an acre: these prices refer to the lands belonging to the Canada Land Company; the crown lands sell at prices varying from 4s. to 7s. 6d. per acre, but the localities of these lands are not so desirable in most instances. The price of clearing wild lands is about £4 5s. per acre, but in many locations, particularly near the railways, the sale of the timber covers the expenses of clearing. As has been previously observed, the soil and climate of Upper Canada are favourable to a great variety of crops. Wheat, however, is probably the most certain and profitable, and, with respect to cereals and other crops, the produce of the land per acre is not less than in England. In addition to tobacco, flax and hemp are occupying the attention of the settlers; and as an annually increasing amount of capital is employed in factories, these last are likely to prove very profitable.

In addition to the capabilities of the soil, Lake Huron and the Georgian Bay present extensive resources in the way of fish, and their borders are peculiarly desirable locations for the emigrant population of the west of Ireland and the west Highlands of Scotland.

With such very great advantages, it is not surprising that the tide of emigration should set increasingly towards this part of the British dominions. The following is a statement of the number of persons who landed at Quebec during the last five years. The emigration returns for 1855 will probably show a very considerable increase:—

1850	32,292
1851	41,076
1852	39,176
1853	36,699
1854	53,183

It may be believed that the greater number of these persons are now enjoying a plenty, many an affluence, which their utmost exertions could not have obtained for them at home. Wherever a farmstead, surrounded by its well-cleared acres, is seen, it is more than probable that the occupant is also the owner. The value of land increases so rapidly, that persons who originally bought their land in its wild state for 4s. per acre, have made handsome fortunes by disposing of it. In Canada, the farmer holds a steady and certain position; if he saves money, a hundred opportunities will occur for him to make a profitable investment; but if, as is more frequently the case, he is not rich as far as money is concerned, he has all the comforts and luxuries which it could procure. His land is ever increasing in value; and in the very worst seasons, or under accidental circumstances of an unfavourable nature, he can never know real poverty, which is a deficiency in the necessaries of life.

But in Canada, as in the Old World, people who wish to attain competence or wealth must toil hard for it. In Canada, with all its capabilities and advantages, there is no royal road to riches—no Midas touch to turn everything into gold. The primal curse still holds good, "though softened into mercy;" and those who emigrate, expecting to work less hard for 5s. a day than at home for 1s. 6d., will be miserably disappointed, for, where high wages are given, hard work is required; those must also be disappointed who expect to live in style from off the produce of a small Canadian farm, and those whose imaginary dignity revolts from plough, and spade, and hoe, and those who invest borrowed capital in farming operations. The fields of the slothful in Canada bring forth thorns and thistles, as his fields brought them forth in England. Idleness is absolute ruin, and drunkenness carries with it worse evils than at home, for the practice of it entails a social ostracism, as well as total ruin, upon the emigrant and his family. The same conditions of success are required as in England—honesty, sobriety, and industry; with these, assisted by all the advantages which Canada possesses, there is no man who need despair of acquiring independence and affluence, although there is always enough of difficulty to moderate the extravagance of exaggerated expectations.

The Government of Canada demands a few remarks. Within the last few years the position of this colony, with respect to England, has been greatly changed, by measures which have received the sanction of the Imperial Parliament. In 1847 the Imperial Government abandoned all control over the Canadian tariff, and the colonial legislature now exercises supreme power over customs duties, and all matters of general and local taxation. This was a very important step, and gave a vast impulse to the prosperity of Canada. The colony now has all the advantages—free from a few of the inconveniences—of being an independent country. England retains the right of nominating the Governor-General, and the Queen has the power, rarely if ever exercised, of putting a veto upon certain of the acts of the colonial legislature. England conducts all matters of war and diplomacy, and provides a regular military establishment for the defence of Canada; and though she is neither required to espouse our quarrels, or bear any portion of our burdens, we should be compelled to espouse *hers* in any question relating to her honour or integrity, at a lavish expenditure of blood and treasure. It appears that the present relations in which Canada stands to England are greatly to her advantage, and there is happily no desire on her part to sever them.

The Governor-General is appointed by the Crown, generally for a term of five years, but is paid by the province; he acts as viceroy, and his assent to the measures of the Legislature is required, in order to render them valid. His executive council, composed of the ministers of the day, is analogous to our English Cabinet. The governor, like our own Sovereign, must bow to the will of a majority in the Legislature, and dismiss his ministers when they lose the confidence of that body. The "second estate" is the Legislative Council. The governor, with the advice of his ministry, appoints the members of this body. They are chosen for life, and their number is unrestricted. At present there are about forty members. The functions of this council are very similar to those of our House of Peers, and consist, to a great extent, in registering the decrees of the Lower House.

The "third estate" is denominated the House of Assembly, and consists of 130 members, 65 for each province.[1] The qualification for the franchise has been placed tolerably high, and no doubt wisely, as, in the absence of a better guarantee

1 The members of the Legislative Council and the House of Assembly receive six dollars (24s. sterling) a day for their attendance. The members of the Executive Council are paid at the rate of £1260 per annum.

for the right use of it, a property qualification, however trifling in amount, has a tendency to elevate the tone of election-eering, and to enhance the value which is attached to a vote. The qualification for electors is a £50 freehold, or an annual rent of £7 10s. Contrary to the practice in the States, where large numbers of the more respectable portion of the community abstain from voting, in Canada the votes are nearly all recorded at every election, and the fact that the franchise is within the reach of every sober man gives an added stimulus to industry.

The attempt to establish British constitutional government on the soil of the New World is an interesting experiment, and has yet to be tested. There are various disturbing elements in Canada, of which we have little experience in England; the principal one being the difficulty of legislating between what, in spite of the union, are two distinct nations, of different races and religions. The impossibility of reconciling the rival, and frequently adverse claims, of the Upper and Lower Provinces, has become a very embarrassing question. The strong social restraints, and the generally high tone of public feeling in England, which exercise a powerful control over the minister of the day, do not at present exist in Canada; neither has the public mind that nice perception of moral truth which might be desired. The population of Upper Canada, more especially, has been gathered from many parts of the earth, and is composed of men, generally speaking, without education, whose sole aim is the acquisition of wealth, and who are not cemented by any common ties of nationality. Under these circumstances, and bearing in mind the immense political machinery which the Papacy can set to work in Canada, the transfer of British institutions to the colony must at present remain a matter of problematical success. It is admitted that the failure of representative institutions arises from the un-worthiness of constituencies; and if the efforts which are made by means of education to elevate the character of the next generation of electors should prove fruitless, it is probable that, with the independence of the colony, American institutions, with their objectionable features, would follow. At present the great difficulties to be surmounted lie in the undue power possessed by the French Roman Catholic population, and the Romanist influences brought to bear successfully on the Government.

There is in Canada no direct taxation for national purposes, except a mere trifle for the support of the provincial lunatic asylums, and for some other public buildings. The provincial revenue is derived from customs duties, public works, crown lands, excise, and bank impost. The customs duties last year came to £1,100,000, the revenue from public works to £123,000, from lands about the same sum, from excise about £40,000, and from the tax on the current notes of the banks £30,000. Every county, township, town, or incorporated village, elects its own council; and all local objects are provided for by direct taxation through these bodies. In these municipalities the levying of the local taxes is vested, and they administer the monies collected for roads, bridges, schools, and improvements, and the local administration of public justice.

According to the census taken in 1851, the population of Upper Canada was 952,000 souls, being an increase since 1842 of 465,945. That of Lower Canada amounted to 890,000, making a total of 1,842,000; but if to this we add the number of persons who have immigrated within the last four years, we have a population of 2,012,134.

Of the population of Lower Canada, 669,000 are of French origin. These people speak the French language, and profess the Romish faith. The land is divided into *seigneuries*; there are feudal customs and antiquated privileges, and the laws are based upon the model of those of old France. The progress of Lower Canada is very tardy. The French have never made good colonists, and the Romish religion acts as a drag upon social and national progress. The *habitans* of the Lower Province, though moral and amiable, are not ambitious, and hold their ancient customs with a tenacity which opposes itself to their advancement. The various changes in the tariff made by the Imperial Government affected Lower Canada very seriously. On comparing the rate of increase in the population of the two provinces in the same period of twelve years, we find that for Upper Canada it was 130 per cent., for Lower Canada only 34 per cent. The disparity between the population and the wealth of the two provinces is annually on the increase.

The progress of Upper Canada is something perfectly astonishing, and bids fair to rival, if not exceed, that of her gigantic neighbour. Her communication between the Lake district and the Atlantic is practically more economical, taking the whole of the year, and, as British emigration has tended chiefly to the Upper Province, the population is of a more homogeneous character than that of the States. The climate also is more favourable than that of Lower Canada. These circumstances, combined with the inherent energy of the Anglo-Saxon races which have principally colonised it, account in great measure for the vast increase in the material prosperity of the Upper Province as compared with the Lower.

In 1830 the population of Upper Canada was 210,437 souls; in 1842, 486,055; and in 1851 it had reached 952,004. Its population is now supposed to exceed that of Lower Canada by 300,000 souls. It increased in nine years about 100 per cent. In addition to the large number of emigrants who have arrived by way of Quebec, it has received a considerable accession of population from the United States; 7000 persons crossed the frontier in 1854. The increase of its wealth is far more than commensurate with that of its population. The first returns of the assessable property of Upper Canada were taken in 1825, and its amount was estimated at £1,854,965. In 1854 it was estimated at £6,393,630; but in seven years after this, in 1852, it presents the astonishing amount of £37,695,931! The wheat crop of Upper Canada in 1841 was 3,221,991 bushels, and in 1851 it was 12,692,852; but the present year, 1855, will show a startling and almost incredible increase. In addition to the wealth gained in the cultivation of the soil, the settlers are

251

seizing upon the vast water-power which the country affords, and are turning it to the most profitable purposes. Saw-mills, grist-mills, and woollen-mills start up in every direction, in addition to tool and machinery factories, iron-foundries, asheries, and tanneries.

Towns are everywhere springing up as if by magic along the new lines of railway and canal, and the very villages of Upper Canada are connected by the electric telegraph. The value of land is everywhere increasing as new lines of communication are formed. The town of London, in Upper Canada, presents a very remarkable instance of rapid growth. It is surrounded by a very rich agricultural district, and the Great Western Railway passes through it. Seven years ago this place was a miserable-looking village of between two and three thousand inhabitants; now it is a flourishing town, alive with business, and has a population of 13,000 souls. The increase in the value of property in its vicinity will appear almost incredible to English readers, but it is stated on the best authority: a building-site sold in September, 1855, for £150 per foot, which ten years ago could have been bought for that price per acre, and ten years earlier for as many pence.

In Upper Canada there appears to be at the present time very little of that state of society which is marked by hard struggles and lawless excesses. In every part of my travels west of Toronto I found a high degree of social comfort, security to life and property, the means for education and religious worship, and all the accessories of a high state of civilization, which are advantages brought into every locality almost simultaneously with the clearing of the land. Yet it is very apparent, even to the casual visitor, that the progress of Canada West has only just begun. No limits can be assigned to its future prosperity, and, as its capabilities become more known, increasing numbers of stout hearts and strong arms will be attracted towards it.

The immense resources of the soil under cultivation have not yet been developed; the settlers are prodigal of land, and a great portion of the occupied territory, destined to bear the most luxuriant crops, is still in bush. The magnificent districts adjoining Lake Huron, the Georgian Bay, and Lake Simcoe, are only just being brought into notice; and of the fertile valley of the Ottawa, which it is estimated would support a population of mine millions, very little is known. Every circumstance that can be brought forward combines to show that Upper Canada is destined to become a great, a wealthy, and a prosperous country.

The census gives some interesting tables relating to the origins of the inhabitants of Canada. I wish that I had space to present my readers with the whole, instead of with this brief extract:—

Canadians, French origin	695,000
Canadians, English origin	651,000
England and Wales	93,000
Scotland	90,000
Ireland	227,000
United States	56,000
Germany	10,000

Besides these there are 8000 coloured persons and 14,000 Indians in Canada, and emigrants from every civilised country in the world.

As far as regards the Church of England, Canada is divided into three dioceses—Toronto, Montreal, and Quebec—with a prospect of the creation of a fourth, that of Kingston. The clergy, whose duties are very arduous and ill-requited, have been paid by the Society for Propagating the Gospel, and out of the proceeds of the clergy reserves. The Society has, in great measure, withdrawn its support, and recent legislative enactments have a tendency to place the Church of England in Canada, to some extent, on the voluntary system. The inhabitants of Canada are fully able to support any form of worship to which they may choose to attach themselves.

Trinity College, at Toronto, is in close connexion with the Church of England.

The Roman Catholics have enormous endowments, including a great part of the island of Montreal, and several valuable seigneuries. Very large sums are also received by them from those who enter the convents, and for baptisms, burials, and masses for the dead. The enslaving, enervating, and retarding effects of Roman Catholicism are nowhere better seen than in Lower Canada, where the priests exercise despotic authority. They have numerous and wealthy conventual establishments, both at Quebec and Montreal, and several Jesuit and other seminaries. The Irish emigrants constitute the great body of Romanists in Upper Canada; in the Lower Province there are more than 746,000 adherents to this faith.

The Presbyterians are a very respectable, influential, and important body in Canada, bound firmly together by their uniformity of worship and doctrine. Though an Episcopalian form of church government and a form of worship are as obnoxious to them as at home, their opposition seldom amounts to hostility. Generally speaking, they are very friendly in their intercourse with the zealous and hard-working clergy of the Church of England; and, indeed, the comparative absence of sectarian feeling, and the way in which the ministers of all denominations act in harmonious combination for the general good, is one of the most pleasing features connected with religion in Canada.

In Upper Canada there are 1559 churches, for 952,000 adherents, being one place of worship for every 612 inhabitants. Of these houses of worship, 226 belong to the Church of England, 135 to the Roman Catholics, 148 to the Presbyterians, and 471 to the Methodists. In Lower Canada there are 610 churches, for 890,261 adherents, 746,000 of whom are Roman Catholics. There is therefore in the Lower Province one place of worship for every 1459 inhabitants. These religious statistics furnish additional proof of the progress of

Upper Canada. The numbers adhering to the five most important denominations are as follows, in round numbers:—

Roman Catholics..	..	..	..	914,000
Episcopalians	..	..	..	268,000
Presbyterians	..	..	..	237,000
Methodists	..	..	..	183,000
Baptists..	..	..	..	49,000

Beside these there are more than 20 sects, some of them holding the most extravagant and fanatical tenets. In the Lower Province there are 45,000 persons belonging to the Church of England, 33,000 are Presbyterians, and 746,000 are Roman Catholics. With this vast number of Romanists in Canada, it is not surprising that under the present system of representation, which gives an equal number of representatives to each province, irrespective of population, the Roman Catholics should exercise a very powerful influence on the colonial Parliament. This influence is greatly to be deplored, not less socially and politically than religiously. Popery paralyses those countries under its dominion; and the stationary condition of Lower Canada is mainly to be attributed to the successful efforts of the priests to keep up that system of ignorance and terrorism, without which their power could not continue to exist.

More importance is attached generally to education in Upper Canada than might have been supposed from the extreme deficiencies of the first settlers. A national system of education, on a most liberal scale, has been organised by the Legislature, which presents in unfavourable contrast the feeble and isolated efforts made for this object by private benevolence in England. Acting on the principle that the first duty of government is to provide for the education of its subjects, a uniform and universal educational system has been put into force in Canada.

This system of public instruction is founded on the co-operation of the Executive Government with the local municipalities. The members of these corporations are elected by the freeholders and householders. The system, therefore, is strictly popular and national, as the people voluntarily tax themselves for its support, and, through their elected trustees, manage the schools themselves. It is probable that the working of this plan may exercise a beneficial influence on the minds of the people, in training them to thought for their offspring, as regards their best interests. No compulsion whatever is exercised by the Legislature over the proceedings of the local municipalities; it merely offers a pecuniary grant, on the condition of local exertion. The children of every class of the population have equal access to these schools, and there is no compulsion upon the religious faith of any. Religious minorities in school municipalities have the alternative of separate schools, and attach considerable importance to this provision. Although what we should term religious instruction is not a part of the common school system, it is gratifying to know that both the Bible and Testament are read in a very large majority of these schools, and that the number where they are used is annually on the increase. There are in Upper Canada 3127 common schools, about 1800 of which are free, or partially free. The total amount available for school purposes in 1853 amounted to £199,674, a magnificent sum, considering the youth and comparatively thin population of the country. The total number of pupils in the same year was 194,136. But though this number appears large, the painful fact must also be stated, that there were 79,000 children destitute of the blessings of education of any kind. The whole number of teachers at the same period was 3539, of whom 885 were Methodists, 850 were Presbyterians, 629 were Episcopalians, 351 were Roman Catholics, and 194 belonged to the Baptist persuasion. The inspection of schools, which is severe and systematic, is conducted by local superintendents appointed by the different municipalities. There is a Board of Public Instruction in each county for the examination and licensing of teachers; the standard of their qualifications is fixed by provincial authority. At the head of the whole are a Council of Public Instruction and a Chief Commissioner of Schools, both appointed by the Crown. There are several colleges, very much on the system of the Scotch Universities, including Trinity College at Toronto, in connection with the Church of England, and Knox's College, a Presbyterian theological seminary. There are also medical colleges, both in Upper and Lower Canada, and a chair of agriculture has been established in University College, Toronto. From these statements it will be seen that, from the ample provision made, a good education can be obtained at a very small cost. There are in Lower Canada upwards of 1100 schools.

Every town, and I believe I may with truth write every village, has its daily and weekly papers, advocating all shades of political opinion. The press in Canada is the medium through which the people receive, first by telegraphic despatch, and later in full, every item of English intelligence brought by the bi-weekly mails. Taking the newspapers as a whole, they are far more gentlemanly in their tone than those of the neighbouring republic, and perhaps are not more abusive and personal than *some* of our English provincial papers. There is, however, very great room for improvement, and no doubt, as the national palate becomes improved by education, the morsels presented to it will be more choice. Quebec, Montreal, and Toronto have each of them several daily papers, but, as far as I am aware, no paper openly professes republican or annexationist views, and some of the journals advocate in the strongest manner an attachment to British institutions. The prices of these papers vary from a penny to threepence each, and a workman would as soon think of depriving himself of his breakfast as of his morning journal. It is stated that thousands of the subscribers to the newspapers are so illiterate as to depend upon their children for a knowledge of their contents. At present few people, comparatively speaking, are more than half educated. The knowledge of this fact lowers the tone of the press, and circumscribes both authors and speakers, as any allusions to

257

history or general literature would be very imperfectly, if at all, understood.

The merchants and lawyers of Canada have, if of British extraction, generally received a sound and useful education, which, together with the admirable way in which they keep pace with the politics and literature of Europe, enables them to pass very creditably in any society. There are very good book-stores in Canada, particularly at Toronto, where the best English works are to be purchased for little more than half the price which is paid for them at home, and these are largely read by the educated Canadians, who frequently possess excellent libraries. Cheap American novels, often of a very objectionable tendency, are largely circulated among the lower classes; but to provide them with literature of a better character, large libraries have been formed by local efforts, assisted by government grants. Canada as yet possesses no literature of her own, and the literary man is surrounded by difficulties. Independently of the heavy task of addressing himself to uneducated minds, unable to appreciate depth of thought and beauty of language, it is not likely that, where the absorbing passion is the acquisition of wealth, much encouragement would be given to the struggles of native talent.

Canada, young as she is, has made great progress in the mechanical arts, and some of her machinery and productions make a very creditable show at the Paris Exhibition; but it must be borne in mind that this is due to the government, rather than to the enterprise of private exhibitors.

Taken altogether, there is perhaps no country in the world so prosperous or so favoured as Canada, after giving full weight to the disadvantages which she possesses, in a large Roman Catholic population, an unsettled state of society, and a mixed and imperfectly educated people. It is the freest land under the sun, acknowledging neither a despotic sovereign nor a tyrant populace; life and property are alike secure—liberty has not yet degenerated into lawlessness—the constitution combines the advantages of the monarchical and republican forms of government—the Legislative Assembly, to a great extent, represents the people—religious toleration is enjoyed in the fullest degree—taxation and debt, which cripple the energies and excite the disaffection of older communities, are unfelt—the slave flying from bondage in the south knows no sense of liberty or security till he finds both on the banks of the St. Lawrence, under the shadow of the British flag. Free from the curse of slavery, Canada has started untrammelled in the race of nations, and her progress already bids fair to outstrip in rapidity that of her older and gigantic neighbour.

Labour is what she requires, and as if to meet that requirement, circumstances have directed the attention of emigrants towards her—the young, the enterprising, and the vigorous, are daily leaving the wasted shores of Scotland and Ireland for her fertile soil, where the laws of England shall still protect them, and her flag shall still wave over them. Large numbers of persons are now leaving the north-east of Scotland for Canada, and these are among the most valuable of the emigrants who seek her shores. They carry with them the high moral sense, the integrity, and the loyalty which characterise them at home; and in many cases more than this—the religious principle, and the "godliness which has promise of the life which now is, and of that which is to come."

Taken as a *whole*, the inhabitants of both provinces are attached to England and England's rule; they receive the news of our reverses with sorrow, and our victories create a burst of enthusiasm from the shores of the St. Lawrence to those of Lake Superior. As might be expected, the Anglo-French alliance is extremely popular: to show the sympathy of Canada, the Legislature made the munificent grant of £20,000 to be divided between the Patriotic Funds of both nations, and every township and village has contributed to swell a further sum of £30,000 to be applied to the same object. The imperial garrisons in Canada have recently been considerably diminished, and with perfect safety; the efforts of agitators to produce disaffection have signally failed; and it is stated by those best acquainted with the temper of the people, that Canada will not become a separate country, except by England's voluntary act.

At present every obstacle to her further development seems to be removed—her constitution has been remodelled within the last few years on an enlarged and liberal basis—her religious endowments have just been placed on a permanent footing—all the points likely to cause a rupture with the United States have been amicably settled—and important commercial advantages have been obtained: the sun of prosperity shines upon her from the Gulf of St. Lawrence to the distant shores of the Ottawa and the Western Lakes. She requires only for the future the blessing of God, so freely accorded to the nations which honour Him, to make her great and powerful. The future of nations, as of individuals, is mercifully veiled in mystery; we can trace the rise and progress of empires, but we know not the time when they shall droop and decay—when the wealthy and populous cities of the Present shall be numbered with the Nineveh and Babylon of the Past. It may be that in future years our mighty nation shall go the way of all that have been before it; but whether the wise decrees of Providence doom it to flourish or decline, we can still look with confident hope to this noble colony in the New World, believing that on her enlightened and happy shores, under the influence of beneficent institutions and of a scriptural faith, the Anglo-Saxon race may renew the vigour of its youth, and realise in time to come the brightest hopes which have ever been formed of England in the New World.

CHAPTER XV

Preliminary remarks on re-entering the States—
Americanisms—A little slang—Liquoring up—Eccentricities in
dress—A 'cute chap down east—Conversation on eating—A
Kentucky gal—Lake Champlain—Delaval's—A noisy serenade—
Albany—Beauties of the Hudson—The Empire City.

It has been truly observed that a reliable book on the United
States yet remains to be written. The writer of such a volume
must neither be a tourist nor a temporary resident. He must
spend years in the different States, nicely estimating the
different characteristics of each, as well as the broadly-marked
shades of difference between East, West, and South. He must
trace the effect of Republican principles upon the various
races which form this vast community, and, while analysing the
prosperity of the country, he must carefully distinguish
between the real, the fictitious, and the speculative. In England
we speak of America as *"Brother Jonathan"* in the singular
number, without any fraternal feeling however, and consider it
as one nation, possessing uniform distinguishing characteristics. I saw *less* difference between Edinburgh and Boston,
than between Boston and Chicago; the dark-haired Celts of the
west of Scotland, and the stirring artisans of our manufacturing
cities, have more in common than the descendants of the
Puritans in New England, and the reckless, lawless inhabitants
of the newly-settled territories west of the Mississippi. It must
not be forgotten that the thirty-two States of which the Union
is composed, may be considered in some degree as separate
countries, each possessing its governor and assembly, and
framing, to a considerable extent, its own laws. Beyond the
voice which each State possesses in the Congress and Senate at
Washington, there is apparently little to bind this vast
community together; there is no national form of religion, or
state-endowed church; Unitarianism may be the prevailing
faith in one State, Presbyterianism in another, and Universal-

ism in a third; while between the Northern and Southern States there is as wide a difference as between England and Russia—a difference stamped on the very soil itself, and which, in the opinion of some, threatens a disseverance of the Union.

Other causes also produce highly distinctive features in the inhabitants. In the long-settled districts bordering upon the Atlantic, all the accompaniments and appliances of civilisation may be met with, and a comparatively stationary, refined, and intellectual condition of society. Travel for forty hours to the westward, and everything is in a transition state: there are rough roads and unfinished railroads; foundations of cities laid in soil scarcely cleared from the forest; splendid hotels within sound of the hunter's rifle and the lumberer's axe; while the elements of society are more chaotic than the features of the country. Every year a tide of emigration rolls westward, not from Europe only, but from the crowded eastern cities, forming a tangled web of races, manners, and religions which the hasty observer cannot attempt to disentangle. Yet there are many external features of uniformity which the traveller cannot fail to lay hold of, and which go under the general name of Americanisms. These are peculiarities of dress, manners, and phraseology, and, to some extent, of opinion, and may be partly produced by the locomotive life which the American leads, and the way in which all classes are brought into contact in travelling. These peculiarities are not to be found among the highest or the highly-educated classes, but they force themselves upon the tourist to a remarkable, and frequently to a repulsive, extent; and it is safer for him to narrate facts and comment upon externals, though in doing so he presents a very partial and superficial view of the people, than to present his readers with general inferences drawn from partial premises, or with conclusions based upon imperfect, and often erroneous, data.

An entire revolution had been effected in my way of looking at things since I landed on the shores of the New World. I had ceased to look for vestiges of the past, or for relics of ancient magnificence, and, in place of these, I now contemplated vast resources in a state of progressive and almost feverish development, and, having become accustomed to a general absence of the picturesque, had learned to look at the practical and the utilitarian with a high degree of interest and pleasure. The change from the lethargy and feudalism of Lower Canada and the gaiety of Quebec, to the activity of the New England population, was very startling. It was not less so from the *reposeful* manners and gentlemanly appearance of the English Canadians, and the vivacity and politeness of the French, to Yankee dress, twang, and peculiarities.

These appeared, as the Americans say, in "full blast," during the few hours which I spent on Lake Champlain. There were about a hundred passengers, including a sprinkling of the fair sex. The amusements were story-telling, whittling, and smoking. Fully half the stories told began with, "There was a 'cute 'coon down east," and the burden of nearly all was some clever act of cheating, "sucking a greenhorn," as the phrase is. There were occasional anecdotes of "bustings-up" on the southern rivers, "making tracks" from importunate creditors, of practical jokes, and glaring impositions. There was a great deal of "liquoring-up" going on the whole time. The best story-teller was repeatedly called upon to "liquor some," which was accordingly done by copious draughts of "gin-sling," but at last he declared he was a "gone 'coon, fairly stumped," by which he meant to express that he was tired and could do no more. This assertion was met by encouragements to "pile on," upon which the individual declared that he "couldn't get his steam up, he was tired some." This word *some* is synonymous in its use with our word *rather*, or its Yankee equivalent "*kinder*." On this occasion someone applied it to the boat, which he declared was "almighty dirty, and shaky some"—a great libel, by the way. The dress of these individuals somewhat amused me. The prevailing costumes of the gentlemen were straw hats, black dress coats remarkably shiny, tight pantaloons, and pumps. These were worn by the sallow narrators of the tales of successful roguery. There were a very few hardy western men, habited in scarlet flannel shirts, and trowsers tucked into high boots, their garments supported by stout leathern belts, with dependent bowie-knives; these told "yarns" of adventures, and dangers from Indians, something in the style of Colonel Crockett.

The ladies wore their satin or kid shoes of various colours, of which the mud had made woeful havoc. The stories, which called forth the applause of the company in exact proportion to the barefaced roguery and utter want of principle displayed in each, would not have been worth listening to, had it not been from the extraordinary vernacular in which they were clothed, and the racy and emphatic manner of the narrators. Some of these voted three legs of their chairs superfluous, and balanced themselves on the fourth; while others hooked their feet on the top of the windows, and balanced themselves on the back legs of their chairs, in a position strongly suggestive of hanging by the heels. One of the stories which excited the most amusement reads very tamely divested of the slang and manner of the story-teller.

A "'cute chap down east" had a "2.50" black mare (one which could perform a mile in two minutes fifty seconds), and, being about to "make tracks," he sold her to a gentleman for 350 dollars. In the night he stole her, cut her tail, painted her legs white, gave her a "blaze" on her face, sold her for 100 dollars, and decamped, sending a note to the first purchaser acquainting him with the particulars of the transaction. "'Cute chap that;" "A wide-awake feller;" "That coon had cut his eye-teeth;" "A smart sell that;" were the comments made on this roguish transaction, all the sympathy of the listeners being on the side of the rogue.

The stories related by Barnum of the tricks and impositions practised by himself and others are a fair sample, so far as roguery goes, of those which are to be heard in hotels, steamboats, and cars. I have heard men openly boast, before a miscellaneous company, of acts of dishonesty which in

England would have procured transportation for them. Mammon is the idol which the people worship; the one desire is the acquisition of money; the most nefarious trickery and bold dishonesty are invested with a spurious dignity if they act as aids to the attainment of this object. Children from their earliest years imbibe the idea that sin is sin—*only when found out.*

The breakfast bell rang, and a general rush took place, and I was left alone with two young ladies who had just become acquainted, and were resolutely bent upon finding out each other's likes and dislikes, with the intention of vowing an eternal friendship. A gentleman who looked as if he had come out of a ball-room came up, and with a profusion of bows addressed them, or the prettiest of them, thus:—"Miss, it's feeding time, I guess; what will you eat?" "You're very po-lite; what's the ticket?" "Chicken and corn-fixings, and pork with onion-fixings." "Well, I'm hungry some; I'll have some pig and fixings." The swain retired, and brought a profusion of viands, which elicited the remark, "Well, I guess that's substantial, anyhow." The young ladies' appetites seemed to be very good, for I heard the observation, "Well, you eat considerable; you're in full blast, I guess." "Guess I am: it's all-fired cold, and I have been an everlastin long time off my feed." A long undertoned conversation followed this interchange of civilities, when I heard the lady say in rather elevated tones, "You're trying to rile me some; you're piling it on a trifle too high." "Well, I did want to put up your dander. Do tell now, where was you raised?" "In Kentucky." "I could have guessed that; whenever I sees a splenderiferous gal, a kinder gentle goer, and high stepper, I says to myself, That gal's from old Kentuck, and no mistake."

This couple carried on a long conversation in the same style of graceful badinage; but I have given enough of it.

Lake Champlain is extremely pretty, though it is on rather too large a scale to please an English eye, being about 150 miles long. The shores are gentle slopes, wooded and cultivated, with

265

the Green Mountains of Vermont in the background. There was not a ripple on the water, and the morning was so warm and showery, that I could have believed it to be an April day had not the leafless trees told another tale. Whatever the boasted beauties of Lake Champlain were, they veiled themselves from English eyes in a thick fog, through which we steamed at half-speed, with a dismal fog-bell incessantly tolling.

I landed at Burlington, a thriving modern town, prettily situated below some wooded hills, on a bay, the margin of which is pure white sand. Here, as at nearly every town, great and small, in the United States, there was an excellent hotel. No people have such confidence in the future as the Americans. You frequently find a splendid hotel surrounded by a few clapboard houses, and may feel inclined to smile at the incongruity. The builder looks into futurity, and sees that in two years a thriving city will need hotel accommodation; and seldom is he wrong. The American is a gregarious animal, and it is not impossible that an hotel, with a *table-d'hôte*, may act as a magnet. Here I joined Mr. and Mrs. Alderson, and travelled with them to Albany, through Vermont and New York. The country was hilly, and more suited for sheep-farming than for corn. Water-privileges were abundant in the shape of picturesque torrents, and numerous mills turned their capabilities to profitable account. Our companions were rather of a low description, many of them Germans, and desperate tobacco-chewers. The whole floor of the car was covered with streams of tobacco-juice, apple-cores, grape-skins, and chestnut-husks.

We crossed the Hudson River, and spent the night at Delaval's, at Albany. The great peculiarity of this most comfortable hotel is, that the fifty waiters are Irish girls, neatly and simply dressed. They are under a coloured manager, and their civility and alacrity made me wonder that the highly-paid services of male waiters were not more frequently dispensed with. The railway ran along the street in which the hotel is situated. From my bedroom window I looked down into the funnel of a locomotive, and all night long was serenaded with screams, ringing of bells, and cries of "All aboard" and "Go ahead."

Albany, the capital of the State of New York, is one of the prettiest towns in the Union. The slope on which it is built faces the Hudson, and is crowned by a large state-house, the place of meeting for the legislature of the Empire State. The Americans repudiate the "centralization" principle, and for wise reasons, of which the Irish form a considerable number, they almost invariably locate the government of each state, not at the most important or populous town, but at some inconsiderable place, where the learned legislators are not in danger of having their embarrassments increased by deliberating under the coercion of a turbulent urban population. Albany has several public buildings, and a number of conspicuous churches, and is a very thriving place. The traffic on the river between it and New York is enormous. There is a perpetual stream of small vessels up and down. The Empire City receives its daily supplies of vegetables, meat, butter, and eggs from its neighbourhood. The Erie and Champlain canals here meet the Hudson, and through the former the produce of the teeming West pours to the Atlantic. The traffic is carried on in small sailing sloops and steamers. Sometimes a little screw-vessel of fifteen or twenty tons may be seen to hurry, puffing and panting, up to a large vessel and drag it down to the sea; but generally one paddle-tug takes six vessels down, four being towed behind and one or two lashed on either side. As both steamers and sloops are painted white, and the sails are perfectly dazzling in their purity, and twenty, thirty, and forty of these flotillas may be seen in the course of a morning, the Hudson river presents a very animated and unique appearance. It is said that everybody loses a portmanteau at Albany: I was more fortunate, and left it without having experienced the slightest annoyance.

On the other side of the ferry a very undignified scramble takes place for the seats on the right side of the cars, as the scenery for 130 miles is perfectly magnificent. "Go ahead" rapidly succeeded "All aboard," and we whizzed along this most extraordinary line of railway, so prolific in accidents that, when people leave New York by it, their friends frequently request them to notify their safe arrival at their destination. It runs along the very verge of the river, below a steep cliff, but often is supported just above the surface of the water upon a wooden platform. Guide-books inform us that the trains which run on this line, and the steamers which ply on the Hudson, are equally unsafe, the former from collisions and "upsets," the latter from "bustings-up;" but most people prefer the boats, from the advantage of seeing both sides of the river.

The sun of a November morning had just risen as I left Albany, and in a short time beamed upon swelling hills, green savannahs, and waving woods fringing the margin of the Hudson. At Coxsackie the river expands into a small lake, and the majestic Catsgill Mountains rise abruptly from the western side. The scenery among these mountains is very grand and varied. Its silence and rugged sublimity recall the Old World: it has rocky pinnacles and desert passes, inaccessible eminences and yawning chasms. The world might grow populous at the feet of the Catsgills, but it would leave them untouched and unprofaned in their stern majesty. From this point for a hundred miles the eyes of the traveller are perfectly steeped in beauty, which, gathering and increasing, culminates at West Point, a lofty eminence jutting upon a lake apparently without any outlet. The spurs of mountain ranges which meet here project in precipices from five to fifteen hundred feet in height; trees find a place for their roots in every rift among the rocks; festoons of clematis and wild-vine hang in graceful drapery from base to summit, and the dark mountain shadows loom over the lake-like expanse below. The hand wearies of writing of the loveliness of this river. I saw it on a perfect day. The Indian summer lingered, as though unwilling that the chilly blasts of winter should blight the loveliness of this beauteous scene. The gloom of autumn was not there, but its glories were on every leaf and twig. The bright scarlet of the maple vied with the brilliant berries of the rowan, and from among the tendrils of the creepers, which were waving in the sighs of the west wind, peeped forth the deep crimson of the sumach. There were very few signs of cultivation; the banks of the Hudson are barren in all but beauty. The river is a succession of small wild lakes, connected by narrow reaches, bound for ever between abrupt precipices. There are lakes more beauteous than Loch Katrine, softer in their features than Loch Achray, though like both, or like the waters which glitter beneath the blue sky of Italy. Along their margins the woods hung in scarlet and gold—high above towered the purple peaks—the blue waters flashed back the rays of a sun shining from an unclouded sky—the air was warm like June—and I think the sunbeams of that day scarcely shone upon a fairer scene. At midday the Highlands of Hudson were left behind—the mountains melted into hills—the river expanded into a noble stream about a mile in width—the scarlet woods, the silvery lakes, and the majestic Catsgills faded away in the distance; and with a whoop, and a roar, and a clatter, the cars entered into, and proceeded at slackened speed down, a long street called Tenth Avenue, among carts, children, and pigs.

True enough, we were in New York, the western receptacle not only of the traveller and the energetic merchant, but of the destitute, the friendless, the vagabond, and in short of all the outpourings of Europe, who here form a conglomerate mass of evil, making America responsible for their vices and their crimes. Yet the usual signs of approach to an enormous city were awanting—dwarfed trees, market-gardens, cockney arbours, in which citizens smoke their pipes in the evening, and imagine themselves in Arcadia, rows of small houses, and a murky canopy of smoke. We had steamed down Tenth Avenue for two or three miles, when we came to a standstill where several streets met. The train was taken to pieces, and to each car four horses or mules were attached, which took us for some distance into the very heart of the town, racing

269

apparently with omnibuses and carriages, till at last we were deposited in Chambers Street, not in a station, or even under cover, be it observed. My baggage, or "plunder" as it is termed, had been previously disposed of, but, while waiting with my head disagreeably near to a horse's nose, I saw people making distracted attempts, and futile ones as it appeared, to preserve their effects from the clutches of numerous porters, many of them probably thieves. To judge from appearances, many people would mourn the loss of their portmanteaus that night.

New York deserves the name applied to Washington, "the city of magnificent distances." I drove in a hack for three miles to my destination, along crowded, handsome streets, but I believe that I only traversed a third part of the city.

It possesses the features of many different lands, but it has characteristics peculiarly its own; and as with its suburbs it may almost bear the name of the "million-peopled city," and as its growing influence and importance have earned it the name of the Empire City, I need not apologise for dwelling at some length upon it in the succeeding chapter.

CHAPTER XVI

*Position of New York—Externals of the city—Conveyances—
Maladministration—The stores—The hotels—Curiosities of the
hospital—Ragged schools—The bad book—Monster schools—
Amusements and oyster saloons—Monstrosities—A restaurant—
Dwelling-houses—Equipages—Palaces—Dress—Figures—
Manners—Education—Domestic habits—The ladies—The
gentlemen—Society—Receptions—Anti-English feeling—
Autographs—The "Buckram Englishman."*

New York, from its position, population, influence, and
commerce, is worthy to be considered the metropolis of the
New World. The situation of it is very advantageous. It is built
upon Manhattan Island, which is about thirteen miles in length
by two in breadth. It has the narrowest portion of Long Island
Sound, called East River, on its east side; the Hudson, called the
North River, environs it in another direction; while these two
are connected by a narrow strait, principally artificial,
denominated the Haarlem River. This insular position of the
city is by no means intelligible to the stranger, but it is obvious
from the top of any elevated building. The dense part of New
York already covers a large portion of the island; and as it *daily*
extends northward, the whole extent of insulated ground is
divided into lots, and mapped out into streets.

But, not content with covering the island, which, when
Hendrick Hudson first discovered it, abounded with red men,
who fished along its banks and guided their bark canoes over
the surrounding waters, New York, under the names of
Brooklyn, Williamsburgh, and four or five others, has spread
itself on Long Island, Staten Island, and the banks of the
Hudson. Brooklyn, on Long Island, which occupies the same
position with regard to New York that Lambeth and Southwark
do to London, contains a population of 100,000 souls.
Brooklyn, Williamsburgh, Hoboken, and Jersey City are the
residences of a very large portion of the merchants of New

York, who have deserted the old or Dutch part of the town, which is consequently merely an aggregate of offices. Floating platforms, moved by steam, with space in the middle part for twelve or fourteen carriages and horses, and luxurious covered apartments, heated with steam-pipes on either side, ply to and fro every five minutes at the small charge of one halfpenny a passenger, and the time occupied in crossing the ferries is often less than that of the detention on Westminster Bridge. Besides these large places, Staten Island and Long Island are covered with villa residences. Including these towns, which are in reality part of this vast city, New York contains a population of very nearly a million! Broadway, which is one of the most remarkable streets in the world, being at once the Corso, Toledo, Regent Street, and Princes Street of New York, runs along the centre of the city, and is crossed at right angles by innumerable streets, which run down to the water at each side. It would appear as if the inventive genius of the people had been exhausted, for, after borrowing designations for their streets from every part of the world, among which some of the old Dutch names figure most refreshingly, they have adopted the novel plan of numbering them. Thus there are ten "Avenues," which run from north to south, and these are crossed by streets numbered First Street, Second Street, and so on. I believe that the skeletons of one hundred and fifty numbered streets are in existence. The southern part of the town still contains a few of the old Dutch houses, and there are some substantial red-brick villas in the vicinity, inhabited by the descendants of the old Dutch families, who are remarkably exclusive in their habits.

New York is decidedly a very handsome city. The wooden houses have nearly all disappeared, together with those of an antiquated or incongruous appearance; and the new streets are very regularly and substantially built of brown stone or dark brick. The brick building in New York is remarkably beautiful. The windows are large, and of plate-glass, and the whole external finish of the houses is in a splendid but chaste style, never to be met with in street-architecture in England. As the houses in the city are almost universally heated by air warmed by a subterranean stove, very few chimneys are required, and these are seldom visible above the stone parapets which conceal the roofs. Anthracite coal is almost universally used, so there is an absence of that murky, yellow canopy which disfigures English towns. The atmosphere is remarkably dry, so that even white marble edifices, of which there are several in the town, suffer but little from the effects of climate.

Broadway is well paved, and many of the numbered streets are not to be complained of in this respect, but a great part of the city is indescribably dirty, though it is stated that the expense of cleaning it exceeds 250,000 dollars per annum. Its immense length necessitates an enormous number of conveyances; and in order to obviate the obstruction to traffic which would have been caused by providing omnibus accommodation equal to the demand, the authorities have consented to a most alarming inroad upon several of the principal streets. The stranger sees with surprise that double lines of rails are laid along the roadways; and while driving quietly in a carriage, he hears the sound of a warning bell, and presently a railway-car, holding thirty persons, and drawn by two or four horses, comes thundering down the street. These rail-cars run every few minutes, and the fares are very low. For very sufficient reasons, Broadway is not thus encroached upon; and a journey from one end to the other of this marvellous street is a work of time and difficulty. Pack the traffic of the Strand and Cheapside into Oxford Street, and still you will not have an idea of the crush in Broadway. There are streams of scarlet and yellow omnibuses racing in the more open parts, and locking each other's wheels in the narrower—there are helpless females deposited in the middle of a sea of slippery mud, condemned to run a gauntlet between cart-wheels and horses' hoofs—there are loaded stages hastening to and from the huge hotels—carts and waggons laden with merchandise—and "Young Americans" driving fast-trotting

273

horses, edging in and out among the crowd—wheels are locked, horses tumble down, and persons pressed for time are distracted. Occasionally, the whole traffic of the street comes to a dead-lock, in consequence of some obstruction or crowd, there being no policeman at hand with his incessant command, "*Move on!*"

The hackney-carriages of New York are very handsome, and, being drawn by two horses, have the appearance of private equipages; but woe to the stranger who trusts to the inviting announcement that the fare is a dollar within a certain circle. Bad as London cabmen are, one would welcome the sight of one of them. The New York hackmen are licensed plunderers, against whose extortions there is neither remedy nor appeal. They are generally Irish, and cheat people with unblushing audacity. The omnibus or stage accommodation is plentiful and excellent. A person soon becomes accustomed to, and enjoys, the occasional excitement of locked wheels or a race, and these vehicles are roomy and clean. They are sixteen inches wider than our own omnibuses, and carry a number of passengers certainly within their capabilities, and the fares are fixed and very low, $6\frac{1}{2}$ cents for any distance. They have windows to the sides and front, and the spaces between are painted with very tolerably-executed landscapes. There is no conductor; the driver opens and closes the door with a strap, and the money is handed to him through a little hole in the roof. The lady passengers invariably give the money to a gentleman for this purpose, and no rule of etiquette is more rigidly enforced than for him to obey the request to do so, generally consisting in a haughty wave of the hand. The thousand acts of attention which gentlemen, by rigid usage, are compelled to tender to ladies, are received by them without the slightest acknowledgment, either by word or gesture. To so great an extent is this *nonchalance* carried on the part of the females, that two or three newspapers have seriously taken up the subject, and advise the gentlemen to withdraw from the performance of such unrequited attentions.

Strangers frequently doubt whether New York possesses a police; the doubt is very justifiable, for these guardians of the public peace are seldom forthcoming when they are wanted. They are accessible to bribes, and will investigate into crime when liberally rewarded; but probably in no city in the civilised world is life so fearfully insecure. The practice of carrying concealed arms, in the shape of stilettoes for attack, and swordsticks for defence, if illegal, is perfectly common; desperate reprobates, called "Rowdies," infest the lower part of the town; and terrible outrages and murderous assaults are matters of such nightly occurrence as to be thought hardly worthy of notice, even in those prints which minister to man's depraved taste for the horrible.[1]

No language can be too strongly expressive of censure upon the disgraceful condition of New York. The evil may be distinctly traced to the wretched system of politics which prevails at the election of the municipal officers, who are often literally chosen from the lowest of the people, and are venal and corrupt in the highest degree. During my visit to New York a candidate for one of these offices stabbed a policeman, who died of the wound. If I might judge from the tone of the public prints, and from conversations on the subject, public feeling was not much outraged by the act itself, but it was a convenient stalking-horse for the other side, and the policeman's funeral procession, which went down Broadway, was nearly a mile in length.

The principal stores are situated in Broadway; and although they attempt very little in the way of window display, the interiors are spacious, and arranged with the greatest taste. An American store is generally a very extensive apartment,

1 The state of New York has improved. Mr. Fernando Wood, who was elected Mayor in November, 1854, has issued stringent regulations for the maintenance of order. A better police-force has been organised, and many of the notorious "Rowdies" and other bad characters have been shut up on Blackwell's Island. His tenure of office has just expired, and it is much to be feared that the mob, which exercises an undue influence upon the municipal elections, has not chosen a successor who will interfere with its privileges.

handsomely decorated, the roof frequently supported on marble pillars. The owner or clerk is seen seated by his goods, absorbed in the morning paper—probably balancing himself on one leg of his chair, with a spittoon by his side. He deigns to answer your inquiries, but, in place of the pertinacious perseverance with which an English shopman displays his wares, it seems a matter of perfect indifference to the American whether you purchase or no. The drapers' and mercers' shops, which go by the name of "dry goods" stores, are filled with the costliest productions of the world. The silks from the looms of France are to be seen side by side with the productions of Persia and India, and all at an advance of fully two-thirds on English prices. The "fancy goods" stores are among the most attractive lounges of the city. Here Paris figures to such an extent, that it was said at the time when difficulties with France were apprehended, in consequence of the Soulé affair, that "Louis Napoleon might as well fire cannon-balls into the Palais Royal as declare war with America." Some of the bronzes in these stores are of exquisite workmanship, and costly china from Sèvres and Dresden feasts the eyes of the lovers of beauty in this branch of art.

The American ladies wear very costly jewellery, but I was perfectly amazed at the prices of some of the articles displayed. I saw a diamond bracelet containing one brilliant of prodigious size and lustre. The price was 25,000 dollars, or £5000 On inquiring who would purchase such a thing, the clerk replied, "I guess some southerner will buy it for his wife."

One of the sights with which the New York people astonish English visitors is Stewart's dry-goods store in Broadway, an immense square building of white marble, six stories high, with a frontage of 300 feet. The business done in it is stated to be above £1,500,000 per annum. There are 400 people employed at this establishment, which has even a telegraph office on the premises, where a clerk is for ever flashing dollars and cents along the trembling wires. There were lace collars 40 guineas each, and flounces of Valenciennes lace, half a yard deep, at 120 guineas a flounce. The damasks and brocades for curtains and chairs were at almost fabulous prices. Few gentlemen, the clerk observed, give less than £3 per yard for these articles. The most costly are purchased by the hotels. I saw some brocade embroidered in gold to the thickness of half an inch, some of which had been supplied to the St. Nicholas Hotel at £9 per yard! There were stockings from a penny to a guinea a pair, and carpetings from 1s. 8d. to 22s. a yard. Besides six stories above ground, there were large light rooms under the building, and under Broadway itself, echoing with the roll of its 10,000 vehicles.

The hotels are among the sights of New York. The principal are the Astor House (which has a world-wide reputation), the Metropolitan, and the St. Nicholas, all in Broadway. Prescott House and Irving House also afford accommodation on a very large scale. The entrances to these hotels invariably attract the eye of the stranger. Groups of extraordinary-looking human beings are always lounging on the door-steps, smoking, whittling, and reading newspapers. There are southerners sighing for their sunny homes, smoking Havana cigars; western men, with that dashing free-and-easy air which renders them unmistakable; Englishmen, shrouded in exclusiveness, who look on all their neighbours as so many barbarian intruders on their privacy; and people of all nations, whom business has drawn to the American metropolis.

The Metropolitan Hotel is the most imposing in appearance. It is a block of building with a frontage of 300 feet, and is six stories high. I believe that it can accommodate 1300 people. The St. Nicholas is the most superb in its decorations; it is a magnificent building of white marble, and can accommodate 1000 visitors. Everything in this edifice is on a style of princely magnificence. The grand entrance opens into a very fine hall with a marble floor, and this is surrounded with settees covered with the skins of wild animals. The parlours are gorgeous in the extreme, and there are two superb dining-rooms to contain 600 people each. The curtains and sofa-

277

covers in some of the parlours cost £5 per yard, and, as has been previously named, one room is furnished with gold brocade purchased at £9 per yard. About 100 married couples reside permanently at the St. Nicholas; it does not, however, bear the very best reputation, as it is said to be the resort of a large number of professed gamblers. Large as these hotels are, they are nothing to a monster establishment at Cape May, a fashionable summer resort in New Jersey. The capacities of this building, the Mount Vernon Hotel, though stated on the best authority, can scarcely be credited—it is said to make up 3000 beds!

Owing to the high rates of house-rent and the difficulty of procuring servants, together with the exorbitant wages which they require, many married couples, and even families, reside permanently at the hotels. Living constantly in public, without opportunity for holding family intercourse, and being without either home cares or home pleasures, nomade, restless, pleasure-seeking habits are induced, which have led strangers to charge the Americans with being destitute of home life. That such is the case to some extent is not to be denied; but this want is by no means generally observed. I have met with family circles in the New World as united and affectionate as those in the Old, not only in country districts, but in the metropolis itself; and in New England there is probably as much of what may be termed patriarchal life as anywhere in Europe.

The public charities of New York are on a gigantic scale. The New York Hospital, a fine stone building with some large trees in front, situated in Broadway, was one which pleased me as much as any. Two of the physicians kindly took me over the whole building, and explained all the arrangements. I believe that the hospital contains 650 beds, and it is generally full, being not only the receptacle for the numerous accident cases which are of daily occurrence in New York, but for those of a large district besides, which are conveniently brought in by railroad. We first went into the recent-accident room, where the unhappy beings who were recently hurt or operated upon were lying. Some of them were the most piteous objects I ever witnessed, and the medical men, under the impression that I was deeply interested in surgery, took pains to exhibit all the horrors. There were a good many of the usual classes of accidents,—broken limbs and mangled frames. There was one poor little boy of twelve years old, whose arms had been torn to pieces by machinery; one of them had been amputated on the previous day, and, while the medical men displayed the stump, they remarked that the other must be taken off on the next day. The poor boy groaned with a more than childish expression of agony on his pale features, probably at the thought of the life of helplessness before him. A young Irishman had been crushed by a railway car, and one of his legs had been amputated a few hours previously. As the surgeon altered the bandages he was laughing and joking, and had been singing ever since the operation—a remarkable instance of Paddy's unfailing lightheartedness.

But, besides these ordinary accidents, there were some very characteristic of New York and of a New York election. In one ward there were several men who had been stabbed the night before, two of whom were mortally wounded. There were two men, scarcely retaining the appearance of human beings, who had been fearfully burned and injured by the explosion of an infernal machine. All trace of human features had departed; it seemed hardly credible that such blackened, distorted, and mangled frames could contain human souls. There were others who had received musket-shot wounds during the election, and numbers of broken heads, and wounds from knives. It was sad to know that so much of the suffering to be seen in that hospital was the result of furious religious animosities, and of the unrestrained lawlessness of human violence.

There was one man who had been so nearly crushed to pieces, that it seemed marvellous that the mangled frame could still retain its vitality. One leg was broken in three places, and the flesh torn off from the knee to the foot; both arms and several ribs were also broken. We went into one of the female wards, where sixteen broken legs were being successfully treated, and I could not but admire a very simple contrivance which remedies the contraction which often succeeds broken limbs, and produces permanent lameness. Two long straps of plaister were glued from above the knee to the ankle, and were then fixed to a wooden bar, with a screw and handle, so that the tension could be regulated at pleasure. The medical men, in remarking upon this, observed that in England we were very slow to adopt any American improvements in surgery or medicine.

There were many things in this hospital which might be imitated in England with great advantage to the patients. Each ward was clean, sweet, and airy; and the system of heating and ventilation is very superior. The heating and ventilating apparatus, instead of sending forth alternate blasts of hot and cold air, keeps up a uniform and easily regulated temperature. A draught of cold air is continually forced through a large apparatus of steam-pipes, and, as it becomes vitiated in the rooms above, passes out through ventilators placed just below the ceiling. Our next visit was to the laundry, where two men, three women, and, last but not least, a steam-engine of 45-horse power, were perpetually engaged in washing the soiled linen of the hospital. The large and rapidly-moving cylinder which churns the linen is a common part of a steam laundry, but the wringing machine is one of the most beautiful practical applications of a principle in natural philosophy that I ever saw. It consists of a large perforated cylinder, open at the top, with a case in the centre. This cylinder performs from 400 to 700 revolutions in a minute, and, by the power of the centrifugal force thus produced, the linen is impelled so violently against the sides, that the moisture is forced through the perforations, when the linen is left nearly dry.

Strange as it may appear to those who associate America with plenty and comfort, there is a very large class of persons as New York living in a state of squalid and abject poverty; and in order that the children belonging to it may receive some education, it has been found necessary by the benevolent to supplement the common school system with ragged or industrial schools. In order not to wound the pride of parents who are not too proud to receive a gratuitous education for their offspring, these establishments are not called Ragged Schools, but "Boys' Meetings," and "Girls' Meetings." I visited two of these, the first in Tompkin Square. There were about 100 children in the school, and nearly all of them were Irish Roman Catholics. They receive a good elementary education, and answered the questions addressed to them with correctness and alacrity. The Bible, of course, is not read, but the pupils learn a Scripture catechism, and paraphrased versions of Scripture incidents. One day, during the absence of the teacher, one of the pupils was looking into an English Bible, and another addressed her with the words, "You wicked girl, you know the priest says that you are never to open that bad book; I will never walk with you again." The child, on going home, told her mother, and she said that she did not think it could be such a bad book, as the ladies who were so kind to them read it. The child said that it was a beautiful book, and persuaded her mother to borrow a Bible from a neighbour; she read it, and became a Protestant. These children earn their clothing by a certain number of good marks, but most of them were shoeless. Each child is obliged to take a bath on the establishment once a-week. Their answers in geography and history were extremely good. In the afternoon the elder girls are employed in tailoring and dressmaking, and receive so much work that this branch of the school is self-supporting.

I visited another industrial school, in a very bad part of the town, adjoining the Bowery, where the parents are of the very worst description, and their offspring are vicious and unmanageable. I think that I never saw vice and crime so legibly stamped upon the countenances of children as upon those in this school. The teachers find it extremely difficult to preserve discipline at all; and the pilfering habits of the pupils are almost incorrigible. They each receive a pint of excellent soup and an unlimited quantity of bread for dinner; but they are discontented and unthankful.

The common school system will be enlarged upon in a succeeding chapter; but I cannot forbear noticing one school which I visited. It was a lofty, four-storied building of red brick, with considerable architectural pretensions. It was faced with brown stone, and had a very handsome entrance-hall and staircase. The people of New York vie with each other in their hospitality to strangers, and in showing them the objects of interest within their city in the very best manner; and it was under the auspices of Dr. Wells, one of the commissioners of education, that I saw this admirable school, or rather educational institution. On inquiring the reason of the extraordinary height of the balustrades, I was told that some weeks previously, as the boys were hurriedly leaving school, forty of them had been pushed over the staircase, out of which number nearly the whole were killed!

In the girls' room about 900 girls between the ages of eight and eighteen were assembled. They were the children of persons in every class in the city except the very wealthiest and the poorest. All these girls were well dressed, some of them tasteful, others fantastic, in their appearance. There was a great deal of beauty among the elder pupils; I only regretted that the bright bloom which many possessed should be so evanescent. The rich luxuriant hair, often of a beautiful auburn hue, was a peculiarity which could not be overlooked. There were about ten female teachers, the principal of whom played some lively airs upon the piano, during which time the pupils marched steadily in from various class-rooms, and took their seats at handsome mahogany desks, which accommodated two each. No expense had been spared in the fittings of the apartment; the commissioners of education are evidently of opinion that the young do not acquire knowledge the more speedily from being placed on comfortless benches, without any means of resting their weak and tired frames.

Each desk contained a drawer or cupboard; and to encourage those habits of order and self-reliance to which so much weight is attached in the States, each pupil is made responsible for the preservation and security of her books and all implements of education. The business of the day commenced by the whole number of girls reverently repeating the Lord's Prayer, which, in addressing God as "Our Father," proclaims the common bond of brotherhood which unites the whole human race. The sound of 900 youthful voices solemnly addressing their Creator was very beautiful and impressive. A chapter from the Bible, read aloud by the teacher, followed, and a hymn beautifully sung, when the pupils filed off as before to the sound of music. We next went to the elementary room, appropriated to infants, who are not sent to the higher school till their proficiency reaches the standard required.

The infant system does not appear to differ materially from ours, except that it is of a more intellectual nature. In this room 1300 children joined in singing a hymn. In the boys' rooms about 1000 boys were receiving instruction under about 12 specimens of "Young America." The restless, the almost fearful energy of the teachers surprised me, and the alacrity of the boys in answering questions. In the algebra-room questions involving the most difficult calculation on the part of the pupils were answered sometimes even before the teacher had worked them out himself.

Altogether, I was delighted with this school and with the earnestness displayed by both teachers and pupils. I was not so well pleased with the manners of the instructors, particularly in the boys' school. There was a boastfulness, an exaggeration, and a pedantry, which are by no means necessary accompaniments of superior attainments. The pupils have a disrespectful, familiar, and independent air, though I understood that the punishments are more severe than are generally approved of in English schools. The course of instruction is very complete. History is especially attended to, with its bearing upon modern politics. The teachers receive from £80 to £300 a year, and very high attainments are required. Besides the common and industrial schools, there are means of education provided for the juvenile portion of the very large foreign population of New York, principally German. There are several schools held under the basements of the churches, without any paid teachers. The ladies of New York, to their honour be it said, undertake, unassisted, the education of these children, a certain number being attached to every school. Each of these ladies takes some hours of a day, and youth and beauty may be seen perseveringly engaged in this arduous but useful task.

The spirit of practical benevolence which appears to permeate New York society is one of its most pleasing features. It is not only that the wealthy contribute large sums of money to charitable objects, but they personally superintend their right distribution. No class is left untouched by their benevolent efforts; wherever suffering and poverty are found, the hand of Christianity or philanthropy is stretched out to relieve them. The gulf which in most cities separates the rich from the poor has been to some extent lessened in New York; for numbers of ladies and gentlemen of education and affluence visit among the poor and vicious, seeking to raise them to a better position.

If there are schools, emigrant hospitals, orphan asylums, and nursing institutions, to mark the good sense and philanthropy of the people of New York, so their love of amusement and recreation is strongly evidenced by the numerous places where both may be procured. There is perhaps as much pleasure-seeking as in Paris; the search after amusement is characterised by the same restless energy which marks the pursuit after wealth; and if the Americans have little time for enjoying themselves, they are resolved that the opportunities for doing so shall be neither distant nor few. Thus, Broadway and its neighbourhood contain more places of amusement than perhaps any district of equal size in the world. These present variety sufficient to embrace the tastes of the very heterogeneous population of New York.

There are three large theatres; an opera-house of gigantic proportions, which is annually graced by the highest vocal talent of Europe; Wood's minstrels, and Christy's minstrels, where blacks perform in unexceptionable style to unwearied audiences; and comic operas. There are *al fresco* entertainments, masquerades, concerts, restaurants, and oyster saloons. Besides all these, and many more, New York contained in 1853 the amazing number of 5980 taverns. The number of places where amusement is combined with intellectual improvement is small, when compared with other cities of the same population. There are however some very magnificent reading-rooms and libraries.

The amount of oysters eaten in New York surprised me, although there was an idea at the time of my visit that they produced the cholera, which rather checked any extraordinary excesses in this curious fish. In the business streets of New York the eyes are greeted continually with the words "Oyster Saloon," painted in large letters on the basement story. If the stranger's curiosity is sufficient to induce him to dive down a flight of steps into a subterranean abode, at the first glance rather suggestive of robbery, one favourite amusement of the people may be seen in perfection. There is a counter at one side, where two or three persons, frequently blacks, are busily engaged in opening oysters for their customers, who swallow them with astonishing relish and rapidity. In a room beyond, brightly lighted by gas, family groups are to be seen, seated at round tables, and larger parties of friends, enjoying basins of stewed oysters; while from some mysterious recess the process of cookery makes itself distinctly audible. Some of these saloons are highly respectable, while many are just the reverse. But the consumption of oysters is by no means confined to the saloons; in private families an oyster supper is frequently a nightly occurrence; the oysters are dressed in the parlour by an ingenious and not inelegant apparatus. So great is the passion for this luxury, that the consumption of it during the season is estimated at £3500 a day.

There are several restaurants in the city, on the model of those in the Palais Royal. The most superb of these, *but not by any means the most respectable*, is Taylor's, in Broadway. It combines Eastern magnificence with Parisian taste, and strangers are always expected to visit it. It is a room about 100 ft. in length, by 22 in height; the roof and cornices richly carved and gilded, the walls ornamented by superb mirrors, separated by white marble. The floor is of marble, and a row of fluted and polished marble pillars runs down each side. It is a perfect blaze of decoration. There is an alcove at one end of the apartment, filled with orange-trees, and the air is kept refreshingly cool by a crystal fountain. Any meal can be obtained here at any hour. On the day on which I visited it, the one hundred marble tables which it contains were nearly all occupied; a double row of equipages lined the street at the door; and two or three hundred people, many of them without bonnets and fantastically dressed, were regaling themselves upon ices and other elegances in an atmosphere redolent with the perfume of orange-flowers, and musical with the sound of trickling water, and the melody of musical snuff-boxes. There was a complete maze of fresco, mirrors, carving, gilding, and marble. A dinner can be procured here at any hour of day or night, from one shilling and sixpence up to half-a-guinea, and other meals in like proportion. As we merely went to see the restaurant, we ordered ices, which were served from large reservoirs, shining like polished silver. These were paid for at the time, and we received tickets in return, which were taken by the doorkeeper on coming out. It might be supposed that Republican simplicity would scorn so much external display; but the places of public entertainment vie in their splendour with the palaces of kings.

It was almost impossible for a stranger to leave New York without visiting the American museum, the property of *Phineas Taylor Barnum*. The history of this very remarkable man is now well known, even in England, where the publication of his 'Autobiography' has been a nine days' wonder. It is said that 60,000 copies were sold at New York in one day, so successful has he been in keeping himself for ever before the public eye. It is painful to see how far a man whose life has been spent in total disregard of the principles of truth and integrity should have earned for himself popularity and fame. His museum is situated in Broadway, near to the City Hall, and is a gaudy building, denoted by huge paintings, multitudes of flags, and a very noisy band. The museum contains many objects of real interest, particularly to the naturalist and geologist, intermingled with a great deal that is spurious and contemptible. But this museum is by no means the attraction to this "Palace of Humbug." There is a collection of horrors or monstrosities attached, which appears to fascinate the vulgar gaze. The principal objects of attraction at this time were, a dog with two legs, a cow with four horns, and a calf with six legs—disgusting specimens of deformity, which ought to have been destroyed, rather than preserved to gratify a morbid taste for the horrible and erratic in nature. But while persons of the highest station and education in England patronised an artful and miserable dwarf, cleverly exhibited by a showman totally destitute of principle, it is not surprising that the American people should delight in yet more hideous exhibitions, under the same auspices.

The magnificence of the private dwellings of New York must not escape mention, though I am compelled to withhold many details that would be interesting, from a fear of "violating the rights of hospitality." The squares, and many of the numbered streets, contain very superb houses of a most pleasing uniformity of style. They are built either of brown stone, or of dark red brick, durably pointed, and faced with stone. This style of brick masonry is extremely tasteful and beautiful. Every house has an entrance-porch with windows of stained glass, and double doors; the outer one being only closed at night. The upper part of the inner door is made of stained glass; the door-handles and bell-pulls are made of highly-polished electro-plate; and a handsome flight of stone steps, with elegant bronze balustrades, leads up to the porch. The entrance-halls are seldom large, but the staircases, which are of stone, are invariably very handsome. These houses are six stories high, and usually contain three reception-rooms; a dining-room, small, and not striking in appearance in any way, as dinner-parties are seldom given in New York; a small, elegantly-furnished drawing-room, used as a family sitting-room, and for the reception of morning visitors; and a magnificent reception-room, furnished in the height of taste and elegance, for dancing, music, and evening parties.

In London the bedrooms are generally inconvenient and uncomfortable, being sacrificed to the reception-rooms; in New York this is not the case. The bedrooms are large, lofty, and airy; and are furnished with all the appurtenances which modern luxury has been able to devise. The profusion of marble gives a very handsome and chaste appearance to these apartments. There are bathrooms generally on three floors, and hot and cold water are laid on in every story. The houses are warmed by air heated from a furnace at the basement; and though in addition open fires are sometimes adopted, they are made of anthracite coal, which emits no smoke, and has rather the appearance of heated metal than of fuel. Ornamental articles of Parisian taste and Italian workmanship abound in these houses; and the mouldings, cornices, and woodwork, are all beautifully executed. The doorways and windows are very frequently of an arched form, which contributes to the tasteful appearance of the houses. Every species of gaudy decoration is strictly avoided; the paint is generally white, with gilt mouldings; and the lofty rooms are either painted in panels, or hung with paper of a very simple pattern.

The curtains and chair-covers are always of very rich damask, frequently worth from two to three guineas a yard; but the richness of this, and of the gold embroidery, is toned down by the dark hue of the walnut-wood furniture. The carpets of the reception-rooms are generally of rich Kidderminster, or velvet pile; an air of elegance and cleanliness pervades these superb dwellings; they look the height of comfort. It must be remembered that the foregoing is not a description of a dwelling here and there, but of fifty or sixty streets, or of 4000 or 5000 houses, those inhabited by merchants of average incomes, storekeepers not of the wealthiest class, and lawyers. The number of servants kept in such mansions as these would sound disproportionately small to an English ear. Two or three female servants only are required. Breakfast is very early, frequently at seven, seldom later than eight. The families of merchants in business in the lower part of the city often dine at one, and the gentlemen return to a combination of dinner with tea at six. It does not appear that at home luxury in eating is much studied. It is not customary, even among some of the wealthier inhabitants of New York, to indulge in sumptuous equipages "Hacks," with respectable-looking drivers and pairs of horses, fill the place of private carriages, and look equally well. Coachmen require high wages, and carriages are frequently injured by collision with omnibuses; these are among the reasons given for the very general use of hired vehicles.

The private equipages to be seen in New York, though roomy and comfortable, are not elegant. They are almost invariably closed, with glass sides and front, and are constructed with a view to keep out the intense heat of the summer sun. The coachmen are generally blacks, and the horses are stout animals, with cropped tails. The majority have broken knees, owing to the great slipperiness of the pavements.

Altogether, the occupants of stages are the most secure of the numerous travellers down Broadway. The driver, on his lofty box, has more control over his horses, and, in case of collision, the weight of his vehicle gives him an advantage; and there is a general inclination, on the part of the conductors of carriages, to give these swiftly-moving vehicles "ample room and verge enough." While threading the way through the intricate labyrinth of waggons, stages, falling horses, and locked wheels, it is highly unpleasant for the denizens of private carriages to find the end of a pole through the back of the equipage, or to be addressed by the coachman, "Massa, dat big waggon is pulling off my wheel."

Having given a brief description of the style of the ordinary dwellings of the affluent, I will just glance at those of the very wealthy, of which there are several in Fifth Avenue, and some of the squares, surpassing anything I had hitherto witnessed in royal or ducal palaces at home. The externals of some of these mansions in Fifth Avenue are like Apsley House, and Stafford House, St. James's; being substantially built of brown stone. At one house which I visited in —— Street, about the largest private residence in the city, and one which is considered to combine the greatest splendour with the greatest taste, we entered a spacious marble hall, leading to a circular stone staircase of great width, the balustrades being figures elaborately cast in bronze. Above this staircase was a lofty dome, decorated with paintings in fresco of eastern scenes. There were niches in the walls, some containing Italian statuary, and others small jets of water pouring over artificial moss.

There were six or eight magnificent reception-rooms, furnished in various styles—the Mediæval, the Elizabethan, the Italian, the Persian, the modern English, &c. There were fountains of fairy workmanship, pictures from the old masters, statues from Italy, "*chefs-d'œuvre*" of art; porcelain from China and Sèvres; damasks, cloth of gold, and *bijoux* from the East; Gobelin tapestry, tables of malachite and agate, and "knick-knacks" of every description. In the Mediæval and Elizabethan apartments, it did not appear to me that any anachronisms had been committed with respect to the furniture and decorations. The light was subdued by passing through windows of rich stained glass. I saw one table the value of which might be about 2000 guineas. The ground was black marble, with a wreath of flowers inlaid with very costly gems upon it. There were flowers or bunches of fruit, of turquoise, carbuncles, rubies, topazes, and emeralds, while the leaves were of malachite, carnelian, or agate. The effect produced by this lavish employment of wealth was not very good. The bedrooms were scarcely less magnificently furnished than the reception-rooms; with chairs formed of stag-horns, tables inlaid with agates, and hangings of Damascus cashmere, richly embossed with gold. There was nothing gaudy, profuse, or prominent in the decorations or furniture; everything had evidently been selected and arranged by a person of very refined taste. Among the very beautiful works of art was a collection of cameos, including some of Cellini's from the antique, which were really entrancing to look upon.

Another mansion, which N. P. Willis justly describes as "a fairy palace of taste and art," though not so extensive, was equally beautiful, and possessed a large winter-garden. This was approached by passing through a succession of very beautiful rooms, the walls of which were hung with paintings which would have delighted a *connoisseur*. It was a glass building with a high dome; a fine fountain was playing in the centre, and round its marble basin were orange, palm, and myrtle trees, with others from the tropics, some of them of considerable growth. Every part of the floor that was not of polished white marble was thickly carpeted with small green ferns. The *gleam* of white marble statues, from among the clumps of orange-trees and other shrubs, was particularly pretty; indeed, the whole had a fairy-like appearance about it. Such mansions as these were rather at variance with my ideas of republican simplicity; they contained apartments which would have thrown into the shade the finest rooms in Windsor Castle or Buckingham Palace. It is not the custom for Americans to leave large fortunes to their children; their wealth is spent in great measure in surrounding themselves with the beautiful and the elegant in their splendid mansions; and it is probable that the adornments which have been collected with so much expense and trouble will be dispersed at the death of their present possessors.

I have often been asked, "How do the American ladies dress? Have they nice figures? Do they wear much ornament? What are their manners like? Are they highly educated? Are they domestic?" I will answer these questions as far as I am capable of doing so.

In bygone times, the "good old times" of America perhaps, large patterns, brilliant colours, exaggerated fashions, and redundant ornament, were all adopted by the American ladies; and without just regard to the severity of their climate, they patronised thin dresses, and yet thinner shoes; both being, as has been since discovered, very prolific sources of ill health. Frequent intercourse with Europe, and the gradual progress of good taste, have altered this absurd style, and America, like England, is now content to submit to the dictation of Paris in all matters of fashion. But though Paris might dictate, it was found that American milliners had stubborn wills of their own, so Parisian *modistes* were imported along with Parisian silks, ribands, and gloves. No dressmaker is now considered orthodox who cannot show a prefix of *Madame*, and the rage for foreign materials and workmanship of every kind is as ludicrous as in England.

Although the deception practised is very blameable, there is some comfort in knowing that large numbers of the caps, bonnets, mantles, and other articles of dress, which are marked ostentatiously with the name of some *Rue* in Paris, have never incurred the risks of an Atlantic voyage. But however unworthy a devotion to fashion may be, it is very certain that the ladies of New York dress beautifully, and in very good taste. Although it is rather repugnant to one's feelings to behold costly silks and rich brocades sweeping the pavements of Broadway, with more effect than is produced by the dustmen, it is very certain that more beautiful *toilettes* are to be seen in this celebrated thoroughfare, in one afternoon, than in Hyde Park in a week. As it is impossible to display the productions of the millinery art in a close carriage in a crowd, Broadway is the fashionable promenade; and the lightest French bonnets, the handsomest mantles, and the richest flounced silk dresses, with *jupons*, ribands, and laces to correspond, are there to be seen in the afternoon. Evening attire is very much the same as in England, only that richer materials are worn by the young. The harmony of colours appears to be a subject studied to some purpose, and the style of dress is generally adapted to the height, complexion, and figure of the wearer.

The figures of the American ladies in youth are very sylph-like and elegant; and this appearance is obtained without the use of those artificial constraints so justly to be condemned. They are almost too slight for beauty, though this does not signify while they retain the luxuriant wavy hair, brilliant complexion, elastic step, and gracefulness of very early youth. But unfortunately a girl of twenty is too apt to look faded and haggard; and a woman who with us would be in her bloom at thirty, looks *passée*, wrinkled, and old. It is then that the sylph-like form assumes an unpleasant angularity, suggestive of weariness and care. It is remarkable, however, that ladies of recent English extraction, under exactly the same circum-stances, retain their good looks into middle life, and advancing years produce *embonpoint*, instead of angularity. I was very agreeably surprised with the beauty of the young ladies of New York; there is something peculiarly graceful and fascinating in their personal appearance.

To judge from the costly articles of jewellery displayed in the stores, I should have supposed that there was a great rage for ornament; but from the reply I once received from a jeweller, on asking him who would purchase a five-thousand-guinea diamond bracelet, "I guess some Southerner will buy it for his wife," I believe that most of these articles find their way to the South and West, where a less-cultivated taste may be supposed to prevail. I saw very little jewellery worn, and that was generally of a valuable but plain description. The young ladies appear to have adopted the maxim, "Beauty when unadorned is adorned the most." They study variety in ornament rather than profusion. "What are their manners like?" is a difficult question to answer. That there is a great difference between the manners of English and American ladies may be inferred from some remarks made to me by the most superior woman whom I met in America, and one who had been in English society in London. In naming a lady with whom she was acquainted, and one who could scarcely be expected to be deficient in affection towards herself, she said, "Her manners were perfectly ladylike, but she seemed to talk merely because conversation was a conventional requirement of society, and I cannot believe that she had any heart." She added, "I did not blame her for this; it was merely the result of an English education, which studiously banishes every appearance of interest or emotion. Emotion is condemned as romantic and vulgar sensibility, interest as enthusiasm."

The system which she reprehended is not followed at New York, and the result is, not that the ladies "wear their hearts on their sleeves for daws to peck at," but that they are unaffected, lively, and agreeable. The *repose* so studiously cultivated in England, and which is considered perfect when it has become listlessness, apathy, and indifference, finds no favour with our lively Transatlantic neighbours; consequently the ladies are very *naïve* and lively, and their manners have the vivacity without the frivolity of the French. They say themselves that they are not so highly educated as the ladies of England. Admirable as the common schools are, the seminaries for ladies, with one or two exceptions, are very inferior to ours, and the early age at which the young ladies go into society precludes them from completing a superior education; for it is scarcely to be expected that, when their minds are filled with the desire for conquest and the love of admiration, they will apply systematically to remedy their deficiencies. And again, some of their own sex in the States have so far stepped out of woman's proper sphere, that high attainments are rather avoided by many from the ridicule which has been attached to the unsuitable display of them in public. The young ladies are too apt to consider their education completed when they are emancipated from school restraints, while in fact only the basis of it has been laid. Music and drawing are not much cultivated in the higher branches; and though many speak the modern languages with fluency, natural philosophy and arithmetic, which strengthen the mental powers, are rather neglected. Yet who has ever missed the higher education which English ladies receive, while in the society of the lively, attractive ladies of New York? Of course there are exceptions, where active and superior minds become highly cultivated by their own persevering exertions; but the aids offered by ladies' schools are comparatively insignificant.

The ladies in the United States appeared to me to be extremely domestic. However fond they may be of admiration as girls, after their early marriages they become dutiful wives, and affectionate, devoted mothers. And in a country where there are few faithful attached servants, far more devolves upon the mother than English ladies have any idea of. Those amusements which would withdraw her from home must be abandoned; however fond she may be of travelling, she must abide in the nursery; and all those little attentions which in England are turned over to the nurse must be performed by herself, or under her superintending eye. She must be the nurse of her children alike by day and by night, in sickness and in health; and with the attention which American ladies pay to their husbands, their married life is by no means an idle one. Under these circumstances, the early fading of their bloom is not to be wondered at, and I cannot but admire the manner in which many of them cheerfully conform to years of anxiety and comparative seclusion, after the homage and gaiety which seemed their natural atmosphere in their early youth.

Of the gentlemen it is less easy to speak. They are immersed in a whirl of business, often of that speculative kind which demands a constant exercise of intense thought. The short period which they can spend in the bosom of their families must be an enjoyment and relaxation to them; therefore, in the absence of any statements to the contrary, it is but right to suppose that they are affectionate husbands and fathers. However actively the gentlemen of New York are engaged in business pursuits, they travel, read the papers, and often devote some time to general literature. They look rather more pale and careworn than the English, as the uncertainties of business are greater in a country where speculative transactions are carried to such an exaggerated extent. They also indulge in eccentricities of appearance in the shape of beards and imperials, not to speak of the "goatee" and moustaches of various forms. With these exceptions, there is nothing in appearance, manner, or phraseology to distinguish them from gentlemen in the best English society, except perhaps that they evince more interest and animation in their conversation.

The peculiar expressions which go under the name of Americanisms are never heard in good society, and those disagreeable habits connected with tobacco are equally unknown. I thought that the gentlemen were remarkably free from mannerisms of any kind. I have frequently heard Americans speak of the descriptions given by Dickens and Mrs. Trollope of the slang and disagreeable practices to be met with in the States; and they never, on a single occasion, denied their truthfulness, but said that these writers mistook the perpetrators of these vulgarities for *gentlemen*. The gentlemen are extremely deferential and attentive in their manners to ladies, and are hardly, I think, treated with sufficient graciousness in return. At New York a great many are actively engaged in philanthropic pursuits. The quiescence of manner attained by English gentlemen, which frequently approaches inanity, is seldom to be met with in America. The exhilarating influences of the climate and the excitement of business have a tendency to produce animation of manner, and force and earnestness of expression. A great difference in these respects is apparent in gentlemen from the southern States, who live in an enervating climate, and whose pursuits are of a more tranquil nature. The dry, elastic atmosphere of the northern States produces a restlessness which must either expend itself in bodily or mental exertion or force of expression; from this probably arise the frequent use of superlatives, and the exaggeration of language, which the more phlegmatic English attribute to the Americans.

Since my return to England I have frequently been asked the question, "What is society like in America?" This word *society* is one of very ambiguous meaning. It is used in England by the titled aristocracy to distinguish themselves, their connexions, and those whose wealth or genius has gained them admission into their circles. But every circle, every city, and even every country neighbourhood, had what it pleases to term "society;" and when the members of it say of an individual, "I never met him in society," it ostracises him, no matter how estimable or agreeable he may be. In England, to "society," in each of its grades, wealth is a sure passport, as has been evidenced of late years by several very notorious instances. Thus it is extremely difficult to answer the question, "What is New York society like?" It certainly is not like that which is associated in our minds with the localities May Fair and Belgravia; neither can it be compared to the circles which form parasitically round the millionaire; still less is it like the dulness of country neighbourhoods. New York has its charmed circles also; a republic admits of the greatest exclusiveness; and, in the highest circles of the city, to say that a man is not in society, is to ostracise him as in England. It must be stated that some of the most agreeable *salons* of New York are almost closed against foreigners. French, Germans, and Italians, with imposing titles, have proved how unworthily they bear them; and this feeling against strangers—I will not call it prejudice, for there are sufficient grounds for it—is extended to the English, some of whom, I regret to say, have violated the rights of hospitality in many different ways. I have heard of such conduct on the part of my countrymen as left me no room for surprise that many families, whose acquaintance would be most agreeable, strictly guard their drawing-room from English intrusion. And, besides this, there are those who have entered houses merely to caricature their inmates, and have received hospitality only to ridicule the manner in which it was exercised, while they have indulged in unamiable personalities, and have not respected the sanctity of private life.

It was through an introduction given me by a valued English friend that I, as an English stranger, was received with the kindest hospitality by some of those who have been rendered thus exclusive by the bad taste and worse conduct of foreigners. I feel, as I write, that any remarks I make on New York society cannot be perfectly free from bias, owing to the overwhelming kindness and glowing hospitality which I met with in that city. I found so much to enjoy in society, and so much to interest and please everywhere, that when I left New York it was with the wish that the few weeks which I was able to spend there could have been prolonged into as many months.

But, to answer the question. The best society in New York would not suffer by comparison in any way with the best society in England. It is not in the upper classes of any nation that we must look for national characteristics or peculiarities. Society throughout the civilized world is, to a certain extent, cast in the same mould; the same laws of etiquette prevail, and the same conventionalisms restrict in great measure the display of any individual characteristics. Balls are doubtless the same in "society" all over the world; a certain amount of black cloth, kid gloves, white muslin, epaulettes if they can be procured, dancing, music, and ices. Everyone acknowledges that dinner-parties are equally dull in London and Paris, in Calcutta and in New York, unless the next neighbour happens to be peculiarly agreeable. Therefore, it is most probable that balls and dinner-parties are in New York exactly the same as in other places, except that the latter are less numerous, and are principally confined to gentlemen. It is not, in fact, convenient to give dinner parties in New York; there are not sufficient domestics to bear the pressure of an emergency, and the pleasure is not considered worth the trouble. If two or three people have sufficient value for the society of the host and hostess to come in to an ordinary dinner, at an ordinary hour, they are welcome. If turtle and venison were offered on such an occasion, it would have the effect of repelling, rather than attracting, the guests, and it would not have the effect of making them believe that their host and hostess always lived on such luxurious viands.

As dinner-parties are neither deemed agreeable nor convenient, and as many sensible people object to the late hours and general dissipation of mind produced by balls and large dancing parties, a happy innovation upon old customs has been made, and early evening receptions have been introduced. Some of the most splendid mansions of New York, as well as the most agreeable, are now thrown open weekly for the reception of visitors in a social manner. These receptions differ from what are known by the same name in London. The crowd in which people become wedged, in a vain attempt to speak to the hostess, is as much as possible avoided; late hours are abandoned; the guests, who usually arrive about eight, are careful to disappear shortly after eleven, lest, Cinderella-like, the hostess should vanish. Then, again, all the guests feel themselves on a perfect equality, as people always ought to do who meet in the same room, on the invitation of the same hostess.[1]

The lady of the house adopts the old but very sensible fashion of introducing people to each other, which helps to prevent a good deal of stiffness. As the rooms in the New York houses are generally large, people sit, stand, or walk about as they feel inclined, or group themselves round someone gifted

---

1 The Americans justly ridicule that species of bad breeding which leads people at parties to draw back from others, from a fear that their condescension should fall upon ground unconsecrated by the dictatorial fiat of "society." An amusing instance of the effect of this pride, which occurred in England, was related. Some years ago the illustrious Baron Humboldt was invited to play the part of lion at the house of a nobleman. A select circle of fashionables appeared, and among the company a man very plainly dressed and not noticeable in appearance. He spoke first to one person, and then to another: some drew themselves up with a haughty stare; others answered in monosyllables; but all repulsed the Baron; and it was not until late in the evening, after he had departed early, disgusted with this ungracious reception, that these people knew that by their conduct they had lost the advantage of the conversation of one of the greatest men of the age.

with peculiar conversational powers. At all of these re-unions there was a great deal of conversation worth listening to or joining in, and, as a stranger, I had the advantage of being introduced to everyone who was considered worth knowing. Poets, historians, and men of science are to be met with frequently at these receptions; but they do not go as lions, but to please and be pleased; and such men as Longfellow, Prescott, or Washington Irving may be seen mixing with the general throng with so much *bonhommie* and simplicity, that none would fancy that in their own land they are the envy of their age, and sustain world-wide reputations. The way in which literary lions are exhibited in England, as essential to the *éclat* of fashionable parties, is considered by the Americans highly repugnant to good taste. I was very agreeably surprised with the unaffected manners and extreme simplicity of men eminent in the scientific and literary world.

These evening receptions are a very happy idea; for people, whose business or inclinations would not permit them to meet in any other way, are thus brought together without formality or expense. The conversation generally turned on Europe, general literature, art, science, or the events of the day. I must say that I never heard one remark that could be painful to an English ear made, even in jest. There was none of that vulgar boastfulness and detraction which is to be met with in less educated society. Most of the gentlemen whom I met, and many of the ladies, had travelled in Europe, and had brought back highly cultivated tastes in art, and cosmopolitan ideas, which insensibly affect the circles in which they move.

All appeared to take a deep interest in the war, and in our success. I heard our military movements in the Crimea criticised with some severity by military men, some of whom have since left for the seat of war, to watch our operations. The conclusion of the Vienna negociations appeared to excite some surprise. "I had no idea," an officer observed to me, "that public opinion was so strong in England as to be able to compel a minister of such strong Russian proclivities as Lord

Aberdeen to go to war with his old friend Nicholas." The arrangements at Balaklava excited very general condemnation; people were fond of quoting the saying attributed to a Russian officer, "You have an army of *lions* led by *asses*."

The Americans are always anxious to know what opinion a stranger has formed of their country, and I would be asked thirty times on one evening, "How do you like America?" Fortunately, the kindness which I met with rendered it impossible for me to give any but a satisfactory reply. English literature was a very general topic of conversation, and it is most gratifying to find how our best English works are "familiar in their mouths as household words." Some of the conversation on literature was of a very brilliant order. I heard very little approximation to either wit or humour, and *badinage* is not cultivated, or excelled in, to the same extent as in England.

On one occasion I was asked to exhibit a collection of autographs, and the knowledge of English literature possessed by the Americans was shown by the information they had respecting not only our well-known authors, but those whose names have not an extended reputation even with us. Thus the works of Maitland, Ritchie, Sewell, Browning, Howitt, and others seemed perfectly familiar to them. The trembling signature of George III. excited general interest from his connection with their own history, and I was not a little amused to see how these republicans dwelt with respectful attention on the decided characters of Queen Victoria. A very characteristic letter of Lord Byron's was read aloud, and, in return for the pleasure they had experienced, several kind individuals gave me valuable autographs of their own *literati* and statesmen. Letters written by Washington descend as precious heirlooms in families, and so great is the estimation in which this venerated patriot is held, that, with all the desire to oblige a stranger which the Americans evince, I believe that I could not have purchased a few lines in his handwriting with my whole collection.

It would be difficult to give any idea of the extremely agreeable character of these receptions. They seemed to me to be the most sensible way of seeing society that I ever met with, and might be well worthy of general imitation in England. When I saw how sixty or a hundred people could be brought together without the inducements of dancing, music, refreshments, or display of any kind; when I saw also how thoroughly they enjoyed themselves, how some were introduced, and those who were not entered into sprightly conversation without fear of lessening an imaginary dignity, I more than ever regretted the icy coldness in which we wrap ourselves. And yet, though we take such trouble to clothe ourselves in this glacial dignity, nothing pleases us better than to go to other countries and throw it off, and mix with our fellow men and women as rational beings should, not as if we feared either to compromise ourselves or to be repulsed by them. This national stiffness renders us the laughing-stock of foreigners; and in a certain city in America no play was ever more successful than the "*Buckram Englishman*," which ridiculed and caricatured our social peculiarities.

The usages of etiquette are much the same as in England, but people appeared to be assisted in the enjoyment of society by them rather than trammeled. Morning visiting is carried to a great extent, but people call literally in the morning, before two o'clock oftener than after. On New Year's Day, in observance of an old Dutch custom, the ladies remain at home, and all the gentlemen of their acquaintance make a point of calling upon them. Of course time will only allow of the interchange of the compliments of the season, where so much social duty has to be performed in one brief day, but this pleasant custom tends to keep up old acquaintanceships and annihilate old feuds. It is gratifying to observe that any known deviation from the rules of morality is punished with exclusion from the houses of those who are considered the leaders of New York society; it is also very pleasing to see that to the best circles in New York wealth alone is not a passport. I have heard cards of invitation to these receptions refused to foreigners bearing illustrious titles, and to persons who have the reputation of being *millionaires*. At the same time, I have met those of humble position and scanty means, who are treated with distinction because of their talents or intellectual powers. Yet I have never seen such a one patronised or treated as a lion; he is not expected to do any homage, or pay any penalty, for his admission into society. In these circles in New York we are spared the humiliating spectacle of men of genius or intellect cringing and uneasy in the presence of their patronising inferiors, whom birth or wealth may have placed socially above them. Of course there is society in New York where the vulgar influence of money is omnipotent, and extravagant display is fashionable; it is of the best that I have been speaking.

It may seem a sudden transition from society to a cemetery, and yet it is not an unnatural one, for many of the citizens of New York carry their magnificence as far as possible to the grave with them, and pile their wealth above their heads in superb mausoleums or costly statues. The *Père la Chaise* of the city is the Greenwood Cemetery, near Brooklyn on Long Island. I saw it on the finest and coldest of November days, when a piercing east wind was denuding the trees of their last scarlet honours. After encountering more than the usual crush in Broadway, for we were rather more than an hour in driving three miles in a stage, we crossed the Brooklyn Ferry in one of those palace ferry-boats, where the spacious rooms for passengers are heated by steam-pipes, and the charge is only one cent, or a fraction less than a halfpenny. It was a beautiful day; there was not a cloud upon the sky; the waves of the Sound and of the North River were crisped and foam-tipped, and dashed noisily upon the white pebbly beach. Brooklyn, Jersey, and Hoboken rose from the water, with their green fields and avenues of villas; white, smokeless steamers were passing and repassing; large anchored ships tossed upon the waves; and New York, that compound of trees, buildings, masts, and spires, rose in the rear, without so much as a single cloud of smoke hovering over it.

A railway runs from Brooklyn to the cemetery, with the cars drawn by horses, and the dead of New York are conveniently carried to this last resting-place. The entrance is handsome, and the numerous walls and carriage-drives are laid with fine gravel, and beautifully swept. We drove to see the most interesting objects, and the coachman seemed to take a peculiar pride in pointing them out. This noble burying-ground has some prettily diversified hill and dale scenery, and is six miles round. The timber is very fine, and throughout art has only been required as an assistance to nature. To this cemetery most of the dead of New York are carried, and after "life's fitful fever," in its most exaggerated form, sleep in appropriate silence. Already several thousand dead have been placed here in places of sepulture varying in appearance from the most splendid and ornate to the simplest and most obscure. There are family mausoleums, gloomy and sepulchral looking, in the Grecian style; family burying-grounds neatly enclosed by iron or bronze railings, where white marble crosses mark the graves; there are tombs with epitaphs, and tombs with statues; there are simple cenotaphs and monumental slabs, and nameless graves marked by numbers only.

One very remarkable feature of this cemetery is the "Potter's Field," a plot containing several acres of ground, where strangers are buried. This is already occupied to a great extent. The graves are placed in rows close together, with numbers on a small iron plate to denote each. Here the shipwrecked, the pestilence-stricken, the penniless, and friendless are buried; and though such a spot cannot fail to provoke sad musings, the people of New York do not suffer any appearances of neglect to accumulate round the last resting-place of those who died unfriended and alone. Another feature, not to be met with in England, strikes the stranger at first with ludicrous images, though in reality it has more of the pathetic. In one part of this cemetery there are several hundred graves of children, and these, with most others of children of the poorer class, have toys in glass cases placed upon them. There are playthings of many kinds, woolly dogs and lambs, and little wooden houses, toys which must be associated in the parents' minds with those who made their homes glad, but who have gone into the grave before them. One cannot but think of the bright eyes dim, the merry laugh and infantine prattle silent, the little hands, once so active in playful mischief, stiff and cold; all brought so to mind by the sight of those toys. There is a fearful amount of mortality among children at New York, and in several instances four or five buried in one grave told with mournful suggestiveness of the silence and desolation of once happy hearths.

There are a few very remarkable and somewhat fantastic monuments. There is a beautiful one in white marble to the memory of a sea-captain's wife, with an exact likeness of himself, in the attitude of taking an observation, on the top. An inscription to himself is likewise upon it, leaving only the date of his death to be added. It is said that, when this poor man returns from a voyage, he spends one whole day in the tomb, lamenting his bereavement.

There is a superb monument, erected by a fireman's company to the memory of one of their brethren, who lost his life while nobly rescuing an infant from a burning dwelling. His statue is on the top, with an infant in his arms, and the implements of his profession lie below. But by far the most extraordinary, and certainly one of the lions of New York, is to a young lady who was killed in coming home from a ball. The carriage-horses ran away, she jumped out, and was crushed under the wheels. She stands under a marble canopy supported by angels, and is represented in her ball-dress, with a mantle thrown over it. This monument has numerous pillars and representations of celestial beings, and is said to have cost about £6000. Several of the marble mausoleums cost from £4000 to £5000. Yet all the powerful, the wealthy, and the poor have descended to the dust from whence they sprung; and here, as everywhere else, nothing can disguise the fact that man, the feeble sport of passion and infirmity, can only claim for his inheritance at last the gloom of a silent grave, where he must sleep with the dust of his fathers. I observed only one verse of Scripture on a tombstone, and it contained the appropriate prayer, "*So teach us to number our days, that we may apply our hearts unto wisdom.*"

Having seen the emigrants bid adieu to the Old World, in the flurry of grief, hope, and excitement, I was curious to see what difference a five-weeks' voyage would have produced in them, and in what condition they would land upon the shores of America. In a city where emigrants land at the rate of a thousand a day, I was not long of finding an opportunity. I witnessed the debarkation upon the shore of the New World of between 600 and 700 English emigrants, who had just arrived from Liverpool. If they looked tearful, flurried, and anxious when they left Liverpool, they looked tearful, pallid, dirty, and squalid when they reached New York. The necessary discomforts which such a number of persons must experience when huddled together in a close, damp, and ill-ventilated steerage, with very little change of clothing, and an allowance of water insufficient for the purposes of cleanliness, had been increased in this instance by the presence of cholera on board of the ship.

The wharfs at New York are necessarily dirty, and are a scene of indescribable bustle from morning to night, with ships arriving and sailing, ships loading and unloading, and emigrants pouring into the town in an almost incessant stream. They look as if no existing power could bring order out of such a chaos. In this crowd, on the shores of a strange land, the emigrants found themselves. Many were deplorably emaciated, others looked vacant and stupified. Some were ill, and some were penniless; but poverty and sickness are among the best recommendations which an emigrant can bring with him, for they place him under the immediate notice of those estimable and overworked men, the Emigration Commissioners, whose humanity is above all praise. These find him an asylum in the Emigrants' Hospital, on Ward's Island, and despatch him from thence in health, with advice and assistance for his future career. If he be in health, and have a few dollars in his pocket, he becomes the instantaneous prey of emigrant runners, sharpers, and keepers of groggeries; but of this more will be said hereafter.

A great many of these immigrants were evidently from country districts, and some from Ireland; there were a few Germans among them, and these appeared the least affected by the discomforts of the voyage, and by the novel and rather bewildering position in which they found themselves. They probably would feel more at home on first landing at New York than any of the others, for the lower part of the city is to a great extent inhabited by Germans, and at that time there were about 2000 houses where their favourite beverage, *lager-beer*, could be procured.

The goods and chattels of the Irish appeared to consist principally of numerous red-haired, unruly children, and ragged-looking bundles tied round with rope. The Germans were generally ruddy and stout, and took as much care of their substantial-looking, well-corded, heavy chests as though they contained gold. The English appeared pale and debilitated, and sat helpless and weary-looking on their large blue boxes. Here they found themselves in the chaotic confusion of this million-peopled city, not knowing whither to betake themselves, and bewildered by cries of "Cheap hacks!" "All aboard!" "Come to the cheapest house in all the world!" and invitations of a similar description. There were lodging-touters of every grade of dishonesty, and men with large placards were hurrying among the crowd, offering "palace" steamboats and "lightning express" trains, to whirl them at nominal rates to the Elysian Fields of the Far West. It is stated that six-tenths of these emigrants are attacked by fever soon after their arrival in the New World, but the provision for the sick is commensurate with the wealth and benevolence of New York.

Before leaving the city I was desirous to see some of the dwellings of the poor; I was therefore taken to what was termed a poor quarter. One house which I visited was approached from an entry, and contained ten rooms, which were let to different individuals and families. On the lowest floor was an old Irish widow, who had a cataract in one eye, and, being without any means of supporting herself, subsisted upon a small allowance made to her by her son, who was a carter. She was clean, but poorly dressed, and the room was scantily furnished. Except those who are rendered poor by their idleness and vices, it might have been difficult to find a poorer person in the city, I was told. Much sympathy was expressed for her, and for those who, like her, lived in this poor quarter. Yet the room was tolerably large, lofty, and airy, and had a window of the ordinary size of those in English dwelling-houses. For this room she paid four dollars or 16s. per month, a very high rent. It was such a room as in London many a respectable clerk, with an income of £150 a year, would think himself fortunate in possessing.

I could not enter into the feelings of the benevolent people of New York when they sympathised with the denizens of this locality. I only wished that these generous people could have seen the dens in which thousands of our English poor live, with little light and less water, huddled together, without respect to sex or numbers, in small, ill-ventilated rooms. Yet New York has a district called the Five Points, fertile in crime, fever, and misery, which would scarcely yield the palm for vice and squalor to St. Giles's in London, or the Saltmarket in Glasgow. A collection of dwellings called the Mud Huts, where many coloured people reside, is also an unpleasing feature connected with the city. But with abundant employment, high wages, and charities on a princely scale for those who from accidental circumstances may occasionally require assistance, there is no excuse for the squalid wretchedness in which a considerable number of persons have chosen to sink themselves.

It is a fact that no Golden Age exists on the other side of the water; that vice and crime have their penalties in America as well as in Europe; and that some of the worst features of the Old World are reproduced in the New. With all the desire that we may possess to take a sanguine view of things, there is something peculiarly hopeless about the condition of this class at New York, which in such a favourable state of society, and at such an early period of American history, has sunk so very low. The existence of a "dangerous class" at New York is now no longer denied. One person in seven of the whole population came under the notice of the authorities, either in the ranks of criminals or paupers, in 1852; and it is stated that last year the numbers reached an alarming magnitude, threatening danger to the peace of society. This is scarcely surprising when we take into consideration the numbers of persons who land in this city who have been expatriated for their vices, who are flying from the vengeance of outraged law, or who expect in the New World to be able to do evil without fear of punishment.

There are the idle and the visionary, who expect to eat without working; penniless demagogues, unprincipled adventurers, and the renegade outpourings of all Christendom; together with those who are enervated and demoralised by sickness and evil associates on board ship. I could not help thinking, as I saw many of the newly-arrived emigrants saunter helplessly into the groggeries, that, after spending their money, they would remain at New York, and help to swell the numbers of this class. These people live by their wits, and lose the little they have in drink. This life is worth very little to them; and in spite of Bible and Tract societies, and church missions, they know very little of the life to come; consequently they are ready for any mischief, and will imperil their existence for a small bribe. Many or most of them are Irish Roman Catholics, who, having obtained the franchise in many instances by making false affidavits, consider themselves at liberty to use the club also.

I was at New York at the time of the elections, and those of 1854 were attended with unusual excitement, owing to the red-hot strife between the Irish Roman Catholics and the "Know-nothings." This society, established with the object of changing the naturalisation laws, and curbing the power of popery, had at this period obtained a very large share of the public attention, as much from the mystery which attended it as from the principles which it avowed. To the minds of all there was something attractive in a secret organisation, unknown oaths, and nocturnal meetings; and the success which had attended the efforts of the Know-nothings in Massachusetts, and others of the States, led many to watch with deep interest the result of the elections for the Empire State. Their candidates were not elected, but the avowed contest between Protestantism and Popery led to considerable loss of life. Very little notice of the riots on this occasion has been taken by the English journalists, though the local papers varied in their accounts of the numbers of killed and wounded from 45 to 700! It was known that an *émeute* was expected, therefore I was not surprised, one evening early in November, to hear the alarm-bells ringing in all directions throughout the city. It was stated that a Know-nothing assemblage of about 10,000 persons had been held in the Park, and that, in dispersing, they had been fired upon by some Irishmen called the Brigade. This was the commencement of a sanguinary struggle for the preservation of order. For three days a dropping fire of musketry was continually to be heard in New York and Williamsburgh, and reports of great loss of life on both sides were circulated. It was stated that the hospital received 170 wounded men, and that many more were carried off by their friends. The military were called out, and, as it was five days before quiet was restored, it is to be supposed that many lives were lost. I saw two dead bodies myself; and in one street or alley by the Five Points, both the side-walks and the roadway were slippery with blood. Yet very little sensation was excited in the upper part of the town; people went out and came in as usual; business was not interrupted; and to questions upon the subject the reply was frequently made, "Oh, it's only an election riot," showing how painfully common such disturbances had become.

There are many objects of interest in New York and its neighbourhood, among others, the Croton aqueduct, a work worthy of a great people. It cost about £5,000,000. sterling, and by it about 60,000,000 gallons of water are daily conveyed into

311

the city. Then there are the prisons on Blackwell's Island, the lunatic asylums, the orphan asylums, the docks, and many other things; but I willingly leave these untouched, as they have been described by other writers. In concluding this brief and incomplete account of New York, I may be allowed to refer to the preface of this work, and repeat that any descriptions which I have given of things or society are merely "sketches," and, as such, are liable to the errors which always attend upon hasty observation.

New York, with its novel, varied, and ever-changing features, is calculated to leave a very marked impression on a stranger's mind. In one part one can suppose it to be a negro town; in another, a German city; while a strange dreamy resemblance to Liverpool pervades the whole. In it there is little repose for the mind, and less for the eye, except on the Sabbath-day, which is very well observed, considering the widely-differing creeds and nationalities of the inhabitants. The streets are alive with business, retail and wholesale, and present an aspect of universal bustle. Flags are to be seen in every direction, the tall masts of ships appear above the houses; large square pieces of calico, with names in scarlet or black letters upon them, hang across the streets, to denote the whereabouts of some popular candidate or "puffing" storekeeper; and hosts of omnibuses, hacks, drays, and railway cars at full speed, ringing bells, terrify unaccustomed foot-passengers. There are stores of the magnitude of bazaars, "daguerrean galleries" by hundreds, crowded groggeries and subterranean oyster-saloons, huge hotels, coffee-houses, and places of amusement; while the pavements present men of every land and colour, red, black, yellow, and white, in every variety of costume and beard, and ladies, beautiful and ugly, richly dressed. Then there are mud huts, and palatial residences, and streets of stately dwelling-houses, shaded by avenues of ilanthus-trees; waggons discharging goods across the pavements; shops above and cellars below; railway whistles and steamboat bells, telegraph-wires, eight and ten to a post, all converging towards Wall Street—the

Lombard Street of New York; militia regiments in many-coloured uniforms, marching in and out of the city all day; groups of emigrants bewildered and amazed, emaciated with dysentery and sea-sickness, looking in at the shop-windows; representatives of every nation under heaven, speaking in all earth's Babel languages; and as if to render this ceaseless pageant of business, gaiety, and change, as far removed from monotony as possible, the quick toll of the fire alarm-bells may be daily heard, and the huge engines, with their burnished equipments and well-trained companies, may be seen to dash at full speed along the streets to the scene of some brilliant conflagration. New York is calculated to present as imposing an appearance to an Englishman as its antiquated namesake does to an American, with its age, silence, stateliness, and decay.

The Indian summer had come and gone, and bright frosty weather had succeeded it, when I left this city, in which I had received kindness and hospitality which I can never forget. Mr. Amy, the kind friend who had first welcomed me to the States, was my travelling companion, and at his house near Boston, in the midst of a happy family-circle, I spent the short remnant of my time before returning to England.

We left New York just as the sun was setting, frosty and red, and ere we had reached Newhaven it was one of the finest winter evenings that I had ever seen. The moisture upon the windows of the cars froze into innumerable fairy shapes; the crescent moon and a thousand stars shone brilliantly from a deep blue sky; auroras flashed and meteors flamed, and, as the fitful light glittered on many rushing gurgling streams, I had but to remember how very beautiful New England was, to give form and distinctness to the numerous shapes which we were hurrying past. I was recalling the sunny south to mind, with its vineyards and magnolia groves, and the many scenes of beauty that I had witnessed in America, with all the genial kindness which I had experienced from many who but a few months ago were strangers, when a tipsy Scotch fiddler broke in upon my reveries by an attempt to play 'Yankee Doodle.' It is curious how such a thing can instantly change the nature of the thoughts. I remembered speculations, 'cute notions, guesses, and calculations; "All aboard," and "Go ahead," and "Pile on, skipper;" sharp eager faces, diversities of beards, duellists, pickpockets, and every species of adventurer.

Such recollections were not out of place in Connecticut, the centre and soul of what we denominate *Yankeeism*. This state has one of the most celebrated educational establishments in the States, Yale College at Newhaven, or the City of Elms, famous for its toleration of an annual fight between the citizens and the students, at a nocturnal *fête* in celebration of the burial of Euclid. The phraseology and some of the moral characteristics of Connecticut are quite peculiar. It is remarkable for learning, the useful arts, successful and energetic merchants and farmers; the mythical Sam Slick, the prince of pedlars; and his living equal, Barnum, the prince of showmen. A love of good order and a pervading religious sentiment appear to accompany great simplicity of manners in its rural population, though the Southerners, jealous of the virtues of these New Englanders, charge upon them the manufacture of wooden nutmegs. This state supplies the world with wooden clocks, for which the inhabitants of our colonies appear to have a peculiar fancy, though at home they are called "Yankee clocks what won't go." I have seen pedlars with curiously constructed waggons toiling along even among the Canadian clearings, who are stated to belong to a race "raised" in Connecticut. They are extremely amusing individuals, and it is impossible to resist making an investment in their goods, as their importunities are urged in such ludicrous phraseology. The pedlar can accommodate you with everything, from a clock or bible to a penny-worth of pins, and takes rags, rabbit and squirrel skins, at two cents each, in payment. His knowledge of "soft sawder and human natur" is as great as that of Sam Slick, his inimitable representative; and many a shoeless Irish girl is induced to change a dollar for some trumpery ornament, by his artful compliments to her personal attractions. He seems at home everywhere; talks politics, guesses your needs, cracks a joke, or condoles with you on your misfortunes with an elongated face. He always contrives to drop in at dinner or tea time, for which he always apologises, but in distant settlements the apologetic formulary might be left alone, for the visit of the cosmopolitan pedlar is ever welcome, even though he leaves you a few dollars poorer. There is some fear of the extinction of the race, as railways are now bringing the most distant localities within reach of resplendent stores with plate-glass windows.

It wanted six hours to dawn when we reached Boston; and the ashes of an extinguished fire in the cheerless waiting-room at the depôt gave an idea of even greater cold than really existed. We drove through the silent streets of Boston, and out into the country, in an open carriage, with the thermometer many degrees below the freezing-point, yet the dryness of the atmosphere prevented any feeling of cold. The air was pure, still, and perfectly elastic; a fitful aurora lighted our way, and the iron hoofs of the fast-trotting ponies rattled cheerily along the frozen ground. I almost regretted the termination of the drive, even though the pleasant villa of ——, and a room lighted by a blazing wood fire, awaited me.

The weather was perfectly delightful. Cloudless and golden the sun set at night; cloudless and rosy he rose in the morning; sharp and defined in outline the leafless trees rose against the piercing blue of the sky; the frozen ground rang to every footstep; thin patches of snow diversified the landscape; and the healthful air braced even invalid nerves. Boston is a very fine city, and the whole of it, spread out as a panorama, can be seen from several neighbouring eminences. The rosy flush of a winter dawn had scarcely left the sky when I saw the town from Dorchester Heights. Below lay the city, an aggregate of handsome streets lined with trees, stately public buildings, and church-spires, with the lofty State House crowning the whole. Bright blue water and forests of masts appeared to intersect the town; green, wooded, swelling elevations, dotted over with white villa residences, environed it in every direction; blue hills rose far in the distance; while to the right the bright waters of Massachusett's bay, enlivened by the white sails of ships and pilot-boats, completed this attractive panorama.

Boston is built on a collection of peninsulas; and as certain shipowners possess wharfs far up in the town, to which their ships must find their way, the virtue of patience is frequently inculcated by a long detention at drawbridges, while heavily-laden vessels are slowly warped through the openings. The equanimity of the American character surprised me here, as it often had before; for, while I was devising various means of saving time, by taking various circuitous routes, about 100 *détenus* submitted to the delay without evincing any symptoms of impatience. Part of Boston is built on ground reclaimed from the sea, and the active inhabitants continually keep encroaching on the water for building purposes.

This fine city appeared to greater advantage on my second visit, after seeing New York, Cincinnati, Chicago, and other of the American towns. In them their progress is evidenced by a ceaseless building up and pulling down, the consequences of which are heaps of rubbish and unsightly hoardings covered with bills and advertisements, giving to the towns thus circumstanced an unfinished, mobile, or temporary look. This is still further increased where many of the houses are of wood, and can be moved without being taken to pieces. I was riding through an American town one afternoon, when, to my surprise, I had to turn off upon the side-walk, to avoid a house which was coming down the street, drawn by ten horses, and assisted by as many men with levers. My horse was so perfectly unconcerned at what was such a novel spectacle to me, that I supposed he was used to these migratory dwellings.

Boston has nothing of all this. Stately, substantial, and handsome, it looks as if it had been begun and completed in a day. There is a most pleasing air of respectability about the large stone and brick houses; the stores are spacious and very handsome; and the public buildings are durably and tastefully built. Scientific institutions, music halls, and the splendid stores possessed by the booksellers and philosophical instrument makers, proclaim the literary and refined tastes of the inhabitants, which have earned for their city the name of the "American Athens." There is an air of repose about Boston; here, if anywhere, one would suppose that large fortunes were realised and enjoyed. The sleek horses do not appear to be hurried over the pavements; there are few placards, and fewer puffs; the very carts are built rather to carry weight than for speed. Yet no place which I visited looked more thriving than Boston. Its streets are literally crammed with vehicles, and the side-walks are thronged with passengers, but these latter are principally New Englanders, of respectable appearance. These walks are bordered by acacia and elm trees, which seem to flourish in the most crowded thoroughfares, and, besides protecting both men and horses from the intense heat, their greenness, which they retain till the fall, is most refreshing to the eye. There are a great many private carriages to be seen, as well as people on horseback. The dwelling-houses have plate-glass windows and bright green jalousies; the side-walks are of granite, and the whole has an English air. The common, or rather the park, at Boston, is the finest public promenade that I ever saw, about fifty acres in extent, and ornamented with avenues of very fine trees. This slopes to the south, and the highest part of the slope is crowned by the State House and the handsomest private residences in the city. Boston is very clean and orderly, and smoking is not permitted in the streets. There is a highly aristocratic air about it, and those who look for objects of historical interest will not be disappointed. There is the old Faneuil Hall, which once echoed to the stormy arguments and spirit-stirring harangues of the leaders of the Revolution. A few antiquated, many-gabled houses, remain in its neighbourhood, each associated with some tradition dear to the Americans. Then there is a dark-coloured stone church, which still in common parlance bears the name of King's

Chapel. It is fitted with high pews of dark varnished oak, and the English liturgy, slightly altered, is still used as the form of worship. Then there is the Old South Meeting house, where the inhabitants remonstrated with the governor for bringing in the king's troops; and, lastly, Griffin's Wharf, where, under the impulse of the stern concentrated will of the New England character, the "Sons of Liberty" boarded the English ships, and slowly and deliberately threw the tea which they contained into the water of the harbour.

I visited the Bunker's Hill monument, and was content to take on trust the statement of the beauty of the view from the summit, as the monument, which is 221 feet in height, is ascended by a very steep staircase. Neither did I deny the statement made by the patriotic Americans who were with me, that the British forces were defeated in that place, not feeling at all sure that the national pride of our historians had not led them to tell a tale more flattering than true; for

> "Some say that we won,
> And some say that they won,
> And some say that none won at a', man."

We visited the naval yard at Charlestown, and the *Ohio*, an old seventy-four, now used as a receiving-ship. There was a very manifest difference between the two sides of the main-deck of this vessel; one was scrupulously clean, the other by no means so; and, on inquiring the reason, I was told that the clean side was reserved for strangers! Although this yard scarcely deserves the name of an arsenal, being the smallest of all which America possesses, the numerous guns and the piles of cannon-balls show that she is not unprepared for aggressive or defensive war.

The Merchants' Exchange, where every change in the weather at New Orleans is known in a few minutes; the Post-Office, with its innumerable letter-boxes and endless bustle; the Tremont Hall, one of the finest music-halls in the world; the water-works, the Athenæum, and the libraries, are all worthy of a visit.

There is a museum, which we visited in the evening, but it is not creditable to the taste of the inhabitants of this fine city. There are multitudes of casts and fossils, and stuffed beasts and birds, and monsters, and a steam-engine modelled in glass, which works beautifully; but all these things are to hide the real character of this institution, and appeared to be passed unnoticed by a large number of respectable-looking people who were thronging into a theatre at the back—a very gloomy-looking edifice, with high pews. A placard announced that Dickens' *Hard Times*, which it appears from this has been dramatised, was about to be acted. The plays are said to be highly moral, but in the melodrama religion and buffoonery are often intermingled; and I confess that I did not approve of this mode of solacing the consciences of those who object to ordinary theatricals, for the principle involved remains the same.

The National Theatre is considered so admirably adapted for seeing, hearing, and accommodation, that it is frequently visited by European architects. An American friend took me to see it in the evening, when none are admitted but those who are going to remain for the performance. This being the rule, the doorkeeper politely opposed our entrance; but on my companion stating that I was a stranger, he instantly admitted us, and pointed out the best position for seeing the edifice. The theatre, which has four tiers of boxes, was handsome in the extreme, and brilliantly lighted; but I thought it calculated to produce the same effect of dizziness and headache, as those who frequent our House of Peers experience from the glare and redundant decoration.

This was one among the many instances where the name of stranger produced a magic effect. It appeared as if doors which would not open to anything else, yielded at once to a request urged in that sacred name. This was the case at the Mount Auburn Cemetery, where the gatekeeper permitted us as strangers to drive round in a carriage, which is contrary to rule, and on no occasion would those who so courteously obliged us accept of any gratuity.

There is some rivalry on the part of the people of Boston and New York with regard to the beauty of their cemeteries. Many travellers have pronounced the cemetery of Mount Auburn to be the loveliest in the world; but both it and that of Greenwood are so beautiful, that it is needless to "hint a fault or hesitate a dislike" with regard to either. Mount Auburn has verdant slopes, and deep wild dells, and lakes shaded by forest-trees of great size and beauty; and so silent is it, far removed from the din of cities, that it seems as if a single footstep would disturb the sleep of the dead. Here the neglectfulness and dreariness of the outer aspect of the grave are completely done away with, and the dead lie peacefully under ground carpeted with flowers, and shaded by trees. The simplicity of the monuments is very beautiful; that to Spurzheim has merely his name upon the tablet. Fulton, Channing, and other eminent men are buried here.

New York is celebrated for frequent and mysterious con-flagrations; so are all the American cities in a less degree. This is very surprising to English people, many of whom scarcely know a fire-engine by sight. Boston, though its substantial erections of brick and stone present great obstacles to the progress of the devouring element, frequently displays these unwished-for illuminations, and has some very well organized fire companies. These companies, which are voluntary associations, are one of the important features of the States. The Quakers had the credit of originating them. Being men of peace, they could not bear arms in defence of their country, and exchanged militia service for the task of extinguishing all the fires caused by the wilfulness or carelessness of their fellow-citizens. This has been no easy task in cities built of wood, which in that dry climate, when ignited, burns like pine-knots. Even now, fires occur in a very unaccountable manner. At New York my slumbers were frequently disturbed by the quick-tolling bell, announcing the number of the district where a fire had broken out. These fire companies have regular organizations, and their members enjoy several immunities, one of which I think is, that they are not compelled to serve as jurymen.

They are principally composed of young men, some of them the wilder members of the first families in the cities. Their dresses are suitable and picturesque, and, with the brilliant painting and highly-polished brasses of their large engines, they form one of the most imposing parts of the annual pageant of the "*Glorious Fourth.*" The fireman who first reaches the scene of action is captain for the night, and this honour is so much coveted, as to lead them often to wait, ready equipped, during the winter nights, that they may be able to start forth at the first sound of the bell. There is sufficient dangerous adventure, and enough of thrilling incident, to give the occupation a charm in the eyes of the eager youth of the cities. They like it far better than playing at soldiers, and are popular in every city. As their gay and glittering processions pass along the streets, acclamations greet their progress, and enthusiastic ladies shower flowers upon their heads. They are generous, courageous, and ever ready in the hour of danger. But there is a dark side to this picture. They are said to be the *foci* of political encroachment and intrigue, and to be the centre of the restless and turbulent spirits of all classes. So powerful and dangerous have they become in many instances, that it has been recently stated in an American paper, that one of the largest and most respectable cities in the Union has found it necessary to suppress them.

The Blind Asylum is one of the noblest charitable institutions of Boston. It is in a magnificent situation, overlooking all the beauties of Massachusett's Bay. It is principally interesting as being the residence of Laura Bridgman, the deaf and blind mute, whose history has interested so many in England. I had not an opportunity of visiting this asylum till the morning of the day on which I sailed for Europe, and had no opportunity of conversing with this interesting girl, as she was just leaving for the country. I saw her preceptor, Dr. Howe, whose untiring exertions on her behalf she has so wonderfully rewarded. He is a very lively, energetic man, and is now devoting himself to the improvement of the condition of idiots, in which already he has been extremely successful.

Laura is an elegant-looking girl, and her features, formerly so vacant, are now animated and full of varying expression. She dresses herself with great care and neatness, and her fair hair is also braided by herself. There is nothing but what is pleasing in her appearance, as her eyes are covered with small green shades. She is about twenty-three, and is not so cheerful as she formerly was, perhaps because her health is not good, or possibly that she feels more keenly the deprivations under which she labours. She is very active is her movements, and fabricates numerous useful and ornamental articles, which she disposes of for her mother's benefit. She is very useful among the other pupils, and is well informed with regard to various branches of useful knowledge. She is completely matter-of-fact in all her ideas, as Dr. Howe studiously avoids all imagery and illustration in his instructions, in order not to embarrass her mind by complex images. It is to be regretted that she has very few ideas on the subject of religion.

One of the most interesting places to me in the vicinity of Boston was the abode of General Washington. It became his residence in 1775, and here he lived while the struggle for freedom was going on in the neighbourhood. It is one of the largest villas in the vicinity of Boston, and has side verandahs resting on wooden pillars, and a large garden in front. Some very venerable elms adjoin the house, and the grounds are laid out in the fashion which prevailed at that period. The room where Washington penned his famous despatches is still held sacred by the Americans. Their veneration for this renowned champion of independence has something almost idolatrous about it. It is very fortunate that the greatest character in American history should be also the best. Christian, patriot, legislator, and soldier, he deserved his mother's proud boast, "I know that wherever George Washington is, he is doing his duty." His character needed no lapse of years to shed a glory round it; the envy of contemporary writers left it stainless, and succeeding historians, with their pens dipped in gall, have not been able to sully the lustre of a name which is one of the greatest which that or any age has produced.

This mansion has, however, an added interest, from being the residence of the poet Longfellow. In addition to his celebrity as a poet, he is one of the most elegant scholars which America has produced, and, until recently, held the professorship of modern languages at the neighbouring university of Cambridge. It would be out of place here to criticise his poetry. Although it is very unequal and occasionally fantastic, and though in one of his greatest poems the English language appears to dance in chains in the hexameter, many of his shorter pieces well upwards from the heart, in a manner which is likely to ensure durable fame for their author. The truth, energy, and earnestness of his 'Psalm of Life' and 'Goblet of Life,' have urged many forward in the fight, to whom the ponderous sublimity of Milton is a dead language, and the metaphysical lyrics of Tennyson are un-intelligible. It appeared to me, from what I heard, that his fame is even greater in England than in his own country, where it is in some danger of being eclipsed by that of Bryant and Lowell. He is extremely courteous to strangers, and having kindly offered, through a friend, to show me Cambridge University, I had an opportunity of making his acquaintance.

I have been frequently asked to describe his personal appearance, and disappointment has frequently been expressed at the portrait which truth compels me to give of him. He is neither tall, black-haired, nor pale; he neither raises his eyes habitually to heaven, nor turns down his shirt-collar. He does not wear a look of melancholy resignation, neither does he live in love-gilded poverty, in a cottage embosomed in roses. On the contrary, he is about the middle height, and is by

323

no means thin. He has handsome features, merry blue eyes, and a ruddy complexion; he lives in a large mansion, luxuriously furnished; and, besides having a large fortune, is the father of six blooming children. In short, his appearance might be considered jovial, were it not so extremely gentlemanly.

Mr. Longfellow met us at the door, with that urbanity which is so agreeable a feature in his character, and, on being shown into a very handsome library, we were introduced to Mrs. Longfellow, a lady of dignified appearance and graceful manner. She is well known as the *Mary* of *Hyperion*; and after a due degree of indignation with the author of that graceful and poetical book, she rewarded his constancy and devotion with her hand. The library was panelled in the old style, and a large collection of books was arranged in recesses in the wall; but the apartment evidently served the purposes of library and boudoir, for there were numerous evidences of female taste and occupation. Those who think that American children are all precocious little men and women would have been surprised to see the door boisterously thrown open by a little blooming boy, who scrambled mirthfully upon his father's knee, as though used to be there, and asked him to whittle a stick for him.

It is not often that the conversation of an author is equal in its way to his writings, therefore I expected in Mr. Longfellow's case the disappointment which I did not meet with. He touched lightly on various subjects, and embellished each with the ease and grace of an accomplished scholar, and, doubtless in kindly compliment to an English visitor, related several agreeable reminiscences of acquaintanceships formed with some of our *literati* during a brief visit to England. He spoke with much taste and feeling of European antiquities, and of the absence of them in the New World, together with the effect produced by the latter upon the American character. He said that nothing could give him greater pleasure than a second visit to Europe, but that there were "six obstacles in the way of its taking place."

With him as a very able *cicerone* I had the pleasure of visiting Cambridge University, which reminded me more of England than anything I saw in America; indeed there are features in which it is not unlike its English namesake. It has no Newtonian or Miltonian shades, but in another century the names of those who fill a living age with lustre will have their memorials among its academic groves. There are several halls of dark stone or red brick, of venerable appearance, and there are avenues of stately elms. The library is a fine Gothic edifice, and contains some valuable manuscripts and illuminated editions of old works. There was a small copy of the four evangelists, written in characters resembling print, but so small that it cannot be read without a magnifying glass. This volume was the labour of a lifetime, and the transcriber completed his useless task upon his deathbed. While Mr. Longfellow was showing me some autographs of American patriots, I remarked that as I was showing some in a Canadian city, a gentleman standing by, on seeing the signature of the Protector, asked, in the most innocent ignorance, who Oliver Cromwell was? A lady answered that he was a successful rebel in the olden time! "If you are asked the question a second time," observed the poet, who doubtless fully appreciated the greatness of Cromwell, "say that he was an eminent brewer."

Altogether there is very much both of interest and beauty in Boston and its environs; and I was repeatedly told that I should have found the society more agreeable than that of New York. With the exception of visits paid to the houses of Longfellow and the late Mr. Abbott Lawrence, I did not see any of the inhabitants of Boston, as I only spent three days in the neighbourhood; but at Mr. Amy's house I saw what is agreeable in any country, more especially in a land of transition and change—a happy American home. The people of this western Athens pride themselves upon the intellectual society and the number of eminent men which they possess, among whom may be named Longfellow, Emerson, Lowell, Dana, and Summer. One of these at least is of the transcendental school.

I very much regretted that I had not more time to devote to a city so rich in various objects of interest; but the northern winter had already begun, and howling winds and angry seas warned me that it was time to join my friends at Halifax, who were desirous to cross the "vexed Atlantic" before the weather became yet more boisterous.

CHAPTER XVIII

Origin of the Constitution—The Executive—Congress—Local Legislatures—The army and navy—Justice—Slavery—Political corruption—The foreign element—Absence of principle—Associations—The Know-nothings—The Press and its power—Religion—The Church—The Clergy.

Before concluding this volume it will be proper to offer a few remarks upon American institutions, and such of their effects as are obvious to a temporary resident in the States. In apology for my own incompetence, I must again remind the reader that these are merely surface observations, offered in accordance with the preface to this work.

The Constitution demands the first notice. When our American colonies succeeded in throwing off the yoke of England, it became necessary for them to choose a form of government. No country ever started under such happy auspices. It had just concluded a successful struggle with one of the greatest empires in the world; its attitude of independence was sympathised with by the enthusiastic spirits of Europe, and had even gained the respect of that upright monarch, who, on receiving the first ambassador from his revolted colonies, addressed him with these memorable words:—"I was the last man in England to acknowledge the independence of America; but, being secured, I shall be the last man in England to violate it." Thus circumstanced, each of the thirteen States, with the exception of Rhode Island, sent delegates to Philadelphia to deliberate on the form of government which should be adopted. This deliberative assembly of a free people presented a sublime spectacle in the eyes of nations. After two years of consideration, and considerable differences of opinion, it was decided that the monarchical traditions of the Old World were effete and obsolete; and accordingly a purely Republican Constitution was promulgated, under which the United States have become a rich and powerful nation. It is gratifying to an English person to know that the Constitution of the States was derived in great measure from that of England, enlarged, and divested of those which were deemed its objectionable features. The different States had previously possessed local assemblies, and governors, and the institutions connected with slavery; the last remain to this day in pretty much the same state as when they were bequeathed by England to America. Washington entered upon the office of President in 1789, and discharged its duties, as he did those of every other station, with that high-souled and disinterested patriotism which render him as worthy to be imitated as admired.

There are three authorities, the President, the Senate, and the House of Representatives, all elected by the people; thus their acts are to a certain extent expressive of the popular will.

The President is elected by universal suffrage, once in four years. He receives a salary of £5000 per annum, and is assisted by five secretaries, who, with two other executive officers, are paid at the rate of £1600 a-year. This officer has considerable power and enormous patronage. He makes treaties, which merely require the ratification of the Senate; he grants pardons, and may place his veto on the acts of the two other estates, provided that they have not been returned by two-thirds of the members of the respective houses.

There are sixty-two Senators, or two from each State. These are elected by the local legislatures for a term of six years, and one-third of the number retire every two years. Each Senator must be thirty years of age; he must be a resident of the State which he represents, and he must have been naturalised for nine years.

The Lower House, or House of Representatives, is perhaps the most purely popular body in the world. The members are elected for two years by universal suffrage, that is, by the votes of all the free male citizens of America who have attained the age of 21. Each member of the Lower House must have been naturalised for seven years, and he must have passed the age of 25. Population has been taken as the basis of representation, in the following very simple manner. The number of Representatives was fixed by Act of Congress at 233, although a new one has recently been added for California. The aggregate representative population (by the last decennial enumeration, 21,767,673) is taken, and divided by 233; and the quotient, rejecting fractions, is the ratio of apportionment among the several States. The representative population of each State is then ascertained, and is divided by the above named ratio, and the quotient gives the number of representatives to each State. The State of New York, being the most populous, possesses 33 representatives; two of the States, namely, Delaware and Florida, require no more than one each. On a rough calculation, each member represents about 90,000 persons. The two houses together are named Congress, and the members of both receive 32s. per diem for their attendance, without deduction in case of sickness, in addition to travelling expenses. All measures of legislation and taxation must receive the approval of the President and the Congress, the majority in Congress representing the popular will. Every State has its assembly and governor, and to a certain extent has power to make its own laws. The members of these assemblies, the governors of the States, and the mayors and municipal officers of the cities, are all elected by universal suffrage.

No system of direct taxation is adopted in the States, except for local purposes. The national revenue is derived from customs duties, on many articles so high as to amount to protective duties; from the sale of wild lands; and from one or two other sources. The annual revenue of the country is about £12,000,000, and the expenditure is under the income. The state officials are rather poorly paid. The chief ambassadors do not receive more than £1800 per annum, and the chief justice, whose duties are certainly both arduous and responsible, only receives a salary of £1000 a year. The principal items of expenditure are connected with the army and navy, and the officers in both these services are amply remunerated. The United States navy is not so powerful as might be expected from such a maritime people. There are only twelve ships of the line and twelve first-class frigates, including receiving-ships and those on the stocks.

The standing army consists of 10,000 men, and is regarded with some jealousy by the mass of the people. The pay in this branch of the service varies from that of a major-general, which is £1000 a year, to that of a private, which is about 1*s.* 6*d.* a day. This last is larger than it appears, as it is not subject to the great deductions which are made from that of an English soldier. The real military strength of America consists of an admirably trained militia force of about 2,200,000 men, supported at an enormous expense. This large body is likely to prove invincible for defensive purposes, as it is composed of citizens trained to great skill as marksmen, and animated by the strongest patriotism; but it is to be hoped that is also furnishes a security against an offensive war on a large scale, as it is scarcely likely that any great number of men would abandon their business and homes for any length of time for aggressive purposes.

The highest court of law in the United States is the Supreme Court, which holds one annual session at Washington. It is composed of a chief justice and eight associate justices, and is the only power not subjected directly or indirectly to the will of the people. The United States are divided into nine judicial circuits, in each of which a Circuit Court is held twice a year by a justice of the Supreme Court, assisted by the district judge of the State in which the court sits. There is, however, a great weakness both about the Executive and the administration of justice, the consequence of which is, that, when a measure is placed upon the statute-book which is supposed to be obnoxious to any powerful class, a *league* is formed by private individuals for the purpose of enforcing it, or in some cases it would become a dead letter. The powerful societies which are formed to secure the working of the "*Maine Law*" will occur at once to English readers.

Each State possesses a distinct governmental machinery of its own, consisting of a Governor, a Senate, and a House of

Representatives. The Governor is elected by a majority of the votes of the male citizens for a term of years, varying in different States from one to four. The Senators are elected for like periods, and the Representatives are chosen for one or two years. The largest number of Representatives for any one State is 356.

Nearly all power in the United States is held to a great extent on popular sufferance; it emanates from the will of the majority, no matter how vicious or how ignorant that majority may be. In some cases this leads to a slight alteration of the Latin axiom, *Salus populi est suprema lex*, which may be read, "the *will* of the people is the supreme law." The American constitution is admirable in theory; it enunciates the incontrovertible principle, "All men are free and equal." But unfortunately, a serious disturbing element, and one which by its indirect effects threatens to bring the machinery of the Republic to a "dead lock," appears not to have entered into the calculations of these political theorists.

This element is slavery, which exists in fifteen out of thirty-one states, and it is to be feared that by a recent act of the legislature the power to extend it is placed in the hands of the majority, should that majority declare for it, in the new States. The struggle between the advocates of freedom and slavery is now convulsing America; it has already led to outrage and bloodshed in the State of Kansas, and appearances seem to indicate a prolonged and disastrous conflict between the North and South. The question is one which cannot be passed over by any political party in the States. Perhaps it may not be universally known in England that slavery is a part of the ratified Constitution of the States, and that the Government is bound to maintain it in its integrity. Its abolition must be procured by an important change in the constitution, which *would* shake, and *might* dislocate, the vast and unwieldy Republic. Each State, I believe, has it in its power to abolish slavery within its own limits, but the Federal Government has no power to introduce a modification of the system in any. The federal compact binds the Government "not to meddle with slavery in the States where it exists, to protect the owners in the case of runaway slaves, and to defend them in the event of invasion or domestic violence on account of it." *Thus the rights and property in slaves of the slaveholders are legally guaranteed to them by the Constitution of the United States.* At the last census the slaves amounted to more than 3,000,000, or about an eighth of the population, and constitute an alien body, neither exercising the privileges nor animated by the sentiments of the rest of the commonwealth. Slavery at this moment, as it is the curse and the shame, is also the canker of the Union. By it, by the very constitution of a country which proudly boasts of freedom, three millions of intelligent and responsible beings are reduced to the level of mere property— property legally reclaimable, too, in the Free States by an act called the Fugitive Slave Act. That there are slaveholders amiable, just, and humane, there is not a doubt; but slavery in its practice as a system deprives these millions of knowledge, takes away from them the Bible, keeps a race in heathen ignorance in a Christian land, denies to the slaves compensation for their labour, the rights of marriage and of the parental relation, which are respected even among the most savage nations; it sustains an iniquitous internal slave-trade—it corrupts the owners, and casts a slur upon the dignity of labour. It acts as an incubus on public improvement, and vitiates public morals; and it proves a very formidable obstacle to religion, advancement, and national unity; and so long as it shall remain a part of the American constitution, it gives a living lie to the imposing declaration, "All men are free and equal."

Where the whole machinery of government is capable of being changed or modified by the will of the people while the written constitution remains, and where hereditary and territorial differences of opinion exist on very important subjects, it is not surprising that party spirit should run very high. Where the highest offices in the State are neither lucrative enough nor permanent enough to tempt ambition—where, in addition, their occupants are appointed by the President merely for a short term—and where the highest dignity frequently precedes a life-long obscurity, the notoriety of party leadership offers a great inducement to the aspiring. Party spirit pervades the middle and lower ranks; every man, almost every woman, belongs to some party or other, and aspires to some political influence.

Any person who takes a prominent part either in local or general politics is attacked on the platform and by the press, with a fierceness, a scurrility, and a vulgarity which spare not even the sanctity of private life. The men of wealth, education, and talent, who have little either to gain or lose, and who would not yield up any carefully adopted principle to the insensate clamour of an unbridled populace, stand aloof from public affairs, with very few exceptions. The men of letters, the wealthy merchants, the successful in any profession, are not to be met with in the political arena, and frequently abstain even from voting at the elections. This indisposition to mix in politics probably arises both from the coarse abuse which assails public men, and from the admitted inability, under present circumstances, to stem the tide of corrupt practices, mob-law, and intimidation, which are placing the United States under a tyranny as severe as that of any privileged class—the despotism of a turbulent and unenlightened majority. Numbers are represented *exclusively*, and partly in consequence, property, character, and stake in the country are the last things which would be deemed desirable in a candidate for popular favour.

Owing to the extraordinary influx of foreigners, an element has been introduced which could scarcely have entered into the views of the framers of the Constitution, and is at this time the great hindrance to its beneficial working. The large numbers of Irish Romanists who have emigrated to the States, and whose feelings are too often disaffected and anti-American, evade the naturalisation laws, and, by surreptitiously obtaining votes, exercise a most mischievous influence upon the elections. Education has not yet so permeated the heterogeneous mass of the people as to tell effectually upon their choice of representatives. The electors are caught by claptrap, noisy declamation, and specious promises, coupled with laudatory comments upon the sovereign people. As the times for the elections approach, the candidates of the weaker party endeavour to obtain favour and notoriety by leading a popular cry. The declamatory vehemence with which certain members of the democratic party endeavoured to fasten a quarrel upon England at the close of 1855 is a specimen of the political capital which is too often relied upon in the States.

The enormous numbers of immigrants who annually acquire the rights of citizenship, without any other qualification for the franchise than their inability to use it aright, by their ignorance, turbulence, and often by their viciousness, tend still further to degrade the popular assemblies. It is useless to speculate upon the position in which America would be without the introduction of this terrible foreign element; it may be admitted that the republican form of government has not had a fair trial; its present state gives rise to serious doubts in the minds of many thinking men in the States, whether it can long continue in its present form.

The want of the elements of permanency in the Government keeps many persons from entering into public life: and it would appear that merit and distinguished talent, when accompanied by such a competence as renders a man independent of the emoluments of office, are by no means a passport to success. The stranger visiting the United States is surprised with the entire absence of gentlemanly feeling in political affairs. They are pervaded by a coarse and repulsive vulgarity; they are seldom alluded to in the conversation of the upper classes; and the ruling power in this vast community is in danger of being abandoned to corrupt agitators and noisy charlatans. The President, the Members of Congress, and to a still greater extent the members of the State Legislatures, are the *delegates* of a tyrannical majority rather than the *re-presentatives* of the people. The million succeeds in exacting an amount of cringing political subserviency, in attempting to obtain which, in a like degree, few despots have been successful.

The absence of a property qualification, the short term for which the representatives are chosen, and the want, in many instances, of a pecuniary independence among them, combined with a variety of other circumstances, place the members of the Legislatures under the direct control of the populace; they are its servile tools, and are subject to its wayward impulses and its proverbial fickleness; hence the remarkable absence of any fixed line of policy. The public acts of America are isolated; they appear to be framed for the necessities of the moment, under the influence of popular clamour or pressure; and sometimes seem neither to recognise engagements entered into in the past, or the probable course of events in the future. America does not possess a traditional policy, and she does not recognise any broad and well-defined principle as the rule for her conduct. The national acts of spoliation or meanness which have been sanctioned by the Legislature may be distinctly traced to the manner in which the primary elections are conducted. It is difficult, if not impossible, for the European governments to do more than guess at the part which America will take on any great question—whether, in the event of a collision between nations, she will observe an impartial neutrality, or throw the weight of her influence into the scale of liberty or despotism.

It is to be feared that political morality is in a very low state. The ballot secures the electors from even the breath of censure by making them irresponsible; few men dare to be independent. The plea of expediency is often used in extenuation of the grossest political dishonesty. To obtain political favour or position a man must stoop very low; he must cultivate the good will of the ignorant and the vicious; he must excite and minister to the passions of the people; he must flatter the bad, and assail the honourable with unmerited opprobrium. While he makes the assertion that his country has a monopoly of liberty, the very plan which he is pursuing shows that it is fettered by mob rule. No honourable man can use these arts, which are, however, a high-road to political eminence. It is scarcely necessary to remark upon the effect which is produced in society generally by this political corruption.

The want of a general and high standard of morality is very apparent. That dishonesty which is so notoriously and often successfully practised in political life is not excluded from the dealings of man with man.

It is jested about under the name of "smartness," and commended under that of "'cuteness," till the rule becomes of frequent and practical application, that the disgrace attending a dishonourable transaction lies only in its detection,—that a line of conduct which custom has sanctioned in public life cannot be very blameable in individual action.

While the avenues to distinction in public life are in great measure closed against men of honour, wealth offers a sure road to eminence, and the acquisition of it is the great object followed. It is often sought and obtained by means from which considerations of honesty and morality are omitted; but there is not, as with us, that righteous censorship of public opinion which brands dishonesty with infamy, and places the offender apart, in a splendid leprosy, from the society to which he hoped wealth would be a passport. It you listen to the conversation in cars, steamboats, and hotels, you become painfully impressed with the absence of moral truth which pervades the country. The success of Barnum, the immense popularity of his infamous autobiography, and the pride which large numbers feel in his success, instance the perverted moral sense which is very much the result of the absence of principle in public life; for the example of men in the highest positions in a state must influence the masses powerfully either for good

or evil. A species of moral obliquity pervades a large clas
the community, by which the individuals composing it
prevented from discerning between truth and falsehoc
except as either tends to their own personal aggrandisemei
Thus truth is at a fearful discount, and men exult in successft
roguery, as though a new revelation had authorised them to
rank it among the cardinal virtues.

These remarks apply to a class, unfortunately a very
numerous one, of the existence of which none are more
painfully conscious than the good among the Americans
themselves. Of the upper class of merchants, manufacturers,
shipbuilders, &c., it would be difficult to speak too highly. They
have acquired a world-wide reputation for their uprightness,
punctuality, and honourable dealings in all mercantile
transactions.

The oppression which is exercised by a tyrant majority is one
leading cause of the numerous political associations which
exist in the States. They are the weapons with which the
weaker side combats the numerically superior party. When a
number of persons hit upon a grievance, real or supposed,
they unite themselves into a society, and invite delegates from
other districts. With a celerity which can scarcely be imagined,
declarations are issued and papers established advocating
party views; public meetings are held, and a complete
organization is secured, with ramifications extending all over
the country. A formidable and compact body thus arises, and it
occasionally happens that such a society, originating in the
weakness of a minority, becomes strong enough to dictate a
course of action to the Executive.

Of all the associations ever formed, none promised to
exercise so important an influence as that of the Know-
nothings, or the American party. It arose out of the terrific
spread of a recognised evil—namely, the power exercised upon
the Legislature by foreigners, more especially by the Irish
Romanists. The great influx of aliens, chiefly Irish and
Germans, who speedily or unscrupulously obtain the

franchise, had caused much alarm throughout the country. It was seen that the former, being under the temporal and spiritual domination of their priests, and through them under an Italian prince, were exerting a most baneful influence upon the republican institutions of the States. Already in two or more States the Romanists had organised themselves to interfere with the management of the public schools. This alarm paved the way for the rapid extension of the new party, which first made its appearance before men's eyes with a secret organization and enormous political machinery. Its success was unprecedented. Favoured by the secresy of the ballot, it succeeded in placing its nominees in all the responsible offices in several of the States. Other parties appeared paralysed, and men yielded before a mysterious power of whose real strength they were in complete ignorance. The avowed objects of the Know-nothings were to establish new naturalization laws, prohibiting any from acquiring the franchise without a residence of twenty-one years in the States—to procure the exclusion of Romanists from all public offices—to restore the working of the constitution to its original purity—and to guarantee to the nation religious freedom, a free Bible, and free schools; in fact, to secure to *Americans* the right which they are in danger of ceasing to possess—namely, that of governing themselves.

The objects avowed in the preliminary address were high and holy; they stirred the patriotism of those who writhed under the tyranny of an heterogeneous majority, while the mystery of nocturnal meetings, and a secret organization, conciliated the support of the young and ardent. For a time a hope was afforded of the revival of a pure form of republican government, but unfortunately the Know-nothing party contained the elements of dissolution within itself. Some of its principles savoured of intolerance, and of persecution for religious opinions, and it ignored the subject of slavery. This can never be long excluded from any party consideration, and, though politicians strive to evade it, the question still recurs,

and will force itself into notice. Little more than a year after the Know-nothings were first heard of, they came into collision with the subject, in the summer of 1855, and, after stormy dissensions at their great convention, broke up into several branches, some of which totally altered or abandoned the original objects of their association.

Their triumph was brief: some of the States in which they were the most successful have witnessed their signal overthrow,[1] and it is to be feared that no practical good will result from their future operations. But the good cause of constitutional government in America is not lost with their failure—public opinion, whenever it shall be fairly appealed to, will declare itself in favour of truth and order; the conservative principle, though dormant, is yet powerful; and, though we may smile at republican inconsistencies, and regret the state into which republican government has fallen, it is likely that America contains the elements of renovation within herself, and will yet present to the world the sublime spectacle of a free people governing itself by just laws, and rejoicing in the purity of its original republican institutions.

The newspaper press is one of the most extraordinary features in the United States. Its influence is omnipresent. Every party in religion, politics, or morals, speaks, not by one, but by fifty organs; and every nicely defined shade of opinion has its voices also. Every town of large size has from ten to twenty daily papers; every village has its three or four; and even a collection of huts produces its one "daily," or two or three "weeklies." These prints start into existence without any fiscal restrictions: there is neither stamp nor paper duty. Newspapers are not a luxury, as with us, but a necessary of life. They vary in price from one halfpenny to threepence, and no workman who could afford his daily bread would think of being without his paper. Hundreds of them are sold in the hotels at breakfast-time; and in every steamer and railway car,

1 At several of the state elections at the close of 1855 the Know-nothings succeeded in placing their nominees in public offices, partly by an abandonment of some of their original aims.

from the Atlantic ocean to the western prairies, the traveller is assailed by news-boys with dozens of them of sale. They are bought in hundreds everywhere, and are greedily devoured by men, women, and children. Almost as soon as the locality of a town is chosen, a paper starts into life, which always has the effect of creating an antagonist.

The newspapers in the large cities spare no expense in obtaining, either by telegraph or otherwise, the earliest intelligence of all that goes on in the world. Every item of English news appears in the journals, from the movements of the court to those of the *literati*; and a weekly summary of parliamentary intelligence is always given. Any remarkable law proceedings are also succinctly detailed. It follows, that a dweller at Cincinnati or New Orleans is nearly as well versed in English affairs as a resident of Birmingham, and English politics and movements in general are very frequent subjects of conversation. Since the commencement of the Russian war the anxiety for English intelligence has increased, and every item of Crimean or Baltic news, as recorded in the letters of the "special correspondents," is reprinted in the American papers without abridgment, and is devoured by all classes of readers. The great fault of most of these journals is their gross personality; even the privacy of domestic life is invaded by their Argus-eyed scrutiny. The papers discern everything, and, as everybody reads, no current events, whether in politics, religion, or the world at large, are unknown to the masses. The contents of an American paper are very miscellaneous. Besides the news of the day, it contains congressional and legal reports, exciting fiction, and reports of sermons, religious discussions, and religious anniversaries. It prys into every department of society, and informs its readers as to the doings and condition of all.

Thus every party and sect has a daily register of the most minute sayings and doings, and proceedings and progress of every other sect; and as truth and error are continually brought before the masses, they have the opportunity to know and compare. There are political parties under the names of Whigs, Democrats, Know-nothings, Freesoilers, Fusionists, Hunkers, Woolly-heads, Dough-faces, Hard-shells, Soft-shells, Silver-greys, and I know not what besides; all of them extremely puzzling to the stranger, but of great local significance. There are about a hundred so-called religious denominations, from the orthodox bodies and their subdivisions to those professing the lawless fanaticism of Mormonism, or the chilling dogmas of Atheism. All these parties have their papers, and each "movement" has its organ. The "Woman's Right Movement" and the "Spiritual Manifestation Movement" have several.

There is a continual multiplication of papers, corresponding, not only to the increase of population, but to that of parties and vagaries. The increasing call for editors and writers brings persons into their ranks who have neither the education nor the intelligence to fit them for so important an office as the *irresponsible guidance* of the people. They make up for their deficiencies in knowledge and talent by fiery and unprincipled partisanship, and augment the passions and prejudices of their readers instead of placing the truth before them. The war carried on between papers of opposite principles is something perfectly terrific. The existence of many of these prints depends on the violent passions which they may excite in their supporters, and frequently the editors are men of the most unprincipled character. The papers advocating the opinions of the different religious de-nominations are not exempt from the charge of personalities and abusive writing. No discord is so dread as that carried on under the cloak of religion, and religious journalism in the States is on a superlatively bitter footing.

But evil as is, to a great extent, the influence exercised by the press, terrible as is its scrutiny, and unlimited as is its power, destitute of principle as it is in great measure, it has its bright as well as its dark side. Theories, opinions, men, and things, are examined into and sifted until all can understand their truth and error. The argument of antiquity or authority is exploded and ridiculed, and the men who seek to sustain antiquated error on the foundation of effete tradition are compelled to prove it by scripture or reason. Yet such are the multitudinous and tortuous ways in which everything is discussed, that multitudes of persons who have neither the leisure nor ability to reflect for themselves know not what to believe, and there is a very obvious absence of attachment to clear and strongly defined principles. The great circulation which the newspapers enjoy may be gathered, without giving copious statistics, from the fact that one out of the many New York journals has a circulation of 187,000 copies.[1] The *New York Tribune* may be considered the "leading journal" of America, but it adheres to one set of principles, and Mr. Horace Greely, the editor, has the credit of being a powerful advocate of the claims or morality and humanity.

It is impossible for a stranger to form any estimate of the influence really possessed by religion in America. I saw nothing which led me to doubt the assertion made by persons who have opportunities of forming an opinion, that "America and Scotland are the two most religious countries in the world."

The Sabbath is well observed, not only, as might be expected, in the New England States, but in the large cities of the Union; and even on the coasts of the Pacific the Legislature of California has passed an act for its better observance in that State. It is probable that, in a country where business pursuits and keen competition are carried to such an unheard-of extent, all classes feel the need of rest on the seventh day, and regard the Sabbath as a physical necessity. The churches of all denominations are filled to overflowing; the proportion of communicants to attendants is very large; and the foreign

1 There are now about 400 daily newspapers in the States: their aggregate circulation is over 800,000 copies. There are 2217 weekly papers, with an aggregate circulation of 3,100,057 copies; and the total aggregate circulation of all the prints is about 5,400,000 copies. In one year about 423,000,000 copies of newspapers were printed and circulated.

missions, and other religious societies, are supported on a scale of remarkable liberality.

There is no established church or dominant religious persuasion in the States. There are no national endowments; all are on the same footing, and live or die as they obtain the suffrages of the people. While the State does not recognise any one form of religion, it might be expected that she would assist the ministers of all. Such is not the case; and, though Government has wisely thought it necessary to provide for the education of the people, it has not thought it advisable to make any provision for the maintenance of religion. Everyone worships after his own fashion; the sects are numerous and subdivided; and all enjoy the blessings of a complete religious toleration.

Strange sects have arisen, the very names of which are scarcely known in England, and each has numerous adherents. It may be expected that fanaticism would run to a great height in the States. Among the 100 different denominations which are returned in the census tables, the following designations occur: Mormonites, Antiburgers, Believers in God, Children of Peace, Disunionists; Danian, Democratic Gospel, and Ebenezer Socialists; Free Inquirers, Inspired Church, Millerites, Menonites, New Lights, Perfectionists, Pathonites, Pantheists, Tunkards, Restorationists, Superalists, Cosmopolites, and hosts of others.

The clergy depend for their salaries upon the congregations for whom they officiate, and upon private endowments. The total value of church property in the United States is estimated at 86,416,639 dollars, of which one-half is owned in the States of Massachusetts, New York, and Pennsylvania. The number of churches, exclusive of those in the newly-organised territories, is about 38,000. There is one church for every 646 of the population. The voluntary system is acted upon by each denomination, though it is slightly modified in the Episcopalian church. In it, however, the bishops are elected, the clergy are chosen by the people, and its affairs are regulated by a convention. It is the oldest of the denominations, and is therefore entitled to the first notice.

It has 38 bishops, 1714 ministers, and 105,350 communicants. It has 1422 churches, and its church property is estimated at 11,261,970 dollars. A large number of the educated and wealthy are members of this body. Its formularies, with the exception of some omissions and alterations, are the same as those of the Church of England. Some of its bishops are men of very high attainments. Dr. McIlvaine, the Bishop of Ohio, is a man of great learning and piety, and is well known in England by his theological writings.

The Methodists are the largest religious body in America. As at home, they have their strong sectional differences, but they are very useful, and are particularly acceptable to the lower orders of society, and among the coloured population. They possess 12,467 churches, 8389 ministers, and 1,672,519 communicants, and the value of their church property exceeds 14,000,000 dollars.

The Presbyterians are perhaps the most important of the religious bodies, as regards influence, education, and wealth. Their stronghold is in New England. They have 7752 congregations, 5807 ministers, and 680,021 communicants. Their church property is of the value of 14,000,000 dollars.

The Baptists are very numerous. They have 8181 churches, 8525 ministers, 1,058,754 communicants, and church property to the amount of 10,931,382 dollars.

The Congregationalists possess 1674 churches, 1848 ministers, and 207,609 communicants. Their property is of the value of 7,973,962 dollars.

The Roman Catholics possessed at the date of the last census 1112 churches, and church property to the amount of 9,000,000 dollars.

There is church accommodation for about 14,000,000 persons, or considerably more than half the population. There are 35,000 Sabbath schools, with 250,000 teachers, and 2,500,000 scholars. Besides the large number of churches, religious services are held in many schools and courthouses, and even in forests and fields. The dissemination of the Bible is on the increase. In last year the Bible Society distributed upwards of 11,000,000 copies. The Society for Religious Publications employed 1300 colporteurs, and effected sales during the year to the amount of 526,000 dollars. The principal of the religious societies are for the observance of the sabbath, for temperance, anti-slavery objects, home missions, foreign missions, &c. The last general receipts of all these societies were 3,053,535 dollars.

In the State of Massachusetts the Unitarians are a very influential body, numbering many of the most intellectual and highly educated of the population. These, however, are divided upon the amount of divinity with which they shall invest our Lord.

The hostile spirit which animates some of the religious journals has been already noticed. There is frequently a good deal of rivalry between the members of the different sects; but the way in which the ministers of the orthodox denominations act harmoniously together for the general good is one of the most pleasing features in America. The charitable religious associations are on a gigantic scale, and are conducted with a liberality to which we in England are strangers. The foreign missions are on a peculiarly excellent system, and the self-denying labours and zeal of their missionaries are fully recognised by all who have come in contact with them. No difficulty is experienced in obtaining money for these objects; it is only necessary to state that a certain sum is required, and, without setting any begging machinery to work, donations exceeding the amount flow in from all quarters.

Altogether it would appear from the *data* which are given that the religious state of America is far more satisfactory than could be expected from so heterogeneous a population. The New England States possess to a great extent the externals of religion, and inherit in a modified degree the principles of their Puritan ancestors; and the New Englanders have emigrated westward in large numbers, carrying with them to the newly settled States the leaven of religion and morality. The churches of every denomination are crowded, and within my observation by as many gentlemen as ladies; but that class of aspiring spirits, known under the name of "*Young America*," boasts a perfect freedom from religious observances of every kind.

There is a creed known by the name of Universalism, which is a compound of Antinomianism with several other forms of error, and embraces tens of thousands within its pale. It often verges upon the most complete Pantheism, and is very popular with large numbers of the youth of America.

There is a considerable amount of excitement kept up by the religious bodies in the shape of public re-unions, con-gregational *soirées*, and the like, producing a species of religious dissipation, very unfavourable, I should suppose, to the growth of true piety. This system, besides aiding the natural restlessness of the American character, gives rise to a good deal of spurious religion, and shortens the lives and impairs the usefulness of the ministers by straining and exhausting their physical energies.

To the honour of the clergy of the United States it must be observed that they keep remarkably clear from party-politics, contrasting in this respect very favourably with the priests of the Church of Rome, who throw the weight of their influence into the scale of extreme democracy and fanatical excesses. The unity of action which their ecclesiastical system ensures to them makes their progressive increase much to be deprecated.

It is owing in great measure to the efforts of the ministers of religion that the unbending principles of truth and right have any hold upon the masses; they are ever to be found on the side of rational and constitutional liberty in its extreme form, as opposed to licence and anarchy; and they give the form of practical action to the better feelings of the human mind. Amid the great difficulties with which they are surrounded, owing to the want of any fixed principles of right among the masses, they are ever seeking to impress upon the public mind that the undeviating laws of morality and truth cannot be violated with impunity any more by millions than by individuals, and that to nations, as to individuals, the day of reckoning must sooner or later arrive.

The voluntary system in religion, as it exists in its unmodified form in America, has one serious attendant evil. Where a minister depends for his income, not upon the contributions to a common fund, as is the case in the Free Church of Scotland, but upon the congregation unto which he ministers, his conscience is to a dangerous extent under the power of his hearers. In many instances his uncertain pecuniary relations with them must lead him to slur over popular sins, and keep the unpalatable doctrines of the Bible in the background, practically neglecting to convey to fallen and wicked man his Creator's message, "Repent, and believe the Gospel." It has been found impossible in the States to find a just medium between state-support, and the apathy which in the opinion of many it has a tendency to engender, and an unmodified voluntary system, with the subservience and "high-pressure" which are incidental to it.

Be this as it may, the clergy of the United States deserve the highest honour for their high standard of morality, the fervour of their ministrations, the zeal of their practice, and their abstinence from politics.

CHAPTER XIX

General remarks continued—The common schools—Their defect—Difficulties—Management of the schools—The free academy—Railways—Telegraphs—Poverty—Literature— Advantages for emigrants—Difficulties of emigrants—Peace or war—Concluding observations.

At a time when the deficiencies of our own educational system are so strongly felt, it may be well to give an outline of that pursued in the States. The following statistics, taken from the last census, show that our Transatlantic brethren have made great progress in moral and intellectual interests.

At the period when the enumeration was made there were 80,958 public schools, with 91,966 teachers, and 2,890,507 scholars; 119 colleges, with 11,903 students; 44 schools of theology; 36 schools of medicine; and 16 schools of law. Fifty millions of dollars were annually spent for education, and the proportion of scholars to the community was as 1 to 5.

But it is to the common-school system that the attention should be particularly directed. I may premise that it has one unavoidable defect, namely, the absence of religious instruction. It would be neither possible nor right to educate the children in any denominational creed, or to instruct them in any particular doctrinal system, but would it not, to take the lowest ground, be both prudent and politic to give them a knowledge of the Bible, as the only undeviating rule and standard of truth and right? May not the obliquity of moral vision, which is allowed to exist among a large class of Americans, be in some degree chargeable to those who have the care of their education—who do not place before them, as a part of their instruction, those principles of truth and morality, which, as revealed in Holy Scripture, lay the whole universe under obligations to obedience? History and observation alike show the little influence practically possessed by principles destitute of superior authority, how small the restraint exercised by conscience is, and how far those may wander into error who once desert "Lift's polar star, the fear of God." In regretting the exclusion of religious instruction from the common-school system, the difficulties which beset the subject must not be forgotten, the multiplicity of the sects, and the very large number of Roman Catholics. In schools supported by a rate levied indiscriminately on all, to form a course of instruction which could bear the name of a religious one, and yet meet the views of all, and clash with the consciences and prejudices of none, was manifestly impossible. The religious public in the United States has felt that there was no tenable ground between thorough religious instruction and the broadest toleration. Driven by the circumstances of their country to accept the latter course, they have exerted themselves to meet this omission in the public schools by a most comprehensive Sabbath-school system. But only a portion of the children under secular instruction in the week attend these schools; and it must be admitted that to bestow intellectual culture upon the pupils, without giving them religious instruction, is to draw forth and add to the powers of the mind, without giving it any helm to guide it; in other words, it is to increase the capacity, without diminishing the propensity, to do evil.

Apart from this important consideration, the educational system pursued in the States is worthy of the highest praise, and of an enlightened people in the nineteenth century. The education is conducted at the public expense, and the pupils consequently pay no fees. Parents feel that a free education is as much a part of the birthright of their children as the protection which the law affords to their life and property.

The schools called common schools are supported by an education rate, and in each State are under the administration of a general board of education, with local boards, elected by all who pay the rate. In the State of Massachusetts alone the sum of 921,532 dollars was raised within the year, being at the rate of very nearly a dollar for every inhabitant. Under the supervision of the General Board of Education in the State, schools are erected in districts according to the educational necessities of the population, which are periodically ascertained by a census.

To give some idea of the system adopted, I will just give a sketch of the condition of education in the State of New York, as being the most populous and important.

There is a "state tax," or "appropriation," of 800,000 dollars, and this is supplemented by a rate levied on real and personal property. Taking as an authority the return made to the Legislature for the year ending in 1854, the total sum expended for school purposes within the State amounted to 2,469,248 dollars. The total number of children in the organised districts of the State was 1,150,532, of whom 862,935 were registered as being under instruction. The general management of education within the State is vested in a central board, with local boards in each of the organised districts, to which the immediate government and official supervision of the schools are intrusted.

The system comprises the common schools, with their primary and upper departments, a normal school for the preparation of teachers, and a free academy. In the city of New York there are 224 schools in the receipt of public money, of which 25 are for coloured children, and the number of pupils registered is given at 133,813. These common or ward schools are extremely handsome, and are fitted up at great expense, with every modern improvement in heating and ventilation. Children of every class, residing within the limits of the city, are admissible without payment, as the parents of all are supposed to be rated in proportion to their means.

There is a principal to each school, assisted by a numerous and efficient staff of teachers, who in their turn are expected to go through a course of studies at the Normal School. The number of teachers required for these schools is very great, as the daily attendance in two of them exceeds 2000. The education given is so very superior, and habits of order and propriety are so admirably inculcated, that it is not uncommon to see the children of wealthy storekeepers side by side with those of working mechanics. In each school there is one large assembly-room, capable of accommodating from 500 to 1000 children, and ten or twelve capacious class-rooms. Order is one important rule, and, that it may be acted upon, there is no overcrowding—the pupils being seated at substantial mahogany desks only holding two.

The instruction given comprises all the branches of a liberal education, with the exception of languages. There is no municipal community out of America in which the boon of a first-rate education is so freely offered to all as in the city of New York. There is no child of want who may not freely receive an education which will fit him for any office in his country. The common school is one of the glories of America, and every citizen may be justly proud of it. It brings together while in a pliant condition the children of people of different origins; and besides diffusing knowledge among them, it softens the prejudices of race and party, and carries on a continual process of assimilation.

The Board of Education of New York has lately thrown open several of these schools in the evening, and with very beneficial results. The number of pupils registered last year was 9313. Of these, 3400 were above the age of 16 and under 21, and 1100 were above the age of 21. These evening-schools entailed an additional expense of 17,563 dollars; the whole expenditure for school purposes in the city being 430,982 dollars. In the ward and evening schools of New York, 133,000 individuals received instruction. Each ward, or educational district, elects 2 commissioners, 2 inspectors, and 8 trustees. The duties of the inspectors are very arduous, as the examinations are frequent and severe.

The crowning educational advantage offered by this admirable system is the Free Academy. This academy receives its pupils solely from the common schools. Every person presenting himself as a candidate must be more than 13 years of age, and, having attended a common school for 12 months, he must produce a certificate from the principal that he has passed a good examination in spelling, reading, writing. English grammar, arithmetic, geography, elementary book-keeping, history of the United States, and algebra. This institution extends to the pupils in the common schools the advantage of a free education in those higher departments of learning which cannot be acquired without considerable expense in any other college. The yearly examination of candidates for admission takes place immediately after the common school examinations in July. There are at present nearly 600 students under the tuition of 14 professors, and as many tutors as may be required. The course of study extends over a period of 5 years, and is very complete and severe. Owing to the principle adopted in their selection, the pupils, representing every social and pecuniary grade in society, present a very high degree of scholarship and ability. In this academy the vestiges of antagonism between the higher and lower classes are swept away. Indeed, the poor man will feel that he has a greater interest in sustaining this educational system than the rich, because he can only obtain through it those advantages for his children which the money of the wealthy can procure from other sources. He will be content with his daily toil, happy in the thought that, by the wise provision of his government, the avenues to fame, preferment, and wealth, are opened as freely to his children as to those of the richest citizen in the land.

In order to secure a supply of properly qualified teachers, the Board of Education has established a normal school, which numbers about 400 pupils. Most of these are assistant-teachers in the common schools, and attend the normal school on Saturdays, to enable themselves to obtain further attainments, and higher qualifications for their profession.

Under this system of popular education, the average cost per scholar for 5 years, including books, stationery, fuel, and all other expenses, is 7 dollars 2 cents per annum. This system of education is followed in nearly all the States; and while it reflects the highest credit on America, it contrasts strangely with the niggard plan pursued in England, where so important a thing as the education of the people depends almost entirely on precarious subscriptions and private benevolence.

With a gratuitous and comprehensive educational system, it may excite some surprise that the citizens of New York and other of the populous cities are compelled to supplement the common schools with those for the shoeless, the ragged, and the vicious, very much on the plan of our Scotch and English ragged-schools. Already the large cities of the New World are approximating to the condition of those in the Old, in producing a subsidence or deposit of the drunken, the dissolute, the vicious, and the wretched. With parents of this class, education for their offspring is considered of no importance, and the benevolent founders of these schools are compelled to offer material inducements to the children to attend, in the shape of food and clothing. At these schools, in place of the cleanly, neat, and superior appearance of the children in the common schools, dirt, rags, shoeless feet, and pallid, vicious, precocious countenances are to be seen. Nothing destroys so effectually the external distinguishing peculiarities of race as the habit of evil. There is a uniformity of expression invariably produced, which is most painful. These children are early taught to look upon virtue only as a cloak to be worn by the rich. This dangerous and increasing class in New York is composed almost entirely of foreign immigrants. The instruction in these schools is given principally by ladies of high station and education. It is a noble feature in New York "high life," and in process of time may diminish the gulf which is widening between the different classes, and may lessen the hideous contrasts which are presented between princely fortunes on the one hand, and vicious poverty on the other.

Taking the various schools throughout the Union, it is estimated that between 4,000,000 and 5,000,000 individuals are at this time receiving education.

To turn from the social to the material features of the United States: their system of internal communication deserves a brief notice, for by it their resources have been developed to a prodigious extent. The system of railways, telegraphs, and canal and river navigation presents an indication of the wealth and advancement of the United States, as wonderful as any other feature of her progress. She contains more miles of railway than all the rest of the world put together.

In a comparatively new country like America many of the items of expense which attend the construction of railways in England are avoided; the initiatory expenses are very small. In most of the States, all that is necessary is, for the company to prove that it is provided with means to carry out its scheme, when it obtains a charter from the Legislature at a very small cost. In several States, including the populous ones of New York and Ohio, no special charter is required, as a general railway law prescribes the rules to be observed by joint-stock companies. Materials, iron alone excepted, are cheap, and the right of way is usually freely granted. In the older States land would not cost more than £20 an acre. Wood frequently costs nothing more than the labour of cutting it, and the very level surface of the country renders tunnels, cuttings, and embankments generally unnecessary. The average cost per mile is about 38,000 dollars, or £7600.

In States where land has become exceedingly valuable, land damages form a heavy item in the construction of new lines, but in the South and West the case is reversed, and the proprietors are willing to give as much land as may be required, in return for having the resources of their localities opened up by railway communication. It is estimated that the cost of railways in the new States will not exceed £4000 per mile. The termini are plain, and have been erected at a very small expense, and many of the wayside stations are only wooden sheds. Few of the lines have a double line of rails, and the bridges or viaducts are composed of logs of wood, with little ironwork and less paint, except in a few instances. Except where the lines intersect cultivated districts, fences are seldom seen, and the paucity of porters and other officials materially reduces the working expenses. The common rate of speed is from 22 to 30 miles an hour, but there are express trains which are warranted to perform 60 in a like period. The fuel is very cheap, being billets of wood. The passenger and goods traffic on nearly all the lines is enormous, and it is stated that most of them pay a dividend of from 8 to 15 per cent.

The primary design has been to connect the sea-coast with all parts of the interior, the ulterior is to unite the Atlantic and Pacific Oceans At the present time there are about 25,000 miles of railway in operation and course of construction, and the average rate of fare is seldom more than 1*d*. per mile. Already the chief cities of the Atlantic have been connected with the vast valley of the Mississippi, and before long the regions bordering on Lake Huron and Lake Superior will be united with Mobile and New Orleans. In addition to this enormous system of railway communication, the canal and river navigation extends over 10,000 miles, and rather more than 3000 steamboats float on American waters alone.

The facilities for telegraphic communication in the States are a further evidence of the enterprise of this remarkable people. They have now 22,000 miles of telegraph in operation, and the cost of transmitting messages is less than a halfpenny a word for any distance under 200 miles. The cost of construction, including every outlay, is about £30 per mile. The wires are carried along the railways, through forests, and across cities, rivers, and prairies. Messages passing from one very distant point to another have usually to be re-written at an intermediate station; though by an improved plan they have been transmitted direct from New York to Mobile, a distance of 1800 miles. By the Cincinnati telegraphic route to New Orleans, a distance from New York of 2000 miles, the news brought by the British steamer to Sandy Hook at 8 in the morning has been telegraphed to New Orleans, and before 11 o'clock the effects produced by it upon speculations there have been returned to New York—the message accomplishing a distance of 4000 miles in three hours. The receipts are enormous, for, in consequence of the very small sum charged for transmitting messages, as many as 600 are occasionally sent along the principal lines in one day. The seven principal morning papers in New York paid in one year 50,000 dollars for despatches, and 14,000 for special messages. Messages connected with markets, public news, the weather, and the rise and fall of stocks, are incessantly passing between the great cities. Any change in the weather likely to affect the cotton-crop is known immediately in the northern cities. While in the Exchange at Boston, I witnessed the receipt of a telegraphic despatch announcing that a heavy shower was falling at New Orleans!

It must not be supposed that there is no poverty in the New World. During one year 134,972 paupers were in the receipt of relief, of whom 59,000 were in the State of New York; but to show the evil influence of the foreign, more especially the Irish, element in America, it is stated that 75 per cent. of the criminals and paupers are foreigners.

The larger portion of the crime committed is done under the influence of spirits; and to impose a check upon their sale, that celebrated enactment, known under the name of the "*Maine Law*," has been placed upon the statute-books of several of the States, including the important ones of New York, Maine, Massachusetts, Connecticut, and Nebraska. This law prohibits, under heavy penalties, the manufacture or sale of alcoholic liquors. It has been passed in obedience to the will of the people, as declared at the elections; and though to us its provisions seem somewhat arbitrary, its working has produced very salutary effects.

When so much importance is attached to education, and such a liberal provision is made for it, it is to be expected that a taste for reading would be universally diffused. And such is the case: America teems with books. Every English work worth reading is reprinted in a cheap form in the States as soon as the first copy crosses the Atlantic. Our reviews and magazines appear regularly at half price, and Dickens' 'Household Words' and 'Chambers' Journal' enjoy an enormous circulation without any pecuniary benefit being obtained by the authors. Everyone reads the newspapers and 'Harper's Magazine,' and everyone buys bad novels, on worse paper, in the cars and steamboats. The States, although amply supplied with English literature, have many popular authors of their own, among whom may be named Prescott, Bancroft, Washington Irving, Stowe, Stephens, Wetherall, Emerson, Longfellow, Lowell, and Bryant. Books are very cheap wherever the editions of English works are concerned, and a library is considered an essential part of the fitting up of a house. In many of the States there are public libraries supported by a rate. In the State of New York, in the year ending 1854, the Commissioners of Education received 90,579 dollars for libraries.

Perhaps the greatest advantage offered to emigrants is the opportunity everywhere afforded of investing small sums of money advantageously. In England, in most branches of trade, the low rate of wages renders it impossible for the operative to save any portion of his earnings; and even when he is able to do so, he can rarely obtain a higher rate of interest for his money than that which the savings-banks offer. Economise as he may, his hard-won savings seldom are sufficient to afford him a provision in old age. In America, on the contrary, the man who possesses £5 or £10 has every hope of securing a competence. He may buy land in newly-settled districts, which sometimes can be obtained at 7s. an acre, and hold it till it becomes valuable, or he may obtain a few shares in any thriving corporate concern. A hundred ways present themselves to the man of intelligence and industry by which he may improve and increase his little fortune. The necessaries of life are abundant and cheap, and, aided by a free education, he has the satisfaction of a well-grounded hope that his children will rise to positions of respectability and affluence, while his old age will be far removed from the pressure of want. The knowledge that each shilling saved may produce ten or twenty by judicious investment is a constant stimulus to his industry.

Yet, from all that I have seen and heard, I should think that Canada West offers a more advantageous field for emigrants. Equally free and unburdened by taxation, with the same social and educational advantages, with an increasing demand for labour of every kind, with a rich soil, extraordinary facilities of communication, and a healthy climate, pauperism is unknown; fluctuations in commercial affairs are comparatively small, and, above all, the emigrant is not exposed to the loss of everything which he possesses as soon as he lands.

An infamous class of swindlers, called "emigrant-runners," meet the poor adventurer on his arrival at New York. They sell him second-class tickets at the price of first-class, forged passes, and tickets to take him 1000 miles, which are only available at the outside for 200 or 300. If he holds out against their extortions, he is beaten, abused, loses his luggage for a time, or is transferred to the tender mercies of the boarding-house keeper, who speedily deprives him of his hard-earned savings. These runners retard the westward progress of the emigrant in every way; they charge enormous rates for the removal of his luggage from the wharf; they plunder him in railway-cars, in steamboats, in lodging-houses; and if Providence saves him from sinking into drunkenness and despair, and he can be no longer detained, they sell him a lot in some non-existent locality, or send him off to the west in search of some pretended employment. Too frequently, after the emigrant has lost his money and property, sickened by disappointment and deserted by hope, he is content to remain at New York, where he contributes to increase that "dangerous class" already so much feared in the Empire City.

One point remains to be noticed, and that is, the feeling which exists in America towards England. Much has been done to inflame animosity on each side; national rivalries have been encouraged, and national jealousies fomented. In travelling through the United States I expected to find a very strong anti-

English feeling. In this I was disappointed. It is true that I scarcely ever entered a car, steamboat, or hotel, without hearing England made a topic of discussion in connexion with the war; but, except on a few occasions in the West, I never heard any other than kindly feelings expressed towards our country. A few individuals would prognosticate failure and disaster, and glory in the anticipation of a "busting-up;" but these were generally "Kurnels" of militia, or newly-arrived Irish emigrants. These last certainly are very noisy enemies, and are quite ready to subscribe to the maxim, "That wherever England possesses an interest, there an American wrong exists." Some of the papers likewise write against England in no very measured terms; but it must be borne in mind that declamatory speaking and writing are the safety-valves of a free community, and the papers from which our opinion of American feeling is generally taken do not represent even a respectable minority in the nation. American commercial interests are closely interwoven with ours, and "Brother Jonathan" would not lightly go against his own interests by rushing into war on slight pretences.

While I was dining at an hotel in one of the great American cities a gentleman proposed to an English friend of his to drink "Success to Old England." Nearly two hundred students of a well-known college were present, and one of them begged to join in drinking the toast on behalf of his fellow-students. "For," he added, "we, in common with the educated youth of America, look upon England as upon a venerated mother." I have frequently heard this sentiment expressed in public places, and have often heard it remarked that kindly feeling towards England is on the increase in society.

The news of the victory of the Alma was received with rejoicing; the heroic self-sacrifice of the cavalry at Balaklava excited enthusiastic admiration; and the glorious stand at Inkermann taught the Americans that their aged parent could still defend the cause of freedom with the vigour of youth. The disasters of the winter, and the gloomy months of inaction which succeeded it, had the effect of damping their sympathies; the prophets of defeat were for a time triumphant, and our fading prestige, and reputed incapacity, were made the subjects of ill-natured discussion by the press. But when the news of the fall of Sebastopol arrived, the tone of the papers changed, and, relying on the oblivious memories of their readers, they declared that they had always prophesied the demolition of Russia. The telegraphic report of the victory was received with rejoicing, and the ship which conveyed it to Boston was saluted with thirty-one guns by the States artillery.

The glory of the republic is based upon its advanced social principles and its successful prosecution of the arts of peace. As the old military despotisms cannot compete with it in wealth and enlightenment, so it attempts no competition with them in standing armies and the arts of war. National vanity is a failing of the Americans, and, if their military prowess had never been proved before, they might seek to display it on European soil; but their successful struggle with England in the War of Independence renders any such display unnecessary. The institutions of the States do not date from the military ages of the world, and the Federal Constitution has made no provision for offensive war. The feeling of the educated classes, and of an immense majority in the Free States, is believed to be essentially English. Despotism and freedom can never unite; and whatever may be the declamations of the democratic party, the opinion of those who are acquainted with the state of popular feeling is that, if the question were seriously mooted, a war with England or a Russian alliance would secure to the promoters of either the indignation and contempt which they would deserve. It is earnestly to be hoped, and I trust that it may be believed, that none of us will live to see the day when two nations, so closely allied by blood, religion, and the love of freedom, shall engage in a horrible and fratricidal war.

Such of the foregoing remarks as apply to the results of the vitiation of the pure form of republican government delivered to America by Washington, I have hazarded with very great diffidence. In England we know very little of the United States, and, however candid the intentions of a tourist may be, it is difficult in a short residence in the country so completely to throw off certain prejudices and misapprehensions as to proceed to the delineation of its social characteristics with any degree of fairness and accuracy. The similarity of language, and to a great extent of customs and manners, renders one prone rather to enter into continual comparisons of America with England than to look at her from the point from which she really ought to be viewed—namely, *herself*. There are, however, certain salient points which present themselves to the interested observer, and I have endeavoured to approach these in as candid a spirit as possible, not exaggerating obvious faults, where there is so much to commend and admire.

The following remarks were lately made to me by a liberal and enlightened American on the misapprehensions of British observers:—"The great fault of English travellers in this land very often is that they see all things through spectacles which have been graduated to the age and narrow local dimensions of things in England; and because things here are new, and all that is good, instead of being concentrated into a narrow space so as to be seen at one glance, is widely diffused so as not to be easily gauged—because, in other words, it is the spring here and not the autumn, and our advance has the step of youth instead of the measured walk of age; and because our refinements have not the precise customs to which they have been accustomed at home, they turn away in mighty dissatisfaction. There are excellences in varieties, and things which differ may both be good."

CHAPTER XX

The America—A gloomy departure—An ugly night—Morning at Halifax—Our new passengers—Babies—Captain Leitch—A day at sea—Clippers and steamers—A storm—An Atlantic moonlight—Unpleasant sensations—A gale—Inkermann— Conclusion.

On reaching Boston I found that my passage had been taken in the Cunard steamer *America*, reputed to be the slowest and wettest of the whole line. Some of my kind American friends, anxious to induce me to remain for the winter with them, had exaggerated the dangers and discomforts of a winter-passage; the December storms, the three days spent in crossing the Newfoundland Banks, steaming at half-speed with fog-bells ringing and foghorns blowing, the impossibility of going on deck, and the disagreeableness of being shut up in a close heated saloon. It was with all these slanders against the ship fresh in my recollection that I saw her in dock on the morning of my leaving America, her large, shapeless, wall-sided hull looming darkly through a shower of rain. The friends who had first welcomed me to the States accompanied me to the vessel, rendering my departure from them the more regretful, and scarcely had I taken leave of them when a gun was fired, the lashings were cast off, and our huge wheels began their ceaseless revolutions.

It was in some respects a cheerless embarkation. The Indian summer had passed away; the ground was bound by frost; driving showers of sleet were descending; and a cold, howling, wintry wind was sweeping over the waters of Massachusetts Bay. We were considerably retarded between Boston and Halifax by contrary winds. I had retired early to my berth to sleep away the fatigues of several preceding months, and was awoke about midnight by the most deafening accumulation of sounds which ever stunned my ears. I felt that I was bruised, and that the berth was unusually hard and cold; and, after groping about in the pitch-darkness, I found that I had been thrown out of it upon the floor, a fact soon made self-evident by my being rolled across the cabin, a peculiarly disagreeable course of locomotion. It was impossible to stand or walk, and in crawling across to my berth I was assailed by my portmanteau, which was projected violently against me. Further sleep for some hours was impossible. Bang! bang! would come a heavy wave against the ship's side, close to my ears, as if trying the strength of her timbers. Crash! crash! as we occasionally shipped heavy seas, would the waves burst over the lofty bulwarks, and with a fall of seven feet at once come thundering down on the deck above. Then one sound asserted its claim to be heard over all the others—a sound as if our decks were being stove—a gun or some other heavy body had broken loose, and could not be secured. The incessant groaning, splitting, and heaving, and the roar of the water through the scuppers, as it found a tardy egress from the deluged deck, was the result of merely a "head-wind" and "an ugly night."

Late on the second evening of our voyage, I walked on deck. It was the "fag-end" of a gale, and the rain was pouring down upon the slippery planks. Brightly a sky-rocket whizzed upwards from a distant ship, and burst in a shower of flame, followed by two others, signalling our old acquaintance the *Canada*, bound from Liverpool to Boston. We sent up some fireworks in return, and soon lost sight of the friendly light on her paddle-box. She was the only ship that we saw till we reached the Irish coast.

With some of the other passengers, I was on deck at five in the morning, to see the lights on the heads of Halifax harbour. It was dark and intensely cold and wet. A shower of rain had frozen on deck during the night, and as it began to melt the water ran off in little sooty rills. Slowly, shivering figures came on deck, men in envelopes of fur, and oilskin capes and coats, with teeth chattering with cold, with wrinkled brows, and blue cold noses. And slowly lightened the clear eastern sky, and the crescent moon and stars disappeared one by one, and gradually the low pine-clad hills of Nova Scotia stood out in dark relief against the light, when, all of a sudden, "like a glory, the broad sun" rose behind the purple moorlands, and soon hill and town and lake-like bay were bathed in the cold glow of a winter sunrise. It was now half-past seven—the morning-gun had boomed from the citadel, and, in honour of such an important event as the arrival of the European steamer, it might have been supposed that the inhabitants of the quiet town of Halifax would have been astir. In this idea a Scotch friend and I stepped ashore with the intention of visiting an Indian curiosity-shop. In dismal contrast to the early habits which prevail in the American cities, where sleep is yielded to as a necessity, instead of being indulged in as a luxury, we found the shops closed, and, except the people immediately connected with the steamer, none were stirring in the streets but ragged negroes and squalid-looking Indians. A few 'cute enterprising Yankees would soon metamorphose the aspect of this city. As an arrogant American once observed to me, "It would take a 'Blue Nose' (a Nova-Scotian) as long to put on his hat as for one of our free and enlightened citizens to go from Bosting to New *Orleens*." The appearance of the town was very repulsive. A fall of snow had thawed, and, mixing with the dust, store-sweepings, cabbage-stalks, oyster-shells, and other rubbish, had formed a soft and peculiarly penetrating mixture from three to seven inches deep.

Eighteen passengers joined the *America* at Halifax, and among them I was delighted to welcome my cousins, a party of seven, *en route* from Prince Edward Island to England. The two babies which accompanied them were rather dreaded in prospect, but I believe that their behaviour gained them general approbation. As dogs are not allowed on the poop or in the saloon, a well-conditioned baby is rather a favourite in a ship; gentlemen of amiable dispositions give it plenty of nursing and tossing, and stewards regard it with benignant smiles, and occasionally offer it "titbits" purloined from dinner.

Among the passengers who joined us at Halifax were

Captain Leitch, and three of the wrecked officers of the steamship *City of Philadelphia*, which was lost on Cape Race three months before. Captain Leitch is a remarkable-looking man, very like the portraits of the Count of Monte Christo. His heroism and presence of mind on the occasion of that terrible disaster were the means of saving the lives of six hundred people, many of whom were women and children. When the ship struck, the panic among this large number of persons was of course awful; but so perfect was the discipline of the crew, and so great their attachment to their commander, that not a cabin-boy left the ship in that season of apprehension without his permission. Captain Leitch said that he would be the last man to quit the ship, and he kept his word; but the excitement, anxiety, and subsequent exposure to cold and fatigue, more especially in his search after the survivors of the ill-fated *Arctic*, brought on a malady from which he was severely suffering.

We had only sixty passengers on board, and the party was a remarkably quiet one. There was a gentleman going to Paris as American consul, a daily, animated, and untiring advocate of slavery; a Jesuit missionary, of agreeable manners and cultivated mind, on his way to Rome to receive an episcopal hat; two Jesuit brethren; five lively French people; and the usual number of commercial travellers, agents, and storekeepers, principally from Canada. There were very few ladies, and only three besides our own party appeared in the saloon. For a few days after leaving Halifax we had a calm sea and fair winds, accompanied with rain; and with the exception of six unhappy passengers who never came upstairs during the whole voyage, all seemed well enough to make the best of things.

A brief description of the daily routine on board these ships may serve to amuse those who have never crossed the Atlantic, and may recall agreeable or disagreeable recollections, as the case may be, to those who have.

During the first day or two those who are sea-sick generally remain downstairs, and those who are well look sentimentally at the receding land, and make acquaintances with whom they walk five or six in a row, bearing down isolated individuals of anti-social habits. After two or three days have elapsed, people generally lose all interest in the novelty, and settle down to such pursuits as suit them best. At eight in the morning the dressing-bell rings, and a very few admirable people get up, take a walk on deck, and appear at breakfast at half-past eight. But to most this meal is rendered a superfluity by the supper of the night before—that condemned meal, which everybody declaims against, and everybody, partakes of. However, if only two or three people appear, the long tables are adorned profusely with cold tongue, ham, Irish stew, mutton-chops, broiled salmon, crimped cod, eggs, tea, coffee, chocolate, toast, hot rolls, &c. &c.! These viands remain on the table till half-past nine. After breakfast some of the idle ones come up and take a promenade on deck, watch the wind, suggest that it has changed a little, look at the course, ask the captain for the fiftieth time when he expects to be in port, and watch the heaving of the log, when the officer of the watch invariably tells them that the ship is running a knot or two faster than her real speed, giving a glance of intelligence at the same time to some knowing person near. Many persons who are in the habit of crossing twice a-year begin cards directly after breakfast, and, with only the interruption of meals, play till eleven at night. Others are equally devoted to chess; and the commercial travellers produce small square books with columns for dollars and cents, cast up their accounts, and bite the ends of their pens. A bell at twelve calls the passengers to lunch from their various lurking-places, and, though dinner shortly succeeds this meal, few disobey the summons. There is a large consumption of pale ale, hotch-potch, cold beef, potatoes, and pickles. These pickles are of a peculiarly brilliant green, but, as the forks used are of electro-plate, the daily consumption of copper cannot be ascertained.

At four all the tables are spread; a bell rings—that "tocsin of the soul," as Byron has sarcastically but truthfully termed the dinner-bell; and all the passengers rush in from every quarter of the ship, and seat themselves with an air of expectation till the covers are raised. Grievous disappointments are often disclosed by the uplifted dish-covers, for it must be confessed that to many people dinner is the great event of the day, to be speculated upon before, and criticised afterwards. There is a tureen of soup at the head of each table, and, as soon as the captain takes his seat, twelve waiters in blue jackets, who have been previously standing in a row, dart upon the covers, and after a few minutes of intense clatter the serious business of eating begins. The stewards serve with civility and alacrity, and seem to divine your wishes, their good offices no doubt being slightly stimulated by the vision of a *douceur* at the end of the voyage. Long bills of fare are laid on the tables, and good water, plentifully iced, is served with each meal. Wine, spirits, liqueurs, and ale are consumed in large quantities, as also soups, fish, game, venison, meat, and poultry of all kinds, with French side-dishes, a profusion of jellies, puddings, and pastry, and a plentiful dessert of fresh and preserved fruits. Many people complain of a want of appetite at sea, and the number of bottles of "Perrin's Sauce" used in the Cunard steamers must almost make the fortune of the maker. At seven o'clock the tea-bell rings, but the tables are comparatively deserted, for from half-past nine to half-past ten people can order whatever they please in the way of supper.

In the *America*, as it was a winter-passage, few persons chose to walk on deck after dinner, consequently the saloon from eight till eleven presented the appearance of a room at a fashionable hotel. There were two regularly organised whist-parties, which played rubbers *ad infinitum*. Cards indeed were played at most of the tables—some played backgammon—a few would doze over odd volumes of old novels—while three chess-boards would be employed at a time, for there were ten persons perfectly devoted to this noble game. The varied employments of the occupants of the saloon produced a strange mixture of conversations. One evening, while waiting the slow movements of an opponent at chess, the following remarks in slightly raised tones were audible above the rest:—"Do you really think me pretty?—Oh flattering man!—Deuce, ace—Treble, double, and rub—That's a good hand—Check—It's your play—You've gammoned me—Ay, ay, sir—Parbleu!—Holloa! steward, whisky-toddy for four—I totally despise conventionalisms—Check-mate—Brandy-punch for six—You've thrown away all your hearts"—and a hundred others, many of them demands for something from the culinary department. Occasionally a forlorn wight, who neither played chess nor cards, would venture on deck to kill time, and return into the saloon panting and shivering, in rough surtout and fur cap, bringing a chilly atmosphere with him, voted a bore for leaving the door open, and totally unable to induce people to sympathise with him in his complaints of rain, cold, or the "ugly night." By eleven the saloon used to become almost unbearable, from the combined odours of roast onions, pickles, and punch, and at half-past the lights were put out, and the company dispersed, most to their berths, but some to smoke cigars on deck.

Though the Cunard steamers are said by English people to be as near perfection as steamers can be, I was sorry not to return in a clipper. There is something so exhilarating in the motion of a sailing-vessel, always provided she is neither rolling about in a calm, lying to in a gale, or beating against a head-wind. She seems to belong to the sea, with her tall tapering masts, her cloud of moving canvas, and her buoyant motion over the rolling waves. Her movements are all comprehensible, and *above-board* she is invariably clean, and her crew are connected in one's mind with nautical stories which charmed one in the long-past days of youth. A steamer is very much the reverse. "Sam Slick," with his usual force and aptitude of illustration, says that "she goes through the water like a subsoil-plough with an eight-horse team." There is so much noise and groaning, and smoke and dirt, so much mystery also, and the ship leaves so much commotion in the water behind her. There do not seem to be any regular sailors, and in their stead a collection of individuals remarkably greasy in their appearance, who may be cooks or stokers, or possibly both. Then you cannot go on the poop without being saluted by a whiff of hot air from the grim furnaces below; men are always shovelling in coal, or throwing cinders overboard; and the rig does not seem to belong to any ship in particular. The masts are low and small, and the canvas, which is always spread in fair weather, looks as if it had been trailed along Cheapside on a wet day. In the *America* it was not such a very material assistance either; for on one occasion, when we were running before a splendid breeze under a crowd of sail, the engines were stopped and the log heaved, which only gave our speed at three miles an hour. One lady passenger had been feeding her mind with stories of steamboat explosions in the States, and spent her time in a morbid state of terror by no means lessened by the close proximity of her state-room to the dreaded engine.

On the sixth day after leaving Halifax the wind, which everybody had been hoping for or fearing, came upon us at last, and continued increasing for three days, when, if we had been beating against it, we should have called it a hurricane. It was, however, almost directly aft, and we ran before it under sail. The sky during the two days which it lasted was perfectly cloudless, and the sea had that peculiar deep, clear, greenish-blue tint only to be met with far from land. There was a majesty, a sublimity about the prospect from the poop exceeding everything which I had ever seen. *There* was the mighty ocean showing his power, and *here* were we poor insignificant creatures overcoming him by virtue of those heavensent arts by which man

"Has made fire, flood, and earth,
The vassals of his will."

I had often read of mountain waves, but believed the comparison to be a mere figure of speech till I saw them here, all glorious in their beauty, under the clear blue of a December

369

sky. Two or three long high hills of water seemed to fill up the whole horizon, themselves an aggregate of a countless number of leaping, foam-capped waves, each apparently large enough to overwhelm a ship. Huge green waves seemed to chase us, when, just as they reached the stern, the ship would lift, and they would pass under her. She showed especial capabilities for rolling. She would roll down on one side, the billows seeming ready to burst in foam over her, while the opposite bulwark was fifteen or eighteen feet above the water, displaying her bright green copper. The nights were more glorious than the days, when the broad full moon would shed her light upon the water with a brilliancy unknown in our foggy clime. It did not look like a wan flat surface, placed flat upon a watery sky, but like a large radiant sphere hanging in space. The view from the wheel-house was magnificent. The towering waves which came up behind us heaped together by mighty winds, looked like hills of green glass, and the phosphorescent light like fiery lamps within—the moonlight glittered upon our broad foamy wake—our masts and spars and rigging stood out in sharp relief against the sky, while for once our canvas looked white. Far in the distance the sharp bow would plunge down into the foam, and then our good ship, rising, would shake her shiny sides, as if in joy at her own buoyancy. The busy hum of men marred not the solitary sacredness of midnight on the Atlantic. The moon "walked in brightness," auroras flashed, and meteors flamed, and a sensible presence of Deity seemed to pervade the transparent atmosphere in which we were viewing "the works of the Lord, and his wonders in the deep."

I could scarcely understand how this conjunction of circumstances could produce any but agreeable sensations; but it is a melancholy fact that the saloon emptied and the state-rooms filled, and the number of promenaders daily diminished. People began to find the sea "an unpleasant fact." I heard no more Byronic quotations about its "glad waters," or comments on the "splendid run"—these were changed into anxious questions as to when we should reach Liverpool? and, if we were in danger? People querulously complained of the ale, hitherto their delight; abused the meat; thought the mulligatawny "horrid stuff;" and wondered how they could ever have thought plum-puddings fit for anything but pigs. Mysterious disappearances were very common; diligent peripatetics were seen extended on sofas, or feebly promenading under shelter of the bulwarks; while persons who prided themselves on their dignity sustained ignominious falls, or clung to railings in a state of tottering decrepitude, in an attempted progress down the saloon. Though we had four ledges on the tables, cruets, bottles of claret, and pickles became locomotive, and jumped upon people's laps; almost everything higher than a plate was upset—pickles, wine, ale, and oil forming a most odoriferous mixture; but these occurrences became too common to be considered amusing. Two days before reaching England the gale died away, and we sighted Cape Clear at eight o'clock on the evening of the eleventh day out. A cold chill came off from the land, we were enveloped in a damp fog, and the inclemency of the air reminded us of what we had nearly forgotten, namely, that we were close upon Christmas.

The greater part of Sunday we were steaming along in calm water, within sight of the coast of Ireland, and extensive preparations were being made for going ashore—some people of sanguine dispositions had even decided what they would order for dinner at the *Adelphi*. Morning service was very fully attended, and it was interesting to hear the voices of people of so many different creeds and countries joining in that divinely-taught prayer which proclaims the universal brotherhood of the human race, knowing that in a few hours those who then met in adoration would be separated, to meet no more till summoned by the sound of the last trumpet.

Those who expected to spend Sunday night on shore were disappointed. A gale came suddenly on us about four o'clock, sails were hastily taken in, orders were hurriedly given and executed, and the stewards were in despair, when a heavy lurch of the ship threw most of the things off the table before dinner, mingling cutlery, pickles, and broken glass and china, in one chaotic heap on the floor. As darkness came on, the gale rose higher, the moon was obscured, the rack in heavy masses was driving across the stormy sky, and scuds of sleet and spray made the few venturous persons on deck cower under the nearest shelter to cogitate the lines—

> "Nights like these,
> When the rough winds wake western seas,
> Brook not of glee."

I might dwell upon the fury of that night—upon the awful blasts which seemed about to sweep the seas of every human work—upon our unanswered signals—upon the length of time while we were

> "Drifting, drifting, drifting,
> On the shifting
> Currents of the restless main"—

upon the difficulty of getting the pilot on board—and the heavy seas through which our storm-tossed bark entered the calmer waters of the Mersey: but I must hasten on.

Night after night had the French and English passengers joined in drinking with enthusiasm the toast "*La prise de Sebastopol*"—night after night had the national pride of the representatives of the allied nations increased, till we almost thought in our ignorant arrogance that at the first thunder of our guns the defences of Sebastopol would fall, as did those of Jericho at the sound of the trumpets of Joshua. Consequently, when the pilot came on board with the newspaper, most of the gentlemen crowded to the gangway, prepared to give three cheers for the fall of Sebastopol!

The pilot brought the news of victory—but it was of the barren victory of Inkermann. A gloom fell over the souls of many, as they read of our serried ranks mown down by the Russian fire, of heroic valour and heroic death. The saloon was crowded with eager auditors as the bloody tidings were made audible above the roar of winds and waters. I could scarcely realise the gloomy fact that many of those whom I had seen sail forth in hope and pride only ten months before were now sleeping under the cold clay of the Crimea. Three cheers for the victors of Inkermann, and three for our allies, were then heartily given, though many doubted whether the heroic and successful resistance of our troops deserved the name of victory.

Soon after midnight we anchored in the Mersey, but could not land till morning, and were compelled frequently to steam up to our anchors, in consequence of the fury of the gale. I felt some regret at leaving the good old steamship *America*, which had borne us so safely across the "vexed Atlantic," although she rolls terribly, and is, in her admirable captain's own words, "an old tub, but slow and sure." She has since undergone extensive repairs, and I hope that the numerous passengers who made many voyages in her in the shape of rats have been permanently dislodged.

Those were sacred feelings with which I landed upon the shores of England. Although there appeared little of confidence in the present, and much of apprehension for the future, I loved her better when a shadow was upon her than in the palmy days of her peace and prosperity. I had seen in other lands much to admire, and much to imitate; but it must not be forgotten that England is the source from which those streams of liberty and enlightenment have flowed which have fertilised the Western Continent. Other lands may have their charms, and the sunny skies of other climes may be regretted, but it is with pride and gladness that the wanderer sets foot again on British soil, thanking God for the religion and the liberty which have made this weather-beaten island in a northern sea to be the light and glory of the world.

Isabella Bird was born in Yorkshire in 1831, and was in her twenties when she made the visit to Canada and the ante-bellum United States described in this book. Not long before, at the age of eighteen, she had undergone an operation to remove a spinal tumour; poor health continued to dog her (and indeed did so throughout her life), and it was on the advice of a doctor that she embarked on these travels. They were her first but by no means her last, in an extraordinary life that took her to Japan and Korea, Tibet and China, South East Asia, Australia and New Zealand, Persia and Kurdistan, and, at the age of seventy, across Morocco in a remarkable thousand-mile horseback journey that would have taxed the stamina of a traveller half her age.

From the moment she sailed from Liverpool—witnessing the embarkation of the light cavalry (p. 16) who later in that same year of 1854 met their death in the Crimean War in the Earl of Cardigan's foolish charge at Balaclava—Isabella Bird was all eyes and ears, observing the places and people she encountered with wide-awake and open-minded curiosity. Whether recording the conversation of the pedantic Mr. Latham (pp. 66–8) or the snobbish name-dropping Mr. Haldimands (pp. 171–2), or dealing with a pickpocket (p. 124), an escaped madman who believes himself the king of Montreal (pp. 203–4), or the poet Longfellow (pp. 323–5), Bird in this book is always notable for the cool aplomb with which she takes new experience in her stride. On board a steamer (pp. 362–3), she awakens during a storm to find she has been pitched out of her berth, and while she is crawling across the floor she is hit by her own portmanteau, but her comment is the very definition of laconic: "Further sleep for some hours was impossible."

Plainly this is still an inexperienced young woman, but equally plainly the capacity for flexible response and for informed and generous judgement that marks her later works is continually in the making. Other English travellers to the United States earlier in the 19th century, notably Charles Dickens, had angered Americans by the breach of hospitality which their critical portrayal of the young nation allegedly constituted. Aware of the over-sensitivity of the American reaction, Isabella Bird was also alert to shortcomings in the behaviour of her own countrymen; and *The Englishwoman in America* gives us a personality finely tuned to the good and the bad, the inspiring and the unacceptable, wherever she finds them. Thus she records American energy, courtesy, dishonesty, uprightness, moral obliquity, national pride, and other characteristics great and small, with even-handed equanimity. Not that her own feelings are ever in doubt: perversions of moral sense are always quick to excite her firm condemnation, none more so than the "gigantic evil" of slavery, to which this distant relative of William Wilberforce turns on more than one occasion (pp. 109-12 and 331-2) with abhorrence.

That "canker of the Union" was to cost the United States four years of bloody civil war before Isabella Bird returned to the country for the delightful second visit that produced *A Lady's Life in the Rocky Mountains* (also available in Könemann Travel Classics).

Michael Hulse